THE SECRET
RESCUE

THE SECRET RESCUE

AN UNTOLD STORY OF
AMERICAN NURSES AND
MEDICS BEHIND NAZI LINES

CATE LINEBERRY

LITTLE, BROWN AND COMPANY
New York   Boston   London

Little, Brown and Company
Hachette Book Group
237 Park Avenue, New York, NY 10017
littlebrown.com

First Edition: May 2013

Little, Brown and Company is a division of Hachette Book Group, Inc. The Little, Brown name and logo are trademarks of Hachette Book Group, Inc.

The publisher is not responsible for websites (or their content) that are not owned by the publisher.

The Hachette Speakers Bureau provides a wide range of authors for speaking events. To find out more, go to hachettespeakersbureau.com or call (866) 376-6591.

Map by David Lambert

ISBN 978-0-316-22022-4
LCCN 2013934814

10 9 8 7 6 5 4 3 2 1

RRD-C

Printed in the United States of America

For the forgotten heroes

Our debt to the heroic men and valiant women in the service of our country can never be repaid. They have earned our undying gratitude. America will never forget their sacrifices.

— President Harry S. Truman,
April 16, 1945

Contents

A Note to the Reader

When survivors of an American transport plane that crash-landed in Nazi-occupied Albania in November 1943 returned to the United States after months trapped behind enemy lines, they were forbidden from sharing details of their harrowing ordeal with anyone outside the military. On February 15, 1944, however, British Lieutenant Gavan "Garry" Duffy, who helped save the party, gave a guarded account to the press. Two days later, Allied headquarters finally released Associated Press correspondent Hal Boyle's story on the grueling journey of the thirteen female nurses, thirteen medics, and four-man flight crew. The story had been delayed by the military for weeks.

Though the piece mistakenly declared that all in the party had been rescued and offered enough details to capture the public's imagination, it could not reveal the full story in order to protect those left behind, future downed airmen needing assistance, and the heroic people who helped the Americans escape—including Albanian partisans, villagers, and British and American officers working for clandestine organizations. The media and even friends and family of the survivors wanted to know more, but the men and women who had lived through the nightmare refused to provide any additional information, as they had been ordered.

One nurse told a reporter, "Too many lives might be taken, too much is at stake to reveal our benefactors or the terrible happenings of those terrible weeks."

When the war ended, Albania fell under the power of the ruthless dictator Enver Hoxha, and the Americans who had escaped from Albania knew that sharing the full story with the public could still jeopardize the brave men and women who had helped them and who now lived in terror. Over the many decades that followed, the survivors continued to keep the specifics of their journey private, sharing their memories only with each other, mostly when they reunited twice in the 1980s, sent cards in the mail, or visited one another.

Those concerns changed after communism in Albania began to crumble in late 1990. In 1999, former nurse Agnes Jensen Mangerich, at almost eighty-five years old, published her memories of the ordeal. Eleven years later, the son of Lawrence Abbott, one of the deceased medics, self-published his father's long-lost memoir.

I stumbled across an old newspaper story about this event in 2011 while doing other research on World War II and was intrigued by many aspects of it. I read the two books and began thinking of telling the larger story. Though the memoirs, along with other materials I collected — including declassified American, British, and German documents, photos, letters, stories passed on to family members, and even military footage of the group returning from Albania — helped tell the story, only someone who had experienced it firsthand could answer the many questions I still had. I then learned that Harold Hayes, the only living member of the original thirty on board the plane, was living in a retirement community in Oregon. At eighty-nine, his memory was as sharp as ever, and he was interested in helping me capture the vivid details he remembered and had collected from the others in the years since their fateful journey. Most important, all of the information and leads he provided that could be corroborated proved accurate. (If significant details from sources differ and could not be confirmed, I have noted them in the back of the book.) Hayes shared with me his own unpublished memoir, invited me to spend a week with him and his wife at his home, and invited me back again when I still had more questions.

For the next year and a half, we communicated almost daily by phone and e-mail, and I shared with him my photos and experiences from when I traveled to Albania in early 2012 to see the places germane to the story, including the crash site and villages that seemed to have changed very little over the years. While there, I presented a letter to Albanian President Bamir Topi from Hayes thanking the Albanian people for risking their lives to save the group and interviewed some village men who had been just boys when they had met the Americans.

With the extraordinary help of Hayes and so many others, here is the untold story, seventy years later, of a band of ordinary Americans facing a series of nearly unbelievable but true challenges and the heroes who helped them along the way.

—*Cate Lineberry*

Those On Board Army Air Forces Aircraft 42-68809
on November 8, 1943

Name	Age*	Hometown

Flight Crew, 61st Troop Carrier Squadron

Pilot:
| 1st Lt. Charles Thrasher | 22 | Daytona Beach, FL |

Copilot:
| 2nd Lt. James "Jim" Baggs | 28 | Savannah, GA |

Crew chief:
| Sgt. Willis Shumway | 23 | Tempe, AZ |

Radio operator:
| Sgt. Richard "Dick" Lebo | 23 | Halifax, PA |

Nurses, 807th Medical Air Evacuation Transport Squadron (MAETS)

Name	Age	Hometown
2nd Lt. Gertrude "Tooie" Dawson	29	Vandergrift, PA
2nd Lt. Agnes "Jens" Jensen	28	Stanwood, MI
2nd Lt. Pauleen Kanable	26	Richland Center, WI
2nd Lt. Ann Kopsco	30	Hammond, LA
2nd Lt. Wilma Lytle	31	Butler, KY
2nd Lt. Ann Maness	32	Paris, TX
2nd Lt. Ann "Marky" Markowitz	27	Chicago, IL
2nd Lt. Frances Nelson	25	Princeton, WV
2nd Lt. Helen Porter	30	Hanksville, UT
2nd Lt. Eugenie "Jean" Rutkowski	27	Detroit, MI
2nd Lt. Elna Schwant	26	Winner, SD
2nd Lt. Lillian "Tassy" Tacina	22	Hamtramck, MI
2nd Lt. Lois Watson	23	Chicago, IL

Name	Age*	Hometown

Medics, 807th MAETS

T/3 (S/Sgt.) Lawrence "Larry" Abbott	23	Newaygo, MI
T/3 (S/Sgt.) Charles Adams	21	Niles, MI
T/3 (S/Sgt.) Paul Allen	19	Greenville, KY
T/3 (S/Sgt.) Robert Cranson	36	New Haven, NY
T/3 (S/Sgt.) James "Jim" Cruise	28	Brockton, MA
T/3 (S/Sgt.) Raymond Ebers	25	Steeleville, IL
T/3 (S/Sgt.) William Eldridge	24	Eldridge, KY
T/3 (S/Sgt.) Harold Hayes	21	Indianola, IA
T/3 (S/Sgt.) Gordon MacKinnon	32	Los Angeles, CA
T/3 (S/Sgt.) Robert "Bob" Owen	20	Walden, NY
T/3 (S/Sgt.) John Wolf	21	Glidden, WI
T/3 (S/Sgt.) Charles Zeiber	26	Reading, PA

Medic, 802nd MAETS

Cpl. Gilbert Hornsby	21	Manchester, KY

*Age at the time of the crash landing.

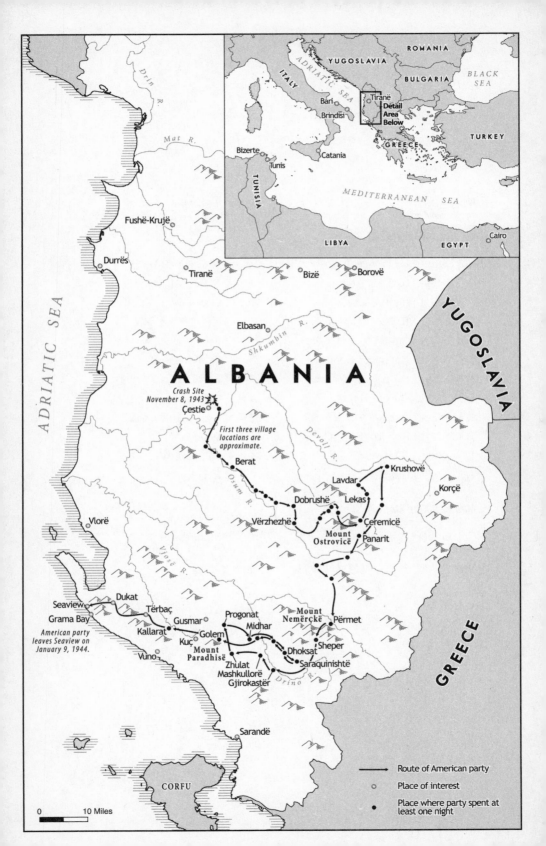

THE SECRET
RESCUE

Prologue

On a chilly, overcast December day in 1943, Gavan "Garry" Duffy, a tough, no-nonsense twenty-four-year-old special operations lieutenant working for Britain, peered through his binoculars from the cover of an Albanian hillside and watched in frustration as waves of German troops and tanks moved through the steep and winding roads of a town on the valley's other side. The town was perched high above an abandoned airfield where American rescue planes were scheduled to land that morning in a risky and dramatic mission to evacuate a group of stranded American men and women. The party had been lost for fifty-two days and was barely surviving the treacherous winter landscape while evading capture by the Nazis.

As Duffy continued to watch the activity across the valley, three German trucks and one armored car drove from the town and parked near the main road that ran in front of the airfield. Now he was certain it was too risky for the rescue planes. With no way for him to communicate directly with the pilots, Duffy's plan had been to signal that it was safe to land by laying out yellow-orange parachute panels from a supply drop to make a large X on the field. Now that the Germans had moved in, there was nothing he could do but wait with the others and watch.

His party of exhausted and ill men and women, riddled with lice and worn out from weeks of traversing Albania's rugged terrain while eluding the enemy, stood near Duffy and his wireless operator as cold wind cut through their filthy, tattered uniforms and blasted their malnourished bodies. They were now so weak from hunger, sickness, and despair that the several miles they had walked from their village hideouts in the rugged mountains that morning to meet the planes had turned into a slow and grueling journey. Some of the men who had volunteered to help Duffy give the prearranged signal to the planes nervously fingered their pieces of parachute. The others continued a silent vigil.

Then, at half past noon, the sudden roar of multiple planes filled the air. Seconds later, three Lockheed P-38 Lightning fighters, nicknamed "fork-tailed devils" by the German Luftwaffe, flew so low over the airfield that the weary group huddled on the hill could see the pilots' faces. A Vickers Wellington, one of Britain's most famous and durable bombers, its machine guns poised for action, suddenly appeared as well, and it buzzed down the airfield ready to provide cover for two C-47s that followed behind. Not only were the Americans coming to their rescue, so were the British. More twin-engined P-38s came in threes until twenty-one planes filled the gray sky.

The men and women stood transfixed by the huge display of airpower. It was the most glorious sight they had ever seen. None of them had expected so many planes—certainly not Duffy. They were amazed at the effort being made to save them, but they were even more affected by the stark reality that they couldn't signal the planes to land. With each passing second their hopes of rescue were further shattered, and they were overcome with feelings that had become inescapable: frustration, loneliness, and heartache.

CHAPTER 1

The Nurses and Medics
of the 807th

More than ninety personnel of the newly formed 807th Medical Air Evacuation Transport Squadron (MAETS) piled into two railroad cars in Louisville, Kentucky, on a sweltering afternoon in the second week of August 1943. As sweat soaked through their summer uniforms, the group, including twenty-five female nurses, stashed their heavy field packs and settled into their assigned seats. The officers, including the nurses, sat in one car, while the enlisted men were assigned to another. Both groups talked with the new friends they'd made over the last few months in Louisville; but with officers and enlisted men prohibited from fraternizing, many in the squadron were almost strangers as they started their journey to uncertain fates overseas.

As new members of the Army Air Forces' MAETS, the men and women were part of an innovative program that transported the wounded and sick from hospitals near the frontlines to better-equipped medical facilities for additional care. In the course of the war, the MAETS would move more than one million troops, with only forty-six patients dying in flight. It was so successful that in 1945, General of the Army Dwight D. Eisenhower deemed air evacuation as important as other World War II medical innovations, including sulfa drugs, penicillin, blood plasma, and whole blood, and credited it with saving thousands of lives.

Among those on board was the 807th's commanding officer, thirty-six-year-old Capt. William P. McKnight. A medical doctor just over six feet tall with a shock of sandy-red hair and a mustache, McKnight was known for quietly but effectively enforcing his authority and was well-respected by the men and women of his squadron. McKnight and the four other doctors in the 807th had been trained as flight surgeons at the School of Aviation Medicine at Randolph Field, Texas, before arriving at Bowman Field Air Base in Louisville and joining the new 807th just a few months before. Despite their titles as flight surgeons, their primary duty when they arrived overseas would be to serve as liaisons between airfields and forward hospitals and to screen patients brought for transport to make sure it was medically safe for them to travel.

First Lt. Grace Stakeman, a thirty-year-old blonde from Terre Haute, Indiana, nicknamed "Teach" by the young women who reported to her, was also finding her seat on the stifling train. As the 807th's head nurse, Stakeman was in charge of the squadron's twenty-four other flight nurses, all second lieutenants who were trained as nurses before joining the military. Like Stakeman, the nurses were allotted relative rank, which, since 1920, had given nurses the status of officers and allowed them to wear insignia but at half the pay of their male counterparts, though as flight nurses they earned an extra sixty dollars per month. Military nurses would be awarded full but temporary rank in 1944 and permanent rank in 1947. Though Stakeman's delicate features gave her a somewhat fragile appearance, she, like the other nurses drawn to volunteer for the Army, was far from frail. After recovering from a car accident in her early twenties that broke six of her vertebrae and required her to wear a full-body cast, she had joined the Army Nurse Corps (ANC) more determined than ever to help others.

The squadron also included twenty-four enlisted men who had just been trained as medics and been promoted to the rank of technician third grade, or T/3. The medics came from a variety of backgrounds and places, with some just out of high school and others with a host of jobs under their belts. While some had enlisted, others had been drafted. The rest of the 807th was made up of a medical administrative corps officer in charge of supplies and dozens of enlisted men who would serve as the squadron's cooks, clerks, and drivers and held ranks between private and master sergeant.

Twenty-one-year-old Harold Hayes, a reserved but inquisitive medic with wire-rimmed glasses, dark hair, and a deep voice that rivaled any radio announcer's, sat in the enlisted men's car and was as anxious as the rest of the squadron to learn of their destination overseas. They were now headed to their port of embarkation, where they would undergo last-minute preparations before shipping out.

Hayes had volunteered for the 807th after working under McKnight at a dispensary at Bowman Field Air Base and was one of the first four medics to join the squadron. He and the three other young men sitting in the car that morning had become fast friends. Twenty-year-old Robert "Bob" Owen from Walden, New York, was a tall, lean, and handsome young man with hazel eyes who still looked like the star high school football player he'd been only a few years before and whose favorite topic of conversation was "Red," the beautiful woman he'd recently met at a USO club in Louisville and would eventually marry. John Wolf from Glidden, Wisconsin, twenty-one years old, was a quiet outdoorsman and avid hunter who had married at seventeen. The oldest at twenty-three and the shortest at just five foot six was Lawrence "Larry" Abbott from Newaygo, Michigan, whose childhood nickname was "Windy" because he liked to talk so much. The four had been nearly inseparable at Bowman and spent their free time swimming, watching movies, drinking beer at Louisville bars, and attending USO dances. These new friends referred to one another fondly as Brother Owen, Brother Wolf, and Brother Hayes, while Owen dubbed Abbott "Little Orville," a reference to his middle name and short stature.

Agnes Jensen, a twenty-eight-year-old brunette with blue eyes and high cheekbones, from Stanwood, Michigan, took her place in the car reserved for the 807th's officers. Nicknamed "Jens," she and Helen Porter, another fresh-faced nurse who was two months shy of turning thirty, from Hanksville, Utah, had been last-minute additions to the 807th after being reassigned from another squadron just ten days earlier. The two considered it a lucky break that they would get to travel overseas earlier than expected.

Also among the nurses was twenty-seven-year-old Eugenie "Jean" Rutkowski, a former airline stewardess raised in Detroit, who had joined the military in May after her fiancé went missing while ferrying a plane to England. Nearby was newly married twenty-three-year-old Lois Watson, a blonde with hazel eyes from Chicago, Illinois. Watson had been a senior in nursing school with plans to become a stewardess when hundreds of Japanese planes attacked the American naval base at Pearl Harbor, trying to destroy the U.S. Navy's Pacific fleet. She and the rest of the country had reeled from the shock and horror of the assault, which left thousands dead, including one of the residents she used to go with on double dates. When she and her father had stopped in an enlistment center in downtown Chicago only to inquire about her joining the Army, she signed up.

By the following December, Watson had found herself at Camp McCoy in Wisconsin and away from home for the first time. Within days of arriving, she met Nolan McKenzie, the young man she would marry just a few months later. Both were interested in flying, and he left in April for training to become a B-25 pilot, while she joined the MAETS in May.

All of the 807th's nurses and medics had just completed a six-week training course in air evacuation at Bowman Field Air Base and were ready to put their skills into practice. The air evacuation program—the first of its kind anywhere in the world—was only months old. The first two MAETS squadrons, the 801st and 802nd, had been activated in early December 1942 and were in demand before they could even finish the training the Army Air Forces (AAF) had rushed to put together. The 802nd had begun its journey to North Africa on Christmas Day, while the 801st left for New Caledonia in the South Pacific in January.

By the time the 807th started its training, the nurses' program included everything from aeromedical physiology and enemy plane identification to chemical warfare and religious procedures in an emergency. They were taught survival skills for the arctic, the jungle, and the desert to prepare them for wherever the war might take them and learned how to unload patients in the event of a water landing. To give them experience in the air, the nurses were flown over the Ohio River. Watson kept telling herself "I won't get airsick" as one flight twisted and turned so much that one of the nurses became ill. To learn what happened to the body without oxygen at ten thousand to fifteen thousand feet, they were put into a low-pressure chamber and watched the dizzying effects on one brave volunteer who went in without an oxygen mask. These training procedures were powerful reminders of the challenges they would face in the air as the unpressurized transport planes traveled at a range of heights and in a variety of weather conditions.

Physical training was as important as the lectures and demonstrations, and the nurses performed daily exercises and long marches, where they were sometimes pelted with flour bombs in simulated air attacks to teach them to take cover. Military drills included navigating obstacle courses that required them to crawl under barbed wire with live machine-gun fire overhead, first on their stomachs and then on their backs. As they practiced on one particularly hot and humid Kentucky day, Watson watched as several of the nurses struggled to finish and passed out on the course after completing it.

Unlike the very first flight nurses, the women of the 807th didn't have to fight to be able to wear pants rather than skirts as part of their uniforms. Months earlier, Col. Florence Blanchfield, the assistant superintendent of the ANC, had ordered flight nurses who were wearing the more practical men's one-piece flight suits without authorization back into their regulation skirts. That policy changed after Blanchfield showed up at Bowman Field wearing the popular "pinks and greens" dress uniform, an olive-drab jacket with a taupe skirt. Having never flown before, the colonel accepted the offer of a demonstration flight. As she awkwardly tried to put on the required parachute while wearing a skirt, the nurses on board explained to her that she would only need to lace it into position in an emergency. Soon after takeoff, the plane experienced engine trouble and the pilot announced that all on board should prepare to jump. Blanchfield fumbled with fastening her parachute until the pilot was able to restart the engine. Shortly after, flight nurses were allowed to forgo their skirts and were given slate-blue uniforms consisting of short Eisenhower jackets with waistbands and matching pants and caps.

Unlike the nurses, the medics, all enlisted men, had received basic military training before volunteering for the air evacuation program. Their specialized instruction in air evacuation covered some of the same material the nurses' program did, including survival skills and additional physical conditioning; but their medical experience, which included working with the nurses for a few weeks in local hospitals, was limited mostly to first aid. Their main focus was learning how to quickly and smoothly load and unload patients, which would be one of their primary tasks. To test their skills and to have a little fun, the medics in the various squadrons often challenged one another to see who could load and unload planes the fastest on practice runs. The 807th couldn't be beat.

Though air evacuation was still new in 1943, medical evacuation itself had only been around since the Civil War. In 1862, the medical director of the Union Army of the Potomac, Maj. Jonathan Letterman, created a system to manage mass casualties, which included first-aid stations on battlefields, mobile field hospitals, and ambulance services. In late August 1862, it took a week to remove injured soldiers from the battlefield at Second Manassas, with many young men succumbing to their injuries as they waited alone and in pain for help to come. Less than a month later, the Battle of Antietam left twenty-three thousand casualties after twelve hours of bloody combat. With Letterman's new triage system in place, medical personnel were able to remove all injured soldiers from the field within twenty-four hours. Though the lifesaving system was refined during the Spanish-American War, it remained virtually unchanged until the age of the airplane.

In 1910, seven years after the Wright brothers made the world's first successful powered flight at Kitty Hawk and one year after the Army received its first plane, Capt. George H. R. Gosman and Lt. Albert L. Rhoades built an aircraft for the sole purpose of transporting wounded soldiers from the battlefield to the hospital. Though the plane they built crashed during its test flight and the War Department turned down Gosman's pleas for financial assistance, the idea of an air ambulance had been born.

Despite the advantages of rapid evacuation that air ambulances could offer, concerns regarding the safety of planes, a technology still in its infancy, would linger for years to come. When Col. A. W. Williams, a retired Army officer, recommended at a meeting of the Association of Military Surgeons in November 1912 that the airplane be used to evacuate patients, the *Baltimore Sun* responded with an editorial stating, "the hazard of being severely wounded is sufficient without the additional hazard of transportation by airplane."

Undaunted by the risks, French physicians and aviation enthusiasts began exploring the use of air ambulances, even proposing a monoplane that carried patients in a box under the fuselage. When French military surgeon Dr. Eugene Chassaing asked for government funds to develop a modified plane, one critic responded, "Are there not enough dead in France today without killing the wounded in airplanes?" Chassaing persevered, however, and using a Dorand AR.2, a French observation biplane, he designed a side opening that allowed room for two stretchers to be placed in the fuselage behind the pilot. In April 1918, two of his planes helped evacuate wounded from Flanders, marking the first successful use of air evacuation on specially equipped aircraft, a victory that helped ensure air evacuation's future.

Though most of the world had been at war since 1914, the United States didn't officially enter the fray until April 1917. With the rush to train thousands of new pilots at temporary flying fields in the States, the inexperienced flyboys crashed regularly, and getting medical care to the injured proved difficult because of poor roads. A surgeon was typically flown to the accident scene and provided medical care on site before transporting the flier to a base hospital in a motor ambulance over bumpy and unpaved roads. It took hours to deliver a patient, and many died along the way.

By 1918, Capt. William C. Ocker, the officer in charge of flight training at Gerstner Field in Louisiana, and reserve medical officer Maj. Wilson E. Driver modified a standard Curtiss JN-4, a biplane called a "Jenny," to allow the craft to carry a patient in a litter, or stretcher, in the rear cockpit. That same year, they transported the first patient to be flown by plane in the United States. News of their success traveled, and air service personnel at nearby Texas airfields replicated their efforts and made their own modifications. On July 23, the Director of the Air Service ordered all flying fields in the United States to employ air ambulances.

Overseas, however, the U.S. Army Medical Department continued to evacuate troops using litter bearers, horse-drawn and motor ambulances, and hospital trains. Many patients, who frequently couldn't be moved from trenches until dark, suffered long and difficult journeys over war-torn roads to get to a hospital.

When the war ended, several European countries continued experimenting with air evacuation and developed equipment and procedures for transporting casualties. The U.S. military, however, still continued to favor ground evacuation. In May 1921, the War Department stated, "In case of accident, the use of airplanes for the transportation of sick and wounded soldiers, when other safer means of transportation is available, could not be justified."

In an effort to promote air evacuation and flight nurses in the United States, Lauretta M. Schimmoler, one of the few female pilots in the country in the 1930s, founded a commercial organization called the Aerial Nurse Corps of America in 1936. She began lobbying the military and the Red Cross to have her organization recognized as a military specialty but was repeatedly turned down. Despite the rejections, Columbia Studios made a movie called *Parachute Nurse* in 1942 in which Schimmoler served as a technical consultant and played a captain. The *New York Times* said the film "hardly makes for either instructional or entertaining fare," but it helped further publicize both air evacuation and flight nurses. The military ultimately recognized Schimmoler's contributions, and three decades later, the Air Force honored her as a pioneer in air evacuation.

The United States' strategy for getting patients from the battlefield to medical facilities finally changed after America entered World War II. The demand for medical air evacuation and its success rate in saving lives overruled any remaining doubts about its safety or practicability. In early 1942, volunteer medics in C-47 cargo planes began mass evacuations of sick and injured construction troops building the Alaska Highway in freezing temperatures. When completed, the 1,500-mile road, which traversed some of the harshest landscape in North America, provided a vital ground route that connected the United States to Alaska through Canada, but it took a significant toll on the men who built it in just eight months. In that year, 223 of them were air evacuated within Alaska and 212 were taken to the continental United States. Some six thousand miles away, Allied soldiers fighting the Japanese were serving in such remote areas of Burma that only cargo and troop carrier planes could reach them. Using American-built C-47s, the Royal Air Force No. 31 Squadron flew some 2,600 sick and wounded patients to airfields in India in early 1942.

As these and other improvised rescues rallied support for air evacuation, the Army took notice. In May 1942 it activated the first U.S. air evacuation unit, the 38th Medical Air Ambulance Squadron, stationed at Fort Benning, Georgia. By the summer, the War Department officially designated responsibility for developing an air evacuation program to the AAF, the successor to the Air Corps and a forerunner of today's modern Air Force.

Commanding General of the AAF Henry "Hap" Arnold asked his air surgeon, Brig. Gen. David N. W. Grant, a Virginian who had entered the Army Medical Service in 1916, to create the new program. A longtime champion of air evacuation, Grant ordered the 38th's officers and enlisted men transferred to Bowman Field Air Base, built in 1940 on the east side of the commercial airport in Louisville. Grant's new program, however, soon had to be scrapped. The AAF Director of Military Requirements insisted that "the activation of any puddle jumper squadrons" to evacuate sick or wounded was unnecessary. It was also at odds with AAF policy, which dictated that aircraft could not be designated only as ambulances—in part because in 1942 the AAF was operating with a vast shortage of planes.

Before the Second World War, the Army had fewer than 2,200 planes and 26,500 men. By January 1939, Hitler's continued aggression and Germany's expanding air force so alarmed President Franklin D. Roosevelt that he asked Congress to appropriate $300 million for the Air Corps. Congress agreed three months later and approved as many as 6,000 serviceable planes. The expansion continued as the country quickly recognized how much of the war would be fought in the skies. In June 1941, the U.S. Army Chief of Staff Gen. George C. Marshall established the AAF to control the Air Corps and the Air Force Combat Command. By the end of the war, the AAF would be considered a major military organization and would boast 63,715 planes and more than two million men and women.

Without the use of dedicated air ambulances, Grant reorganized the fledgling air evacuation program into the Medical Air Evacuation Transport Squadron (MAETS), which would be renamed the Medical Air Evacuation Squadron (MAES) in July 1944. Under Grant's revised plan, first issued in late November 1942, which included the use of flight nurses for the first time, medical personnel would accompany their patients on available transport planes that were already delivering troops and supplies to forward areas. The transport planes could be converted into air ambulances in a matter of minutes on return flights by folding up their bucket seats and adding either web-strapped or metal-bracket litters to hold patients.

Though the medics and nurses of the 807th would have to rely solely on their medical kits during their first few months, each plane would eventually carry a chest of supplies that included everything the medical personnel might need to treat patients, including medications, bandages, equipment for administering intravenous medications and blood plasma, oxygen tanks, and chemically heated pads for flying at high altitudes. Most of the in-flight medical work allocated to the nurses would include adjusting dosages of certain drugs based on the effects of altitude, applying and readjusting splints, giving sedatives and stimulants, treating shock, and administering oxygen. Because the planes served dual functions, however, they could not be marked with a red cross on a white background as outlined by the Geneva Conventions and would be fair game for the enemy.

Medics were assigned from existing troops, but to fill the MAETS rosters with nurses, Grant had to publicize his need for registered nurses willing to fly at a time when most people in the country had never been on a plane. It wasn't until January 1943, several months later, that sixty-year-old Roosevelt became the first American president to travel by aircraft on official business when he crossed the Atlantic to attend the Casablanca Conference with Allied leaders, a meeting which resulted in the demand for nothing less than "unconditional surrender" of Axis powers. With the waters of the Atlantic infested with German U-boats, Roosevelt's advisors had reluctantly agreed to let him travel to the meeting on a Pan Am Boeing 314 flying boat accompanied by fighter planes.

On top of concerns over flying, Grant also faced a nursing shortage. The day the Japanese attacked Pearl Harbor, the Army's roster listed only 7,043 available nurses. A massive propaganda campaign urging young women to join the Army or Navy nurse corps had been unleashed to help fill the need. Posters with slogans like "Become a nurse: Your country needs you" and "Save his life...and find your own" were distributed throughout the country. High school and college students watched filmstrips like *Uncle Sam Needs Nurses* and *No Greater Glory,* while radio and magazine advertisements and stories bombarded young women with patriotic appeals. The January 5, 1942, cover of *Life* magazine pictured the face of a young nurse and the line "Wanted: 50,000 nurses." Even First Lady Eleanor Roosevelt, who had four sons serving in the military, pleaded in an editorial in the *American Journal of Nursing* in August 1942 for young women to join. "I ask for my boys what every mother has the right to ask — that they be given full and adequate nursing care should the time come when they need it. Only you nurses who have not yet volunteered can give it.... You must not forget that you have in your power to bring back some who otherwise surely will not return."

Despite well-publicized risks to nurses and the country's overall nursing shortage, Grant had little trouble recruiting young women for the program, officially designated the School of Air Evacuation in June 1943. Five hundred nurses had put their names on the waiting list to join by that summer despite the deaths of two of the program's recent graduates.

The first member of air evacuation killed was a flight surgeon and member of the 801st MAETS. First Lt. Burton A. Hall, a married thirty-year-old from Philadelphia, Pennsylvania, with a three-year-old son, died in January 1943 in a plane crash over the South Pacific. His body was never recovered. In late July, 2nd Lt. Ruth Gardiner, a 29-year-old from Indianapolis, Indiana, became the first flight nurse to die when she was killed in a plane crash while on an air evacuation mission near Naknek, Alaska, with the 805th. Gardiner, who posthumously became the first woman or nurse to have an Army hospital named after her, had graduated with the first class of flight nurses in February.

Though accidents were a major threat and would take the lives of several air evacuation personnel in the course of the war, the dangers of being captured or caught in the line of fire were also very real for all medical personnel. One of the most publicized events occurred when dozens of military nurses became Japanese prisoners of war in 1942 as Bataan and Corregidor fell. Malnourished and ill, they remained POWs until February 1945 while they cared for other sick captives under grueling conditions.

To help ensure that the nurses willing to volunteer for air evacuation could handle the physical demands of the job, they were required to be between 21 and 36 years old, weigh between 105 and 135 pounds, and stand between 62 and 72 inches tall. The AAF also wanted women who had experience flying, but it wasn't deemed essential, as the instructors quickly figured out in training who was suited for the rigors of flight and who wasn't. As with the nurses in the 807th, those who showed interest were "taken aloft and flown through various maneuvers until they have proved themselves 'air-worthy' and capable of giving efficient service."

With their instruction at Bowman behind them and the sound of whistles from nearby trains filling the air, the men and women of the 807th were one step closer to their journey overseas. As the train chugged out of the Louisville station, the squadron's commanding officer, Captain McKnight, revealed the 807th's port of embarkation — Camp Kilmer, New Jersey. Word spread fast through the two cars as those on board settled in for the long ride.

CHAPTER 2

Destination Unknown

The squadron traveled for nearly twenty-four hours in the scorching summer temperatures before arriving at Camp Kilmer. When their last train finally stopped in New Jersey, their uniforms were covered with soot. They'd had to choose between opening the cars' screened windows to get fresh air and getting blasted by the coal-fired locomotive's smoke or keeping the windows closed and suffering in the heat.

It was about ten in the morning when they first glimpsed Camp Kilmer, a 1,500-acre staging area for troops going overseas that had been completed in mid-1942. Named after the World War I poet Joyce Kilmer who was killed in action in the Aisne-Marne offensive, Camp Kilmer and its rows of wooden barracks functioned more like a small city, with a post office, telephone centers, chapels, theaters, libraries, and a thousand-bed hospital. To help keep the troops entertained, young female volunteers, dubbed "Kilmer Sweethearts," served food and danced with soldiers at a

USO club. The USO also hosted shows, which included occasional performances by Hollywood stars such as bombshell Betty Grable and the "King of Swing," Benny Goodman.

During their six-day stay, those in the 807th were given final medical exams, their gear and records were double-checked, and they received instructions on what not to reveal in letters back home in case their correspondence was to fall into enemy hands. After being repeatedly told to avoid giving any details, one of the nurses sitting near Jens at dinner announced, "I wrote my boyfriend today and told him the wind was blowing, but damn if I'll tell him which direction." Even the long-distance calls they were allowed to make were monitored, with military operators prepared to end them if those on the phone mentioned the camp or their orders. The 807th still, however, did not know exactly where they were headed.

It was a busy few days, but after passing final inspections they were given twelve-hour passes. "Many fellows took advantage of passes...and the only regret was that the time limit was against them and they couldn't put enough liquor on board for the long journey ahead," wrote one of the 807th's enlisted men. While some spent their time blowing off steam, others, like Jens and Rutkowski, visited the sites in New York City. Patriotic well-wishers surrounded Rutkowski and another nurse when they stopped for cheesecake at the landmark restaurant Reuben's and enjoyed a night at the celebrated 21 Club, where they chatted with new friends until four thirty in the morning. They barely made it back to Camp Kilmer by their curfew at six a.m. The break was short-lived, however, and when the members of the 807th returned, they were restricted to the camp in anticipation of their departure.

Close to midnight on the evening of August 16, they received word that they were leaving for the ship that would take them overseas. Nurses, medics, and everyone else in the 807th strapped on their helmets, slung their canvas musette bags and gas masks over their shoulders, and grabbed their barracks bags. If any of them had any doubts about whether they were going off to war, all they had to do was glance in a mirror.

After a mile hike to the train station, a train ride, and a ferry ride across the Hudson River to a pier in New York, the 807th arrived just as the sun rose over an eerily dark city. The U.S. Army had ordered a nightly dim-out along the East Coast to prevent ships in the harbor from being silhouetted against the bright lights after Germany had deployed a series of successful U-boat attacks in attempts to damage the vital supply line to Britain. The attacks had started with the mid-January 1942 assault on the British steamer *Cyclops* as it sailed near Cape Cod and continued throughout the Atlantic. U-boat commanders called their victories the "American Shooting Season" and the "Second Happy Time," referring to their earlier success in the second half of 1940 when U-boats had sunk three million tons of Allied shipping. In the first six months of 1942, U-boats destroyed 171 ships off the East Coast of the United States, 62 in the Gulf of Mexico, and 141 in the Caribbean Sea. Most of the ships attacked were slower supply ships, but troopships were also targeted.

At the Casablanca Conference in January 1943, President Roosevelt and British Prime Minister Winston Churchill had agreed that winning the U-boat battle had to be the Allies' priority if they were to complete the buildup of troops and supplies necessary to liberate Europe. Within months, the Allies had a new strategy in place that incorporated increased sea and air escorts and advanced radar. Though the tactic was successful in curtailing the attacks on the American East Coast, German submarines continued to pose a threat to Allied ships.

Loaded down with gear, the 807th approached the gangplank that led to the *Santa Elena,* a former Grace Line cruise ship. A brass band on the pier belted out the hit song "Pistol Packin' Mama" while young women serving as Red Cross volunteers handed the men and women coffee and doughnuts.

Once on board, the nurses and flight surgeons were crammed into staterooms. A few of the nurses were assigned quarters in the brig, while the medics bunked in one of the ship's holds, which, in its civilian days, would have stored cargo. Though the officers had their own bunks, the enlisted men were assigned two to a bed and had to take shifts sleeping.

For the next twenty-four hours, more troops boarded the *Santa Elena* in the August heat until several thousand were squeezed onto a ship built for a few hundred, and it took on the smells of a locker room. By noon, the ship's lines to the pier were finally raised, the sound of whistles pierced the air, and the *Santa Elena* gave a slight lurch before sailing into the harbor and becoming part of a large convoy of ships.

Navy airplanes and blimps flew over the convoy initially as it sliced its way through the water. The sight of the Statue of Liberty faded in the distance as emotions on board ran high. Some, including Rutkowski, were filled with thoughts of their parents who had told stories of first seeing the Statue of Liberty when they arrived in the country as immigrants, while others wondered what it would be like to go to war.

The convoy soon entered the open sea and began to zigzag across water as smooth as glass to make it more difficult for U-boats to project its course and successfully fire on it. On board the *Santa Elena,* wild speculations on its final destination ran from one end of the ship to the other.

Time on the ship passed slowly, with the exception of the required abandon-ship and battle-station drills, which kept the passengers on alert. Officers walked the decks reserved for their use, while enlisted men cleaned their weapons or played poker games in the ship's former library. Though they couldn't officially play for money, they stuffed cash into tin boxes under the tables. To avoid sleeping in the suffocating hold, many of the enlisted men fought for space outside each night, while the officers sweated in their fatigues; the portholes in their rooms were covered because of blackout regulations.

By the time the *Santa Elena* passed through the Strait of Gibraltar, the narrow channel between Spain and northern Africa that connected the Atlantic Ocean with the Mediterranean Sea, ten days later, the large convoy had broken into smaller ones. Those still traveling with the *Santa Elena* were joined by two camouflaged British aircraft carriers for increased security. When the former cruise line ship was well into the Mediterranean, the personnel were given olive-drab bags filled with cans of foot and louse powder, a booklet of Arabic, French, and Italian phrases, and a copy of *Reader's Digest* magazine that featured an article on penicillin. It was the first time Hayes had read about the use of this newly available antibiotic.

In the early evening of September 1, as many on board watched a movie featuring beloved actress Alice Faye, other ships in the convoy sent up red flares into the night sky. Some on the decks of the *Santa Elena* marveled at their beauty, unaware of their significance as warning signals. Jens was sitting on one of the boxes stashed with life preservers and was trying to glimpse the coast of Africa when she heard aircraft approach. Seconds later, fighter planes dove toward the convoy and fired at them, and the ship reverberated as its guns fired back. Alarm bells pierced the night as a voice came over the loudspeaker and ordered, "Clear the decks! Clear the decks! Air raid! Get below!" Those who weren't wearing their life jackets as ordered rushed to put them on. Jens sprinted down a staircase, and Hayes, who was already below deck, reported to his battle-aid station. The station was below the anti-aircraft guns, and every time the powerful guns fired, the room shook.

Another short burst of gunfire exploded into the air before the raid ended. One of the destroyers in the convoy had received a direct hit, and several men were wounded. Though the *Santa Elena* was unharmed, the baptism of fire left those in the 807th wide-eyed and wondering what else was coming their way.

The following night at dusk, they found their answer as the ringing of another alarm sent everyone on board running for cover. As the moments passed, there was no sign of enemy planes, but word spread that they were under a submarine attack. After an all clear sounded, they learned that a torpedo fired by a submarine had just missed the bow of the ship as it changed course.

The *Santa Elena* may have had luck on her side on that trip, but three months later that luck ran out when a German plane dropped a torpedo that struck her hull while she navigated the Mediterranean. Roughly seventeen hundred Canadians, including some one hundred nurses, were forced to abandon her and were rescued by another ship traveling in the convoy. The following morning the

Santa Elena was accidentally rammed by another transport under tow and sank, killing several crewmen.

The *Santa Elena* arrived in the Bay of Bizerte outside Tunis in the morning on September 4 with five other ships from their convoy, and it was only then that the men and women of the 807th learned it was where they would disembark.

When the members of the squadron finally stood on firm ground later that day for the first time in weeks and piled their barracks bags on the dock, they stood in awe of the destruction all around them. Bizerte's strategic location along the Mediterranean allowed whoever controlled it to also control the Strait of Sicily. In German hands in 1942, Bizerte had fallen to British and American forces in May 1943 after bitter fighting during the North African Campaign, and the area now lay in ruins.

A handful of men from the squadron, including Hayes, remained on the docks to watch over the 807th's bags, while McKnight and the others boarded a nearby barge that took them across a channel to waiting jeeps and toward the loud whistles and gasps of tanned soldiers who noticed the twenty-five nurses headed their way.

After traveling over bumpy roads and hiking a short distance, the squadron arrived at its temporary desert campsite, home to thousands of men waiting for their next orders. The camp was chaotic, with tents pitched in every direction, mess kits hanging from trees, and wet clothes strewn about to dry.

As they found a spot to rest, those in the 807th opened their first C rations and swigged water from their canteens while flies buzzed around them. The rations consisted of two tin cans, one filled with stew, hash, or chili, and the other containing biscuits, candy, a few sheets of toilet paper, some powdered coffee, and cigarettes. Originally intended for troops to eat for a day or two, the bland and monotonous C rations would feed them and soon make them cringe.

It didn't take long for the squadron to realize that the nurses were the only women at the camp, and there was no getting away from the extra attention they attracted. While the enlisted men set up their pup tents, the nurses were welcomed with their own large tent already outfitted with twenty-five cots and electric lights from a generator. Other soldiers dug latrines for the nurses, and a few even dug foxholes for them. That same evening, British officers came by and invited the nurses to their tents across the road for tea and offered them the use of the shower they had rigged. One member of the 807th wrote, "It was soon apparent that our area would be besieged by soldiers coming to see what an American woman looked like, having so much time elapse from their last contact with them."

The differences between the men and the women, however, were quickly forgotten the following night when those in the camp found themselves thinking only of their survival. When they first heard gunfire, some of the nurses and doctors were on duty in the sick tent they'd established. With many of the enlisted men spending their free time swimming in the Mediterranean and walking on the beach, the medical personnel had kept busy removing old shrapnel from swimmers' feet and giving immunizations. Others in the 807th were sleeping in their tents or watching a movie outside.

As the noise grew and red flares erupted in the night sky, they realized they were in the middle of an air raid and scrambled for cover as shrapnel fell to the ground. "Still being rookies as far as war was concerned," one enlisted man of the 807th wrote, "it was taken more or less as a joke, but in less time than it takes to tell, each and every one had wished that [their foxhole] had been many times deeper and made of the heaviest timber available, because more hell broke loose than any of us had ever experienced." Those who hadn't dug their own foxholes as ordered tried to find room in someone else's as they choked on the sand swirling in the air. Jens crawled into the snug foxhole she'd built and covered it with branches as the British soldiers had taught her, to protect herself from the fragments of anti-aircraft shells that fell like rain. One of the flight surgeons kept yelling, "I'd like to get that guy that talked me into this!"

As Rutkowski ran for cover, a British lieutenant grabbed her arm and yelled, "Keep pumping!" The lieutenant guided her to an old German bunker now packed with a cot, a table, two chairs, and an opening in one wall through which soldiers were shooting anti-aircraft guns. He offered Rutkowski a chair and a glass of wine, and she eagerly accepted both. She hoped the wine would help calm her shaking hands. Watching the raid through the opening, she saw one of the flight surgeons, adrenaline pumping, lift a large log onto his shoulder, run toward a foxhole yelling, "Timber!" and throw the log over the top before jumping into the hole. When she saw him the next day, he was unable to move the log by himself.

The onslaught, aimed mostly at the ships in the harbor, finally ended after an hour, and the all clear was sounded, though further warnings continued throughout the night. One bomb had hit an oil tanker close to the *Santa Elena,* and though the blast rocked the ship and frightened those on board, including Hayes and the other men from the 807th, it was undamaged.

Those in the camp who'd chosen to play cards or go swimming over digging shelters as previously ordered furiously dug foxholes over the next few days. It was during this time that the 807th — along with the rest of the world — learned that Italy had capitulated to the Allies. Announced by Gen. Dwight D. Eisenhower on September 8, the surrender had been signed five days before by Marshal Pietro Badoglio, Italy's prime minister since the overthrow of Italian dictator Benito Mussolini in July. President Roosevelt warned the American people that, despite this triumph, the war in the Mediterranean had not yet been won. "The great news that you have heard from General Eisenhower does not give you license to settle back in your rocking chairs and say 'Well, that does it. We've got 'em on the run. Now we can start the celebration.' The time for celebration is not yet."

After several days in the camp trudging through ankle-deep sand, swatting at flies, and bathing in the ocean, the entire 807th, including those who had been ordered to stay with the ship, climbed in the back of military trucks and took a forty-mile ride through the desert to their next temporary home in eastern Tunisia near the capitol of Tunis. As the trucks drove along the desolate roads, they passed ancient Roman arches and a German fighter plane lying abandoned in the sands.

Word that twenty-five nurses were on their way reached the small town of Fochville before they did, and flyboys in P-47 Thunderbolts, P-38 Lightnings, and C-47 Skytrains, apparently eager to show off their skills and welcome the young women, buzzed the convoy as it arrived.

While most in the 807th settled into their new camp and waited anxiously for their next orders, the squadron's flight surgeons were sent to various stations in the Mediterranean to watch the more experienced 802nd — the first squadron activated from Bowman — in action. The rest of the men and women had little to do as they waited for the arrival of transportation and supplies.

An old apartment building in the town functioned as the 807th's temporary headquarters and as barracks for the men, while the nurses were billeted nearby in two small houses. Sports, movies, and gambling filled much of the men's time, while local children camped out in front of their barracks hoping they would be given candy bars for themselves and cigarettes for their parents. With a continuous supply of young officers offering to escort the nurses wherever they wanted to go, the women spent their days shopping in the few stores still open in the nearby capital of Tunis, going to see one of the AAF bands playing at a local club, or swimming on one of the beaches littered with debris from the war.

More than three weeks after its arrival in Fochville, the 807th finally learned it was being sent to Catania, a small town on the eastern side of Sicily. Catania would serve as its headquarters, and from there the nurses and medics would fly to evacuation stations around the Mediterranean to pick up patients and accompany them on flights to better equipped medical facilities. It was a welcome relief for those growing impatient to help the war effort.

As the 807th packed its gear and chartered planes to relocate the unit to Catania, the squadron was called into action. Lt. Edith A. Belden, a nurse from Illinois, and medic Lawrence Abbott flew from Fochville to Corsica to pick up patients and successfully delivered them to Algiers.

It was early October 1943 when the 807th arrived in Catania, and the Allies' recent victories were irrefutable. They had turned the tide in the Pacific by winning the Battle of Midway in 1942. By February 1943 they had achieved another series of victories in the southern Solomon Islands, and Hitler had suffered his first major defeat at Stalingrad. Three months later, the Allies had taken North Africa from the Germans and Italians, and on July 9, they had launched Operation Husky, which led to the successful invasion of Sicily. Mussolini had been deposed from power, and on September 3, the Allies' 15th Army Group, composed of the U.S. 5th Army and the British 8th Army, had landed on mainland Italy and forced Italy to surrender to the Allies.

In response to the invasion, Hitler had rushed more troops into Italy, including into Rome, sent in paratroopers to rescue Mussolini from prison, and appointed him as the leader of the German-controlled state in northern Italy. The Allies were now struggling to capture the Italian capital, slogging their way north through the country while battling a brutal enemy.

As the fighting exploded in Italy, the 807th set up its headquarters in a former military school that had recently housed German soldiers. From there, McKnight and the other flight surgeons assigned the nurses and medics to go to specific evacuation stations. The medics were also stationed in the same building while the nurses and other officers were billeted in a villa overlooking the Mediterranean in a town just north of Catania on the island's east coast. The setting was so picturesque that it was easy for some to forget, for just a moment, that the world was at war.

The nurses and medics began routinely evacuating patients from near the front lines to more fully equipped hospitals around the Mediterranean and were finally doing the work they had been trained to do. McKnight's four flight surgeons oversaw six flight teams consisting of one nurse and one medic who cared for up to twenty-four patients per flight. While in the air, responsibility for the patients ultimately fell to the registered nurses, who had far more medical training and experience than the medics. Heavy fighting and the resulting casualties, however, quickly required the teams to split up and handle flights on their own, with the nurses receiving the more severe cases. The 807th's primary responsibility was to care for British troops from the 8th Army advancing on the eastern side of Italy, while the 802nd was assigned to support American troops from the 5th Army as it made its way up Italy's western side.

To help with the casualties pouring in from the front lines near Foggia on the heel of Italy, McKnight sent flight surgeon Capt. Edward Phillips and a few enlisted men to start an evacuation station at Grottaglie, a small town less than 120 miles from the fighting. Wounded and sick patients who had already received some medical care were taken by plane from Grottaglie to designated facilities.

McKnight sent Hayes a short time later to temporarily help the British operate a station at Bari—just seventy miles from the fighting and as near to the front lines as transport planes could safely reach—until flight surgeon Capt. Philip Voigt could arrive and take over. While Voigt secured the use of transport planes that flew into Bari, and a Royal Air Force medical officer ran the holding unit, the men faced significant challenges with coordinating planes and patients, and dealing with the unpredictable autumn weather. "Weather, no planes, no patients; too many patients, too many planes, delays in arrival of patients . . . lack of cooperation on the part of the hospitals, failure to have planes gassed up, delay in unloading freight, all conspire to make the job a hectic one," wrote one member of the 807th.

Flights also required the nurses and medics to be ready for

anything, and they were. On one of Hayes's first runs, one of the plane's engines stopped, and the pilots, who seemed unfazed by the development, calmly adjusted their flight plan to pick up another plane. On one of Rutkowski's flights from Naples, she found the door of the plane missing. When she asked the pilot about it, he responded, "Yeah, we lost it on the way up." Her patients on that flight included one German prisoner of war along with seventeen British soldiers. During the flight, the British patients noticed the German POW, and, while eyeing the open door, the men "started on how best to assist him to walk home from seven thousand feet over the Mediterranean." The battle-weary British soldiers had just been in a fight with German troops a few hours before, and to Rutkowski's growing concern, they seemed to be seriously contemplating taking action against the POW. It took her a moment to realize she outranked them, but when she did, she hurled threats at them and reminded them that they were soldiers, not murderers, until they settled down.

After transporting their patients, the nurses and medics were on their own to find available flights back to the 807th's headquarters in Catania. They could usually board a plane within a few hours, but they all traveled with their canvas musette bags that carried personal items in case they had to stay for a night or two at one of the stations. A few of the medics and nurses, eager to get back to headquarters, caught rides on combat planes rather than waiting for space on a transport plane.

By the end of October, despite the difficulties faced by the flight surgeons coordinating personnel and planes and dealing with the weather, the 807th's hard work was paying off. In its first three weeks, the squadron evacuated 1,651 patients to more advanced hospitals for further care.

CHAPTER 3

Flying Blind

In the early morning hours of November 8, as they brushed away thoughts of sleep, thirteen of the 807th's flight nurses, ranging from twenty-two to thirty-two years old, boarded jeeps outside their Sicilian villa. Almost all wore grayish-green field coats over their slate-blue wool uniforms and carried musette bags packed with a few extra clothes, books, and magazines. The sky was clear for the first time in days, but most of the women, if not all, wore galoshes over their military shoes to protect them from the muddy airfield.

Capt. Robert Simpson, a thirty-two-year-old flight surgeon from Washington, DC, traveled with the nurses to the airfield that morning to find out the latest weather forecast from the pilots. Storms had grounded the 807th for the past three days, and patients needing to be evacuated were piling up in Bari and Grottaglie. With so much work to be done, McKnight had decided to send half the squadron's medical personnel to help. It was the first, and last, time he sent so many on one plane.

The nurses and Simpson arrived at the Operations building, where they were joined by twelve of the 807th's medics dressed in their khaki wool uniforms, dark-green field jackets, and peaked hats with maroon piping that indicated they were part of the Medical Department. Knowing the muddy field's condition, most of the medics wore military leggings over their pants to keep them clean. Like many of the nurses, the medics had been driven to the airfield several times over the past few days only to have to return to their barracks when their flights were canceled. On one of the mornings, Hayes's driver, a former medic who refused to fly after experiencing bad weather weeks earlier and had been demoted, warned Hayes that one of these times he wouldn't come back. "I'd rather be a private than a dead T/3," he'd told Hayes, who dismissed the comment.

Though he knew none of the others, a medic from the 802nd, Cpl. Gilbert Hornsby, a twenty-one-year-old with a Kentucky drawl, was also joining the flight. After collecting his pay at the 802nd's headquarters in Palermo, Hornsby had flown to Catania and was hitching a ride to his assigned station at Bari.

The thirteen nurses and thirteen medics checked into Operations so their names could be added to the flight manifest and they could be weighed to ensure that their transport plane was under its weight limit. Their plane that morning was a C-53D Skytrooper, a variant of the rugged Douglas C-47 Skytrain. Nicknamed "the Gooney Bird" by American soldiers and dubbed a "Dakota" by the British, the C-47 was later considered by Eisenhower to be one of the most vital pieces of military equipment used in the campaigns in Africa and Europe. The aircraft served in every theater in the war. Almost identical to the C-47, the C-53 was designed specifically to carry paratroops and tow troop-carrying gliders and, as a result, lacked the C-47's large cargo door and reinforced floor.

Since the War Department had been given the responsibility of evacuating sick and wounded men to the AAF, the AAF had used C-53s and C-47s, among a few other planes, to pick up patients and medical personnel on their return flights from forward areas. Thousands of C-47s were built during the war, but only a few hundred of the C-53s were ever constructed. Both versions lacked firepower; and, if attacked by the enemy while traveling without an escort, the pilots knew their only chance was to try to outwit the enemy.

The four-man flight crew waiting near the plane had never flown together before this mission but were all members of the 61st Troop Carrier Squadron of the 314th Troop Carrier Group, which had dropped paratroops into Sicily during the invasion in July. The crew had flown the plane from their new base in Castel-vetrano on the other side of the island to Catania the day before, expecting to transport the 807th personnel. The pilot, First Lt. Charles Thrasher, had canceled the trip, however, because of bad weather and reports that a B-25 pilot had been forced to turn back.

A dark-haired twenty-two-year-old, Thrasher was from a prom-inent Daytona Beach, Florida, family and had attended Bolles Military Academy, where he was one of its top athletes and was known for his jitterbug moves on the dance floor. He had enlisted in 1941 and had just been promoted the previous month from second lieutenant to first lieutenant, which made him the senior officer on board that morning's flight—despite also being the youngest officer.

His copilot was 2nd Lt. James Baggs, a charming and outgoing twenty-eight-year-old from Savannah, Georgia, who enlisted in 1942 and kept a photo of his five-year-old nephew Hunter in the cockpit whenever he flew to remind him of home. Like Thrasher, Baggs had also attended a military school, the Academy of Richmond County, in Augusta, Georgia. He later trained as a fighter pilot at Foster Field in Texas before being selected for special training as a troop carrier pilot and had already flown one hundred missions.

Sgt. Willis Shumway, a six-foot-tall, twenty-three-year-old from Tempe, Arizona, who dreamed of becoming a photographer, filled in for the plane's regular crew chief. Sgt. Richard "Dick" Lebo, another twenty-three-year-old from Halifax, Pennsylvania, an avid athlete who raced pigeons and liked to write in his spare time, served as the radio operator.

Jens was the first of the medical personnel to board the plane, and she sat toward the front in one of the metal bucket seats lining each side of the aircraft. Headstrong and independent, Jens had been looking for adventure when she left her nursing job at Henry Ford Hospital in Detroit and joined the Army in February 1941, ten months before the Japanese attacked Pearl Harbor. The Army immediately sent her to work at the station hospital at Fort Benning, a sprawling post near Columbus, Georgia. She'd never flown before and had paid extra to travel by plane instead of by train from Michigan just for the experience. She liked it so much that she and a fellow nurse had taken advantage of loose regulations to hitch rides at Lawson Army Airfield at Fort Benning during training flights, making sure they were back on base before anyone noticed their absence.

When she began her duties at the Army hospital, Jens did so without any military training. The training of ANC nurses at the time defaulted to whatever instruction their chief nurse could provide. As the Army's nursing recruitment efforts to remedy a major nursing shortage began to pay off, chief nurses became overwhelmed with the demands of training the newly enlisted on top of their other responsibilities. By the time the country entered the war, many of those who were appointed chief nurses were as new to the military as their trainees and lacked the necessary experience in teaching and protocol. In late 1942, the Office of the Surgeon General recognized the need for more formal instruction of nurses and issued guidelines that required them to have a month of instruction on everything from military courtesy and customs to physical training defense against chemical, mechanized, and air attacks.

As months of dinner dates and dancing ticked by, Jens had realized that life for her had changed very little since joining the Army, even as the rest of the world erupted into chaos. When the AAF put out a call for graduate nurses to join the air evacuation program in late 1942, she was excited at the prospect of a job that promised travel, adventure, and flying.

Several of the other nurses who followed Jens on board the plane that morning had worked as airline stewardesses before the war, including Rutkowski. For years, some airlines had required stewardesses to be nurses after they recognized that many skittish passengers fearful of flying took comfort in having the trained women on flights. Gertrude "Tooie" Dawson from Vandergrift, Pennsylvania, Pauleen Kanable from Richland Center, Wisconsin, and Ann E. Kopsco from Hammond, Louisiana, who was almost always referred to as Ann E., were also former stewardesses. Others who piled into the plane that morning had worked in hospitals or in private nursing before they joined the Army and had responded to the country's pleas for nurses to join the military.

The youngest of the women was curly-haired Lillian Tacina, who, like Jens and Rutkowski, had grown up in Michigan. Tacina, or "Tassy" as the other nurses called her, was from Hamtramck and was one of five children. Like many of those on board that morning, she had siblings who were also in the military. Elna Schwant from Winner, South Dakota, had a younger brother Willard, a lieutenant junior grade in the Navy Reserve who had been missing in action since August. He had been a copilot on a patrol bomber in the Atlantic Ocean when the crew reported seeing an enemy submarine and was preparing to destroy it. The plane was never heard from again.

Also on board were Ann Maness from Paris, Texas; Ann "Marky" Markowitz who, like Watson, was from Chicago; Frances Nelson from Princeton, West Virginia; Helen Porter from Hanksville, Utah; and Wilma Lytle from Butler, Kentucky. Of the thirteen, only Watson and Nelson were married.

The thirteen medics, including Hayes, Owen, Abbott, and Wolf, followed the nurses into the cabin and filled the empty seats. Hayes had always loved planes. He'd been fascinated by them since his dad, who had served in World War I as an airplane mechanic, first pointed at one that was flying over their home when Hayes was just four years old. In high school Hayes had dreamed of becoming an aeronautical engineer. He'd first wanted to be a pilot, but he knew his poor eyesight ruled that out.

When Hayes graduated in 1940, his family couldn't afford to send him to college, so he held a series of odd jobs until he was drafted and reported for duty in Indianola on November 3, 1942. He was immediately sent to Camp Barkeley, Texas, where he learned, to his disappointment, that he had been assigned to the Medical Department. He started his training as a sanitary technician, a specialty within the Medical Department designed to help prevent the spread of diseases, and found, much to his surprise, that he enjoyed it. He finished the program, and the Army shipped him to Bowman Field, where he started working with McKnight in setting up a dispensary. When McKnight was made commanding officer of the 807th, he asked Hayes to join as a flight medic, a request Hayes gladly accepted.

Paul Allen from Greenville, Kentucky, the youngest in the group at only nineteen, boarded the plane and sat across from Jens. Also from Kentucky, from a small town that shared his last name, was William Eldridge, who'd worked for the Pennsylvania Railroad before the war. The oldest of the men was thirty-six-year-old Robert Cranson from New Haven, New York, one of four medics who were married. The other three included Wolf, Gordon MacKinnon from Los Angeles, California, and Charles Zeiber, an easygoing twenty-six-year-old newlywed from Reading, Pennsylvania. Also on board were Jim Cruise from Brockton, Massachusetts; Raymond Ebers from Steeleville, Illinois; the odd man out, Hornsby from the 802nd; and Charles Adams of Niles, Michigan, whose brother had been taken prisoner by the Japanese on Wake Island in December 1941 and was being held in a prison camp in Shanghai.

Two of the passengers were never intended to be on the flight. Abbott had switched places at the last minute with one of the other 807th's medics so he could repay a twenty-five-dollar loan to Voigt, the 807th flight surgeon at Bari; and Rutkowski had learned early that morning that Stakeman, their chief nurse, had accidentally added her to the roster for the day. Rutkowski brought the number of nurses on board to thirteen instead of the twelve McKnight had requested. Since she had already gotten up early, however, she decided to go and help the others.

With the differences in rank and having completed most of their training separately, the nurses and medics exchanged polite but friendly hellos as they settled into their seats and buckled their belts for the roughly two-hour flight to Bari. Flight surgeon Simpson, who had come with the nurses that morning, had also boarded the plane to get an update on the weather, and the pilots came into the cabin to speak with him. Checking the weather along and adjacent to the planned line of flight was as critical a task for all pilots before takeoff as checking the fuel supply. Thrasher told Simpson the weather reports were favorable enough to fly, with scattered showers but no mention of thunderstorms. Bari was open and Grottaglie, currently closed, was expected to open. Satisfied, Simpson took his leave, and the pilots returned to the cockpit.

Crew chief Shumway secured the passenger door as the pilots took their seats in the cockpit, and Lebo settled into his separate radio compartment behind the cockpit. Around eight thirty a.m., Thrasher received clearance and pushed the throttles forward, bringing the plane's two engines to life. The passengers sat back in their seats and listened to the familiar roar of the engines as the C-53D took to the sky. During the climb, they could see the island's rolling hills pass below them as they edged northeast toward the toe of Italy. The plane reached its initial cruising altitude quickly, and within fifteen minutes the coast of Calabria in southern Italy was in their sight.

Most of the nurses and medics had already traveled on a handful of evacuation flights, and they quickly relaxed. Some paged through magazines or books, while others talked or tried to catch a few extra minutes of rest. Watson read a book and looked forward to the dinner she and other nurses traveling to Bari planned to have with some of the men from a B-25 squadron. During her previous stays at Bari, they had spent the evenings with them dancing or playing poker in a small room where a single record with "Tuxedo Junction" on one side and "A String of Pearls" on the other was played over and over. She'd run into a few of the men from the squadron in Catania that morning and had wanted to accompany them on their flight, but had been denied, since the 807th had an entire plane designated for their use that day.

In the short time it took the plane to reach the Italian peninsula, ominous clouds had formed in the path ahead. The pilots continued on, hoping the weather would improve, but as time passed and conditions grew worse, they became even more concerned. The nurses and medics in the cabin were also growing worried as they continued to peer out the plane's windows.

At about ten thirty a.m., the flight crew contacted the control tower at Bari to obtain an updated weather report. With weather-related information less than seven days old classified as confidential, aircraft had to have the proper IFF code. Recently developed by the British, the Identification Friend or Foe (IFF) system used a simple shortwave radio that sent coded signals when interrogated by a ground station to help identify which planes were friendly. If the aircraft did not send back the correct signal, it was assumed to be hostile. For unknown reasons, Lebo and the pilots did not have the codes and were refused.

Rather than continue up the toe as they had planned, Thrasher decided to turn right in a more northeasterly direction in an attempt to fly around the system they were currently in. The plan was to make it to the heel of Italy's boot and then follow the coastline northwest to Bari. When they reached the heel, however, even darker, more menacing clouds awaited them. Though they contacted the control tower repeatedly, their requests for weather information continued to be denied because they were not able to provide the codes.

As they changed course once again and followed the coastline, the murky waters churned beneath them. In an attempt to stay below the cloud ceiling, they continued to descend to as low as four hundred feet above sea level. Thick fog soon rolled in and quickly covered the shoreline as thunderstorms and high winds began to rock the plane and the nerves of the nurses and medics.

They were getting closer to Bari, and the weather and visibility had not improved. At ten fifty and again at eleven twenty, the crew asked the station to activate its beacon to help guide them in landing, but without the codes the control tower at Bari again refused to assist. At approximately eleven thirty-five, with no airport in sight and poor visibility continuing, the flight crew again contacted Bari control and asked for a radio fix so they could determine the direction of the airport and fly toward it. This time Bari control replied that it did not have the equipment to provide a fix. At eleven forty-five, more than three hours after takeoff, the crew asked the control tower yet again to turn on the beacon. The tower finally agreed and turned the beacon on for about ten minutes. This was the last message they received from Bari control.

Soon after the approval was received, the plane lost all radio communication. Lebo tried desperately to reestablish it, while the pilots realized the apparently faulty magnetic compass was no longer functioning properly. The flight crew was now acutely aware of the difficult situation they faced. They had lost all radio communication, they had no beacon signal from the airport, they had a nonfunctioning magnetic compass, and they had poor visibility with little ground reference to navigate. They were flying blind.

Someone from the cabin shouted, "Look out there!" and several turned to see two waterspouts about three hundred feet from the plane. Hayes had heard about waterspouts, powerful tornadoes that formed over water, and had even seen pictures, but he'd never imagined how violent they could be. He watched as the large columns of water rose up from the Adriatic Sea. They had appeared suddenly, and he began to worry that if another formed closer to the plane they would all be killed. Thrasher came back to the cabin to talk with the passengers, while Baggs flew the plane. He told them they were going to try to climb above the clouds and away from the immediate threat. Shortly after, the C-53D once again ascended as the passengers watched the wingtips appear and disappear in the thick clouds until they finally broke through. Bright sunlight suddenly lit up the cabin, and, for the moment, they were out of danger.

Their luck did not last for long. At the higher altitude the unheated cabin grew cold quickly, and some began to shiver in their seats. The crew all had flying jackets and all but three of the nurses wore thicker field coats with liners, but the medics only had their lighter field jackets. They were above eight thousand feet, but they couldn't stay there for long. At this altitude, the outside temperature was about thirty degrees Fahrenheit. The wings were starting to ice. If too much ice formed and disrupted the flow of air, the plane wouldn't be able to stay aloft. Transport planes were usually equipped with de-icing boots—rubber shoes on the leading edges of the wings. When turned on, the de-icing boots inflated and deflated to break up the ice. The plane's de-icing boots, however, were lying in the back of the cabin along with the 807th's medical and musette bags. The regular crew chief had removed them for the summer to make flying more efficient and had not yet reinstalled them, adding to the numerous problems those on board already faced.

The pilots found an opening in the clouds and managed to navigate down through it as the passengers braced themselves in their seats against the sudden descent and sharp bank made by the plane. After several minutes, the aircraft leveled out just under the ceiling. They were now flying over water and were about a quarter mile away from a rugged coastline of mountains that soared hundreds of feet in the air. In the middle of this endless expanse of cliffs stood a small strip of beach no bigger than the plane. Thrasher once again came back to the cabin and told the passengers that he suspected that they were somewhere off the western coast of Italy though he didn't know which side of the combat line they were on. He thought they should try to make a water landing and head for the beach given the severe weather, the amount of fuel they had left, and his concerns over what they would face if they continued flying.

Parachuting out of the plane wasn't an option; there were only a handful of parachutes on board in addition to an emergency parachute that could be used for dropping supplies to someone on the ground. Though each of the nurses and medics had been issued a parachute at Bowman Field, the chutes were among equipment that had been shipped to them in Italy but had never arrived. Only 20 out of 155 boxes had eventually turned up in

Catania, and everything from flashlights to the parachutes had been lost or stolen.

The passengers took an inventory of the life preservers hanging on a cable at the back of the cargo bay. There were twenty-eight Mae Wests. That wouldn't be enough to help the thirty souls on board. Hayes and Owen, both experienced swimmers, volunteered to go without life jackets since they'd had the most water-survival training in Kentucky, while Shumway, the crew chief, moved to a seat by the passenger door to be in position to open it when they landed. They were as ready as they would ever be.

Just then, the pilots spotted an airfield, and Thrasher told the passengers they were going to try to land there instead. The field was about five miles inland and sandwiched between mountains. As they edged closer, the pilots flew over the runway to check the conditions. Some who peered out the window could see small buildings on the west side of the field and German fighter planes along the other side. Having seen their fair share of abandoned German planes, they didn't give them much thought. They were more anxious to get out of the severe weather. The pilots circled the field and decided to take their chances. They set up on final approach, lowered the landing gear, and locked it into position. When they neared the end of the runway and were about fifty feet from the ground, a bullet suddenly hit the tail of the plane as anti-aircraft fire erupted from below. Someone was shooting at them. At the same time, the once idle fighter planes came to life and scrambled on the runway.

Thrasher jammed the throttle forward and began a sharp climb in a desperate attempt to get out of firing range. In the excitement of preparing to land on the airfield, however, the pilots had forgotten to switch the fuel tanks. The main tank was running on the small amount of gas that remained, and the engines were stopping. The pilots quickly flipped the switch to change tanks, and the plane bucked at the demand before climbing back into the air.

As the plane gained altitude, a mountainside loomed ahead. The aircraft was within a few hundred feet of slamming into a rocky cliff, but Thrasher turned the plane steeply to the right so that its wings were parallel to the jagged bluff. It was a close call. As the pilots intentionally flew through more clouds, hoping to elude the fighter planes, mountains popped into their view, and they made several more steep turns just in time to avoid them.

When they thought they might be in the clear, they ascended high enough to regain their bearings and could see patches of blue sky. That's when one of the passengers yelled, "What's that plane doing?" A Focke-Wulf Fw190, a German fighter plane dubbed the "Butcher Bird," flew toward them. Without any fire-power, the American pilots' only chance was to outmaneuver the other plane. Thrasher plunged the C-53D into the clouds again, where it remained for fifteen minutes, but when it emerged, the plane was once again in the direct path of a Focke-Wulf. Unsure whether it was the same one or another fighter, the pilots knew they were in trouble. They once again retreated to the clouds, but they couldn't stay hidden forever. The landscape below had changed from rugged mountains to rolling hills, but there was only a clearance of roughly four hundred feet between the tops of the hills and the cloud ceiling. They passed another airfield but decided the chance of a German presence made it too risky to attempt another landing.

Just when it seemed that their luck had run out, the pilots spotted a small lake. It appeared to have reached all the way to the surrounding hills when it was full, but at that time the water had retreated, which left a small patch of open ground. When Thrasher announced they were going to try to land, some of the passengers wondered whether the patch was large enough for a transport plane, but they had no choice but to put their confidence in the pilots. It was around one thirty p.m., and they'd been in the air for about five hours.

Shumway stashed away the de-icing boots and the passenger-loading ladder in the bathroom to prepare for the crash landing and remained in the back of the plane. The nurses and medics remained quiet as they tried to deal with the fears and uncertainties plaguing each of them and do as they had been trained. They braced themselves as best they could. Jens was among those who put her head on her knees and wrapped her arms around her legs, while the pilots lowered the landing gear.

The plane approached the lake and followed the contour of the hill to the landing site. When the wheels finally touched, the plane seemed less than a few hundred feet from the waterline. Both pilots stood on the brakes as the plane careened along the ground still saturated with water. The landing gear slowly sank in the mud until it was completely submerged, bringing the plane to a violent stop. The passengers felt like they'd hit a wall. The force embedded the plane's nose in the marshy land, and as the tail flipped up, the medical and musette bags plummeted through the cabin. The fuselage hovered upright for a few seconds before falling back to the ground in a belly flop.

Though the seatbelts kept the other passengers buckled in, Shumway had buttressed himself against the fuselage frame toward the back of the plane, and the sudden stop loosened his grip. He flew through the air, hitting Watson in the face with his foot before landing in the front of the cabin while a toolbox weighing seventy pounds bounced down the center of the plane and narrowly missed him. Shumway lay on the floor against the bulkhead, disoriented and unable to move. His knee seemed to have taken the brunt of the collision. The impact of his foot left Watson with a split lower lip, a cut under her right eye, loose upper teeth, and the beginnings of a black eye.

The other dazed passengers tried to get their bearings as the shock of the crash landing sank in. Fearing the possibility of a fire and following their training, some rushed to unbuckle their seatbelts and exit the plane. After they pushed the door open, they quickly stepped into the muddy ground, sinking with each step. Rain fell from a dark-gray sky as they moved away from the plane. Behind them lay the fuselage that was level with the ground and standing in several inches of water with no signs of smoke. The plane's propellers were bent, its nose was smashed, and one hole from gunfire was visible in the vertical stabilizer. As more of the medics and nurses piled out, they could see the damage to the plane, and they silently marveled at the fact that they had survived the attack and the crash landing. Beyond the lake bed where the plane had come to rest were dense, forested hills, and beyond those was what looked like an endless expanse of mountains. The men and women had been in the air for so long and become so disoriented that none of them knew where they were.

CHAPTER 4

In Enemy Territory

A few in the group, including Hayes, who were still inside the cabin, picked up Shumway as gently as they could and moved him so the pilots could get out of the cockpit and radio compartment and exit the plane. The nurses feared that Shumway had internal injuries and likely gave him a shot of morphine from their medical kits to help manage the pain. There was little else they could do. When the pilots emerged, one of them carried a Thompson submachine gun. The "tommy gun" was the only weapon among the group.

Concerned that the Germans might have spotted the plane when it flew over the second airfield and would send a patrol to investigate, the pilots and several of the medics decided to do a reconnaissance of the surrounding area. If it looked safe, they would head out and see what they could find.

Hayes and the rest of the scouting party had walked several hundred feet away from the plane when they saw a band of rugged-looking men come out of the woods. The strangers carried rifles on their backs and daggers at their sides and wore fezzes, or flat-crowned hats, emblazoned with red stars on the front. Their dark clothing consisted mostly of coarse woolen shirts and drawstring pants that ballooned at the hips and buttoned at the knees. Some wore thick socks with sandals made of old tire carcasses and jackets that looked like short capes with sleeves.

A stocky man with a handlebar mustache stepped forward and began speaking in an unfamiliar language. His face was so weathered it was difficult for the Americans to tell his age, though they would later learn he was only twenty-two years old. He asked in stilted, broken English if they were British. When Baggs, the copilot, replied they were Americans, he smiled and introduced himself as Hasan Gina, the leader of a group of partisans. He then answered the question they'd all been waiting for: they had landed in Albania.

Though the young Americans knew little about Albania, they would soon learn it was a small but wild land that had changed very little over the last several hundred years. The predominantly Muslim country, about the size of Maryland, was made up of countless poverty-stricken villages, a handful of towns, very few roads, and no railways. Deadly blood feuds and thievery proliferated, few homes had running water or electricity, clothes and shoes were mostly handmade, and pack mules and horses remained the main modes of transportation. Winters were especially brutal, and, for many people, starvation was a constant threat. Even so, the Albanians were proud of their homeland, which they affectionately called "the land of the eagle."

Just two months earlier, thousands of German troops had

occupied the country after Italy surrendered to the Allies, adding to a long list of foreign powers that had ruled Albania for most of its history. During the Ottoman Empire, which lasted for some five hundred years, much of the population had converted to Islam, though the country also included members of the Greek Orthodox Church, mostly in the south, and the Catholic Church, predominantly in the north. The country broke away from the Ottoman Empire in 1912 and declared its independence. The Great Powers of Europe—Austria-Hungary, Britain, Germany, Italy, France, and Russia—formally recognized an independent Albania the following year, but they refused to acknowledge the provisional government and appointed a German prince as its ruler. Prince Wilhem of Wied arrived in March 1914, but after just six months and with the outbreak of World War I, his regime collapsed, and chaos erupted throughout the country as local leaders fought for power.

European powers tried to divide Albania among its neighbors at the Paris Peace Conference in 1919, but in March 1920, U.S. President Woodrow Wilson blocked the plan, ensuring the country's territorial integrity. The United States also recognized an official Albanian representative to Washington; and later that year, Albania was admitted to the newly formed League of Nations, further cementing its independence.

Fighting within the country, however, continued until a clan chief named Ahmet Zogu officially became president in January 1925. He rewrote the constitution, eliminated his opponents, and, by 1928, had crowned himself King Zog. In the meantime, Mussolini had made himself dictator in Italy. When Albania needed economic aid and was refused a loan by the League of Nations, Zog turned to Mussolini, whose help came with substantial political and economic strings. Over the next decade, Italy's influence in the country grew, and on Good Friday, April 7, 1939, more than twenty thousand Italian troops invaded and occupied the country with almost no resistance. King Zog, his wife, and two-day-old son fled to Greece.

Albania remained under Italy's control until Italy's surrender to the Allies in September 1943. Germany, Italy's former partner, immediately invaded the country with little resistance from the Italian divisions still stationed there or from the Albanian people. To curry favor with the ruling elite, the Germans quickly set up a regency council made up of prominent Albanians from the country's major religions and offered Albania a level of self-governance much greater than it had under the Italians.

With the arrival of the Germans, tensions between the two main resistance factions, both of which had developed within the country during the Italian occupation, escalated quickly. Communists such as former schoolteacher Enver Hoxha, the country's future ruthless dictator, and Mehmet Shehu, who had bragged that he had "personally cut the throats of seventy Italian [military police] who had been taken prisoner," had created the partisan movement known as the Lëvizja Nacional Çlirimtarë, or National Liberation Movement. They were estimated to have a force of up to five thousand troops and could rally up to ten thousand. Those who were anticommunist and antimonarchist, many of whom were part of the ruling class, had created the Balli Kombëtar (BK, or Ballists), or National Front, in response and were thought to be able to muster about three thousand soldiers. The BK fought for a return to a Greater Albania, which would bring together all ethnic Albanians. A newly formed third group, the Legality Party, wanted to reinstate King Zog, but only numbered between one thousand and two thousand forces.

In early November, the differences between the partisans and the BK had erupted into a bloody battle—largely to see who would control Albania after the war. Meanwhile the Germans were launching the first of several antipartisan operations in what would become known as the Winter Offensive. The Americans of the 807th didn't know it yet, but they were not only trapped behind Nazi lines, they were also caught in the middle of a civil war.

As the Americans tried to recall anything they knew about Albania, Baggs asked Gina and the other partisans if they were friends of Draža Mihailović, the leader of a resistance group battling the Germans in Yugoslavia. Though Mihailović was fighting the Germans, he was also fighting the communist-dominated partisans in Yugoslavia, Gina's brothers-in-arms. Gina frowned in disapproval at the question and turned away to speak to his men. When he addressed the Americans once again, he responded sternly that the partisans were not friends with Mihailović, and if they thought the Americans were they would shoot them.

The severe reply shocked the Americans, who were still trying to take in the surreal scene before them. Just that morning they had been at headquarters in Catania, and now they were in the hands of Gina and his battle-hardened men who could easily kill them without anyone ever knowing their fate. Though they knew they were hardly the first military personnel to be stranded in enemy territory, the gravity of their situation was becoming apparent.

Gina, who had a habit of adding "my dear" to all of his statements regardless of whom he addressed, further revealed to the men and women that he and his men had been preparing to shoot down their plane with a machine gun they had in the woods until they saw a white star painted on the fuselage. Gina thought the white star might be a symbol used on American planes, as he'd seen in newspapers and magazines, and had ordered his men not to shoot.

The Americans later learned that Gina had learned English at the prestigious Albanian Vocational School, which, for many years, had been run by American Harry T. Fultz and was often referred to as the Fultz School. When the American Junior Red Cross founded it in 1921, Albania had only two secondary schools, neither of which offered technical or vocational courses. The Albanian Vocational School and other schools, however, were later nationalized to diminish foreign influence on the country, but by then Fultz's school had produced more than one hundred and fifty graduates, including Gina, who were versed in some English.

Though everything Gina had said unnerved them, the Americans recognized that the partisans may have information they could use, and they asked Gina about the last airfield they had flown over. He confirmed it was in German hands and agreed that the Germans might come looking for them, and they should leave the area immediately. He and his men offered to lead them to a village about two hours away where they would take care of them while they decided what to do next. Though the Americans had no idea if they could trust them, they had few options. The pilots and the others surmised that their best chance of finding some shelter, some food, and maybe a way out in the unfamiliar terrain stood with these strangers.

As they prepared to leave, Thrasher yelled to Lebo, the radio operator, to turn off the IFF. Lebo walked to the back of the plane and activated a charge that set off a small explosion and destroyed the classified equipment that sent coded signals.

Thrasher then called to the copilot, who was in the cockpit turning off switches. "Hey, Baggs, hurry it up!" With their nerves already frayed, some of the nurses still in the plane, who, like the rest of the passengers, were unaware of the flight crew's names, thought Thrasher was referring to them. After a few indignant moments, they realized their mistake and prepared to leave, grabbing their personal gear and exiting by the passenger door.

The rest of the medical personnel grabbed their musette and medical bags from the plane. All but three of the nurses had water-resistant field coats with them, and most of the medics had stashed their raincoats in their musette bags, which they pulled out and put on. Before they could leave, however, they had to figure out a way to transport Shumway, who was unable to put any weight on his hurt leg. Hayes helped other medics unbolt three attached bucket seats in the aircraft to make a stretcher for him. It was clumsy, but it would work. They placed him on it, and several men hoisted it onto their shoulders. One of the medics found a blanket in the plane's survival gear, which he used to cover Shumway from the cold rain, but they couldn't do much for his feet, which dangled off the edges.

With Shumway ready to go, the nurses and medics joined the flight crew and the band of partisans. Baggs carried the machine gun in a sling on his shoulder as the thirty apprehensive Americans, now bonded in their struggle for survival, followed their new guides into the wooded hills beyond the lake. With them, they carried desperate hopes that they were in trustworthy hands and that the Germans weren't searching for them.

They walked through the dark woods as the medics took turns carrying Shumway on the makeshift stretcher. The slippery terrain led them uphill, and their pants and shoes were wet from the rain and covered in dirt. With each step, their unknown futures loomed ahead of them.

After about an hour, the partisans stopped at a small stone hut built into the hillside, which housed a lone ox. To the surprise of the Americans, the partisans hitched the ox to a nearby cart with oversized wooden wheels and slatted sides made of tree saplings and motioned for the medics carrying Shumway to put him in the cart. It was an unnecessary but kind gesture, and it offered some reassurance to the Americans that they could trust these men.

Just as the weather was clearing, they arrived at a simple, two-story house with a roof covered in overlapping stone. This single building with about two dozen residents made up the Muslim village, thought to be Gjolen, which Gina had mentioned earlier. It was certainly much smaller than the Americans had pictured when he'd spoken of a village, but they welcomed the chance to rest and get out of the rain.

Male partisans already at the house escorted the Americans to the second floor using an outside staircase, while some of the medics carried Shumway up the steps. The Muslim women of this particular village, who kept their distance from the Americans, wore long black dresses, headscarves, and face veils, though the party would learn that not all Muslim women in Albania followed the custom.

When the partisans told the Americans to leave their musette and medical bags on the porch at the top of the steps, the weary Americans did so without much thought. They walked past a primitive bathroom that consisted of a hole in the wooden floor before entering a barren room furnished only with a fireplace and a dirty, handmade woolen rug that looked as if it had once been white. It was difficult to breathe in the room, which was still smoky from previous fires and barely big enough to hold them all. They squeezed in the best they could, discarded their wet jackets, and collapsed onto the cold wooden floor. They sat wherever they could find room as a partisan brought in a simple lamp made from a flat dish filled with oil and a wick and placed it on the mantel.

It was the first time the Americans had been alone since the crash landing, and there was much to discuss. A few of the nurses tended to Shumway and examined Watson's cuts, while conversations about what had happened and what to do were intermingled with people learning each other's names. They knew there were no American troops in Albania, and it would likely be some time before anyone in their squadron realized they were missing. Most of the communication between the evacuation stations was hand delivered by medics or nurses traveling between them. They also knew that though they had landed in a place that felt as foreign to them as almost any place could, they were not that far from Italy, which was just across the Adriatic Sea. The partisans seemed to be doing their best to help them, and going it alone in such a rugged country didn't seem safe or even possible. After a long discussion, the group figured its best chance of escape was to get to the coast with the aid of the partisans and find a boat that could take them back to Italy.

By late that afternoon, the Americans had grown hungry, and Baggs asked Gina if there was any food for them. Meanwhile some of the medics thought it would be best to offer the crude toilet to the nurses while they made use of the outdoors. When Gina came back to the room several hours later, he carried a tray filled with chunks of flat cornbread made solely from cornmeal and water. A few of the men helped Shumway sit up so he could eat as they all took pieces. Though Hayes was hungry and grateful for the food, he gagged when he first tried the bread, which he thought tasted like a handful of dried field corn rather than the cakelike cornbread his mother had made in Indianola. Some of the nurses and medics also had difficulty eating the bread, which would end up sustaining them in the coming weeks, but they were glad to have something in their bellies.

As they ate, a young boy came in and played a few notes on a kaval, a long, end-blown flute, doing his best to piece together a song. The group politely applauded him when he was finished, recognizing the efforts the boy and the partisans were making to help them. Gina then brought a tray of small chunks of sour white cheese, which was as unpalatable to the Americans as the cornbread, but they ate it with gratitude.

The evening wore on, and the fire that flickered in the fireplace and cast shadows on the walls helped warm them as the temperature dropped. Some of the nurses gave the liners from their field coats to the medics to use as blankets, since their thinner field jackets didn't provide much warmth. Hayes stretched out as best he could in the cramped quarters and decided to leave his glasses on rather than risk someone stepping on them. Worn out from the day's events, he was soon asleep. Jens, one of a few who had to sleep sitting up with their backs to the wall, detached the hood of her field coat and used it as a makeshift pillow. She fell asleep, but was eventually awakened by the sound of a man's voice. Fearing for a few moments that the Germans had found them, she started to panic but quickly realized that one of the medics, Hornsby from the 802nd, was talking in his sleep. She had to resist throwing a shoe at him. She looked at the glowing dial from her Army watch and saw that it was about one thirty in the morning and wondered how many more nights they would spend in Albania. The room had gotten colder, and she reached across the row of bodies lying next to her to get a piece of wood for the fire. She hoped sleep, which usually came so easily to her, would offer some comfort from the many worries running through her mind.

The same day the plane crash-landed, the 807th in Catania received radiograms from Philip Voigt, the 807th flight surgeon stationed at Bari, and Edward Phillips, the 807th flight surgeon manning the station in Grottaglie, asking again for attendants. It didn't make any sense to those in Catania, who replied by stating that the plane had left that morning. When word later came that the nurses and medics still hadn't arrived, worry set in. McKnight flew from Catania to Bari the next day to see what he could learn, while reconnaissance planes searched for any signs of the Americans or the missing C-53D.

As the disheveled and exhausted group woke in the village in the morning and found that the rain had cleared, one of the medics stumbled onto the porch and yelled, "Someone has been in my musette bag!" Others quickly poured onto the porch to see what else was missing. Soap, socks, underwear, razors, toothbrushes, and mess gear had all been taken. Only a few items, like toothpaste, shaving cream, and the nurses' makeup, were left behind. Though some scissors had been taken, most of the medical kits were intact. Whoever had stolen their belongings, it seemed, had taken only the items he recognized. When the Americans informed Gina, he calmly explained that Albanians didn't steal and quickly ended the conversation. There was nothing more the Americans could do, and their already uneasy faith in the partisans was deeply shaken.

The Americans didn't know it, but had the partisans caught the perpetrator, they likely would have killed him. Under the partisans' code, the penalty for stealing or failing to share what had been captured from the enemy was punishable by death. When five boys who had found and sold drugs in one village had been caught, the partisans had sentenced them to be shot. They had been spared only because of their young ages and the desperate pleadings of their families. A man who had stolen cigarette papers from a fellow partisan wasn't as lucky and had been immediately executed.

Hayes's bag still contained the louse powder from the Red Cross, a paperback, his raincoat, and a few other items. Most important, he still had the canteen strapped to his belt, the prayer book his minister in Indianola had sent to him in Sicily in his pocket, and a knit cap, which would help keep him warm if needed. Frustrated that someone had taken things the Americans would desperately need if they were stranded there for any period of time, he decided to keep everything he had with him. He wasn't going to let any of it out of his sight.

After the excitement subsided, a couple of partisans gave the group a pitcher of water and a basin. It took the Americans a moment to understand that the water the men were offering was to be used by all of them to wash their hands and faces. They each took their turn, hoping that the washing was in preparation for another meal, but more food never came. It had only been a day since the crash landing, and they were already dirty, hungry, and tired. More than anything, they were anxious to find their way back to Allied lines.

CHAPTER 5

Unlikely Comrades

When the Americans told Gina their plan to get to the coast and pressed him for information about how he could help them, Gina explained that he needed to consult his commandant in the next village before taking the group anywhere else. He had sent a messenger, and they would soon know more. He added that if they were to pursue their idea, they needed to go to the seaport of Vlorë to get a boat, which was up to a two-week walk. Owen, the former high school football star, replied excitedly to Hayes that they'd have some story to tell the guys back in Catania if they were in enemy territory for that long.

While they waited, Thrasher decided that he, Baggs, and Lebo should go back and destroy the plane to keep the Germans from salvaging anything if they found it. It had been impossible to even consider burning it the day before with the rain and the Germans possibly searching for them. Hayes, Owen, and a few other medics decided to join them rather than sit around waiting, and

Thrasher didn't seem to mind. Before they left, Gina sent a man to scout the area ahead of them to make sure there were no signs of German soldiers.

The group headed back to the crash site with a few armed partisans leading the way. As they revisited the rocky trail they'd been on the day before, they remained on guard. The theft of their supplies had done little to calm their concerns about whether they could trust the partisans, and the threat from the Germans was ever present.

The trip that had taken two hours in the rain while they carried Shumway took only an hour that morning. When they reached the edge of the woods, they waited for a signal from the scout that the area was safe before they ventured toward the plane. Given the all clear, the men climbed on board and looked around to see what they could take. Owen grabbed a blanket and a small tarp from a survival kit, while Hayes took four packs of K rations, or emergency meals, along with one of the canvas first-aid kits fastened to the wall of the plane. No one else wanted to take them, but Hayes figured they might just get hungry enough not to care how unappetizing the rations were, especially if the food they'd already been given was any indication of things to come. Abbott grabbed the D rations, emergency rations made into chocolate bars, and a box of sugar cubes that were also part of the emergency supplies. They also found a parachute in the survival kit that they cut into pieces using someone's pocketknife and divided it and the ropes that connected the harness to the canopy among them. Hayes and some of the others then tied pieces of the yellow cotton around their necks as scarves.

The survival kit also contained an inflatable raft and a Gibson Girl emergency radio transmitter, so named for its hourglass shape, but the men decided to leave both behind. They probably wouldn't need the raft, which could not hold all of them, and the Germans would probably be the ones to pick up any emergency signal they sent. They also left behind some of the other first-aid kits attached to the walls of the plane. Had they known just how long they would be in Albania, they might have reconsidered. Either that day or the day before, someone had also unscrewed the clock from the instrument panel and taken it with them.

While they checked for other supplies on the plane, one of the partisans who had climbed in with the Americans picked up a Mae West. When Baggs saw him looking at it, he put it on the man and showed him how to inflate it. The partisan pulled the cord and the vest rapidly filled with air. With a look of surprise and fear, he quickly yanked it off. As new as Albania was to the Americans, much about the Americans was new to the partisans helping them.

When they were sure they had everything they wanted, they were ready to burn the plane. It was disappointing to think of destroying it when it could have easily been fixed with the proper equipment, but they had no choice. Lebo climbed under one of the wings and opened the valve of the fuel tank to let several gallons of gasoline run onto the water under the plane. Baggs found a container on board and filled it with some of the draining gasoline, doused the cockpit with it, and poured it in a trail to the door. He struck a match, but before he could throw it, the fumes ignited, and the explosion knocked him from the ledge of the doorway onto his back and into the mud. He was momentarily stunned, but he wasn't hurt. While Baggs recovered, Thrasher lit matches and threw them onto puddles of gasoline under the plane, but to his growing irritation nothing happened. He then took a stick, wrapped a piece of cloth around it, soaked it in gasoline, and threw it under the airplane wing. A small flame flickered for a moment but quickly died. Either in frustration or out of curiosity, one of the partisans took an ax and hit the ailerons on the trailing edge of the wing, and the men watched with anticipation to see if it would start a spark, but, again, nothing happened. Having run out of ideas and patience, the men decided to go back to the village to see if there was any word from the man Gina called his commandant.

Shortly after the men returned, Gina's messenger arrived and said the commandant would be there in the morning. Until then the Americans would have to wait. The partisans had already brought those in the village with ailments to see the nurses, but there wasn't much the nurses could do for them. A group of female partisans who carried guns and hand grenades had also come to see the nurses and insisted on singing partisan songs. To the Americans' growing concern, word of their arrival was spreading.

To pass the time while they waited for the commandant, Jens started writing a brief diary using the white space in an English–Italian dictionary she had brought in her musette bag. Others anxiously smoked, talked, or watched the villagers come and go from the second-story porch and hoped for good news.

Thrasher and a few of the men traveled back to the plane that evening, but Hayes thought it was safer to stay with the other medics and nurses in the village rather than going out at night in unfamiliar territory. Having eaten only a few pieces of cornbread that evening, he was hungry and thinking about food. Though he had the K rations from the plane, he wouldn't allow himself to use them. As the hours passed by slowly, he busied himself using his share of the shroud lines from the parachute to extend the straps on his musette bag so he could wear it as a backpack and tied the first-aid kit to one of the loops on his belt. He then packed the K rations into his now empty medical bag and tucked the bag under his head to keep anyone from getting into it.

When the men returned that evening around eleven, Thrasher proudly announced to the group that they had finally set the plane ablaze. They had once again opened the valve under the wing and let gasoline flow onto the ground before throwing a lit torch into the liquid. This time it had worked. If the Germans found the C-53D now, they wouldn't be able to salvage much, if anything.

Gina's commandant, a man named Kahreman Ylli, rode up to the village midmorning on a shiny black horse as the Americans, tired from another uncomfortable night's sleep on the hard wooden floor in the small room, watched from the porch. Half a dozen men on foot followed on either side of the commandant, and everything from the black cape he wore to the way the partisans seemed to revere him indicated that he was in charge.

Thrasher and Baggs went outside to greet him. Gina, as the only English-speaking Albanian present, interpreted for the commandant, who immediately wanted to know why the Americans were in Albania. Baggs explained they had crash-landed and asked if the commandant could help them get back to Italy. The commandant pulled Gina off to the side to talk privately. When they came back, Gina tried to explain that the commandant was considering two options, though the pilots had trouble deciphering some of Gina's English. Baggs's interpretation was that the partisans could take them to a British pilot who had parachuted out of a plane and was hiding in the hills, or they could take them to Berat, which was a two-day walk. Berat was now under partisan control, and the commandant thought they would find additional help there in getting the Americans to the coast.

While the commandant mulled over his decision, he announced they should have a feast. It was welcome news to the Americans, who were famished. But before they could get too excited, Gina added that a water buffalo or an ox that would be killed for the celebration had to feed the entire village for several days. What had been called a feast would amount to a few bites of meat for each person with cornbread and onions on the side. The Americans were still grateful for the food, however, and Rutkowski gave the partisans a watch to thank them.

Three men pushed and pulled the struggling animal into the yard in front of the building, tied it to a tree, and used a large knife to slit its throat. It took numerous attempts before it died, and to many of the Americans, including Jens and Hayes, the way the men killed it seemed needlessly cruel. Moments after it was slaughtered, the men suspended its carcass from a tree branch and began to dress it. Wolf, an avid hunter from Wisconsin, jumped in to help them using a hunting knife he carried in a leather sheath on his belt.

While they waited for the meat to cook, the commandant announced his decision through Gina. The partisans would leave for Berat early the next morning. The Americans could only hope that they would find someone there who would lead them to the coast.

It was a mild fall day as Gina and his men, loaded down with an assortment of weapons they kept at the ready, led the party of Americans from the village through thick woods blazing with autumn colors. Baggs carried the machine gun while Shumway rode a white horse Gina had proudly offered him that morning. Shumway's pain was mostly limited to his leg by then, and while the nurses' fears of Shumway having internal injuries had passed, they didn't want him walking. Watson's injuries were starting to heal, though her loosened teeth still bothered her.

The peaceful beauty of the forest belied its hidden dangers, and the Americans remained watchful. Those who had been friends before the crash landing walked together on the path, navigating the rocky terrain and taking comfort in the familiar faces around them. Since the theft of their razors, the men's beards were beginning to grow along with their suspicions, and they all longed for showers and a meal, but they were glad to be moving. Sitting around waiting had only given them more time to think about what could happen.

By noon they had arrived in another one-building village where the residents were expecting them. Gina had sent a messenger ahead to arrange for the Albanians to share what little food they had. After a brief conference between Gina and the leaders of the village, the party sat down in front of a long table and ate as the villagers stole curious glances at the uniformed Americans. When someone asked Gina what it was they were eating, he told them, "Never mind. Just eat it."

It wasn't luck that the villagers were once again so generous. It was *Besa,* an ancient Albanian code of honor, which dictated that Albanians help all those in need despite the risks to themselves. Though the Americans weren't aware of this code, it would help save their lives and those of nearly two thousand Jews, mostly from other European countries, sheltered in Albania during the war.

The group's stay in the village was brief, as Gina and his men were anxious to make more progress before darkness arrived, but the food helped give them the energy they needed to keep going. They plodded along the trail, with those needing to relieve themselves stepping off the path momentarily and then catching up with the others.

They soon approached a churning river about a hundred feet wide and several feet deep. When Hayes saw it, he immediately thought of refilling his canteen, but his hopes disappeared when he saw that the water was too muddy. For the past few days, they'd been drinking water from their canteens, last filled in Catania, and now they were running low. They needed to find more water soon.

As they approached the shore of the river, the Americans noticed two Albanian men waiting with a few mules, a meeting Gina had arranged ahead of time to help the party get across. It was slow going as the mules ferried a few women and men over at a time, with the exceptions of Shumway, who rode his horse, and the partisans, who waded across on their own. Though the process took valuable time, the Americans appreciated the help. Other than a few bites of cornbread, sour cheese, and meat, they'd had nothing since the morning of the flight three days earlier; none of them had slept well, and they were covering a lot of ground. With the mules continuing on the journey with them, a few of the Americans hitched rides.

As daylight faded, Gina and his men led them to a small village of stone houses with stone roof tiles, possibly Poshnje. The male leaders of the village who made up the village council came out to greet them, with the same curious looks the Americans had received earlier in the day. Gina spoke with them and asked permission to stay the night. It wasn't a small request. If the Germans caught the Albanians hiding the Americans, they could be killed. At the very least, the village would be burned, but in all likelihood, the retaliation would be much more brutal. The Americans' stay would also deplete the village's small stores of food and would likely mean that some in the village wouldn't eat that night. Despite the risk and the sacrifice, the village council agreed, and the Americans were divided into three groups with men and women in each.

Owen, Hayes, and Abbott were assigned to the same house along with a few of the nurses, including Rutkowski. Whenever possible, Hayes, Owen, Wolf, and Abbott stuck together as they had during training at Bowman Field, but Gina had become their de facto leader, and he decided how the groups were divided. The two Albanian men who hosted them were friendly and tried to make conversation, but it was nearly impossible for either the Americans or the Albanians to understand one another without Gina there to help translate.

Their hosts served a meal on a round table that stood just inches off the floor, and after a course of cornbread and raw onions, they brought the Americans a bowl of some kind of sweet soup that they put in the center of the table along with a single spoon. Unsure what they were supposed to do, the Americans stared at the soup for a moment until Rutkowski filled the spoon, sipped it, and passed it on to the next person. They liked it so much and were still so hungry that their hosts refilled the bowl several times, and Abbott tried unsuccessfully to learn the name of it so they could ask for it again. When dinner was over, their hosts, who had no bedding to offer, moved the table so the men and women could sleep on the floor next to a smoldering fire.

*   *   *

With Shumway still on horseback and the mules in tow, Gina led the party through the woods the next day as they slowly made their way toward Berat. None of the Americans had been offered anything to eat that morning, and what they'd had the night before dominated the conversation that morning as their hunger took over their thoughts. One group had been served a similar meal to that of the others, but the third group described a dish with some kind of meat that made the others envious. Watson kept thinking of the cake her mother would be having that day to celebrate her fifty-first birthday while unaware that her only daughter was stranded in enemy territory.

They finally stumbled upon a nearby stream. The water looked clear enough to drink, and they thought they were far enough away from a village that it would be relatively free of contaminants. The nurses and medics filled their canteens, relieved to at least have a supply of water with them. For added protection they sterilized the water using a few drops of iodine from glass ampoules in their medical kits.

The hours passed, and they continued on while some of the partisans traveling with them seemed to come and go as Gina sent them off to scout areas or relay messages. In the early afternoon, one of the men came running back to the group. While he tried to catch his breath, he told Gina that a German patrol was in the area. Though the Germans tended to stay near the roads where they could protect their communications, they sometimes ventured into the hills and mountains, particularly when they wanted to exact revenge for attacks on their troops. When partisans had attacked a German convoy in July before the German invasion, the Germans had retaliated by killing 107 civilians in the town of Borovë near the Greek border and burning down the village with flamethrowers. Most victims were women, children, and the elderly. The youngest was just four months old.

Gina warned the Americans to be as quiet as possible as they continued on the trail. They listened for any sound or movement as they walked for the next half hour or so until they reached the edge of the woods. As they neared an exposed hillside, they heard an explosion of five or six rounds of gunfire. It seemed to have come from the right side of the hill ahead, and the shells had landed somewhere far in front of them to their left. They listened for more shooting, but all they heard was silence. After waiting several minutes, they had no choice but to cross the hillside so they could continue on the trail. After a few of the partisans led the way, Gina decided it was safest to send one American across at a time. When Hayes's turn came, he walked past Gina, who said to him, "I am the commandant, yes?" Hayes wasn't sure if it was a statement or a question, but he agreed and kept moving. As Hayes ran across the field, he could hear his canteen rattling against the cup on his belt. It seemed like the loudest noise he'd ever heard. He grabbed the canteen cover to keep it from shaking and finished his dash. When he got to the other side, he was certain everyone had heard it, but no one had noticed.

With everyone safely across, they continued on their way, but Hayes's curiosity about Gina's role as leader of the band of partisans nagged at him. He caught up with Gina and asked him how he had been chosen to lead. Gina explained matter-of-factly that he had won the title by killing the most Germans. If someone else were to kill more, he would be replaced. It was another reminder of the brutal and chaotic world the Americans had unwittingly entered.

Following the path of a stream, they reached the edge of another village, where they watched a miller grinding cornmeal with a water-powered millstone in a small building. They continued on, passing an open-air building where a blacksmith pounded on a piece of iron and his apprentice used bellows to pump air into a fire. As the sun was beginning to set, they found the village council, who spoke with Gina and agreed to let the Americans stay the night. Gina once again separated the Americans into groups and assigned them to various homes — a protocol they would follow at every village they came to in the coming weeks.

Food and firewood were scarce that night. Nurse Kopsco, Hayes, and another medic, in fact, had none of either as they shivered in a room above a stable, but they had a roof over their heads, which helped protect them as the temperature plummeted. Winter weather was quickly approaching, and the men and women knew they didn't have what they would need to survive it.

As the Americans regrouped early the next morning, Gina announced they would arrive in Berat by the afternoon. After five days in Albania, the Americans were desperate to reach the town, and the news cheered them. By now they figured the AAF knew they were missing and were looking for them; but few, if any, had hopes they would be found, given that they had crashed so far off their intended course. They had to get themselves home, and they still thought their best chance was to locate someone in Berat who would take them to the coast. With any luck, they would be back before the AAF sent telegrams to inform their families they were missing.

As they made their way down a hill later that morning, horse and mules in tow, they came upon a wide valley stretching before them for three or four miles. Gina told them Berat was beyond the valley and west of the mountains surrounding it. To get there, first they would have to cross the valley, which would require them to pass the far end of a runway on a German airfield in the middle of the grassy expanse. He'd already sent partisans ahead, and they'd had no trouble. Despite some of the Americans' apprehension about his plan, they had no other options, and they were fiercely determined to get to Berat and, ultimately, home.

Just as they approached the edge of the valley, six B-25s heading east flew over them and disappeared behind mountains. Transfixed by the unexpected appearance of American planes, the group came to a standstill. Moments later, they heard what sounded like bombs exploding and saw a large column of black smoke rise into the air. Though the Americans didn't know it at the time, the planes had just bombed an Albanian oil refinery prized by the Wehrmacht. Three German Messerschmitt Bf109s scrambled on the airfield in response to the American planes, and Gina nudged the elated and distracted Americans to keep moving. With the planes in the air, now was the time to skirt the airfield.

As they approached, they passed a wire fence about four feet high near the end of the runway. Suddenly, roughly a dozen P-38 American fighter planes flew over them following the path of the other planes. At the sight of the P-38s, the German fighter planes unexpectedly turned back to the field and came in to land. Fearing that the German pilots might spot them, the Americans took cover as their training dictated. To the relief of the group, the pilots were too focused on their landings to notice some of the Americans and partisans lying facedown in a ditch about ten feet from the fence, or nurses Jens and Porter hiding under a small tree. The sight of the American planes reminded Jens of home and made her more determined than ever to get back.

Fortunately for the party, the Americans and partisans didn't stay down for too long before moving on to Berat. After bombing the refinery, an attack that killed some two hundred and eighty people, including those hit by partisan snipers in the hills, the P-38s came back and attacked the field, showering it with fragmentation bombs. The Americans had once again narrowly escaped catastrophe.

CHAPTER 6

Under Attack

Early that afternoon, the Americans followed Gina down the main street of Berat, a town of about 10,000 flanked by the Osum River on one side and a terraced hill of white homes with large windows and red-tiled roofs on the other. Overlooking it all loomed a thirteenth-century castle. One of the country's oldest settlements, Berat dated to between 2600 and 1800 B.C. and was long occupied by merchants and craftsman. Its strategic location along trade and military routes during the Ottoman Empire had made it an important town, and many of the buildings from that period were still well preserved.

Hundreds of people cheered, sang, and waved as the large group, including Shumway sitting astride his horse and a few medics and nurses riding mules, passed by. Some threw flowers and saluted the party, while at least one man snapped pictures. Confused by the unexpected and passionate welcome, some of the Americans basked in the attention. One medic even returned a salute. Others, however, worried that if this many people knew they were in Albania, the Germans were sure to find out, as well — if they didn't already know.

The Americans soon learned the reason for the enthusiasm. Gina had sent a messenger ahead to alert the town that the Americans were coming, and the townspeople thought they were the first of a long-awaited Allied invasion force sent to liberate them from the Germans. Seeing the nurses hadn't dissuaded them from the idea, since they were used to female partisans fighting side by side with men. For the Americans who were counting on finding their own liberators in Berat, it was deeply unsettling to realize that these people were looking to them for help.

As the party made its way down the street, they passed several shops before Gina stopped in front of a simple, three-story hotel that despite its humble appearance was named the Grand Hotel Kolumbo. A round-faced man in his late thirties wearing a short black coat, gray trousers, and black boots that came up almost to his knees greeted them in English and spoke with Gina and the pilots for a few moments before motioning for the others to follow him into the hotel. His name was Kostaq Stefa, a partisan who, like Gina, had learned English at the Albanian Vocational School and taught there for several years. The father of four children at the time, Stefa had remained in Berat during the war to take care of his family, including his elderly parents. He served as the partisan chairman of the historic quarter of Berat while his brother and three brothers-in-law were fighting with the partisans.

While several partisans carried Shumway upstairs to a room in the hotel to rest, Stefa escorted the others into the dining room and announced to the great delight of the American men and women that the hotel would serve them a meal. While they sat at a long table and waited for food to be served, Stefa suggested they pool whatever American money they had so they could buy a few items they might need. He would exchange it on their behalf and take some for the cost of the meal. They agreed; and when Stefa returned, he gave the Albanian money to Thrasher, the pilot and senior officer in the group.

The Americans ate a lunch of mutton, cornbread, vegetables, and the sweet soup Hayes, Rutkowski, and the others had enjoyed so much before. It was the most the Americans had eaten since arriving in Albania, and they savored every bite. When they finished, Stefa, rather than Gina, assigned them to various homes in town and quartered some of the nurses, including Watson, in the hotel. Jens and Lytle, a nurse from Kentucky, would go with Stefa, who seemed to have been designated the Americans' new leader and who perhaps, the group thought, could lead them safely to the coast where they hoped to find a boat to take them back to Italy.

Hayes was paired with medics Owen, Abbott, and Cruise, and they were briefly introduced to their host, an Albanian named George, who told them to meet him outside the hotel in a few minutes. In the meantime, they ran upstairs to check on Shumway, who was settled in a bed in a barren room with white plastered walls. Though the room was cold, Shumway appeared comfortable. It was the first bed any of them had seen since they'd been in Albania, and the men suspected Shumway would rest easier that night than any of them.

Assured their friend was safe, they took their leave and stood outside the hotel, watching people roam the streets. Many of the men who appeared to be partisans carried various weapons and wore homespun woolen clothes and parts of German and Italian uniforms they'd found or taken. Almost everything about Albania was so strange and different to the medics that they weren't surprised to also see Italian officers and enlisted men in uniform milling about the town despite Italy's surrender to the Allies a few months before. These soldiers were as stranded as the Americans. After the Germans had invaded, tens of thousands of Italians had run into the mountains fearing that they would be captured or killed, and many now earned just enough from doing menial tasks to keep themselves from starving. Between one thousand and two thousand Italians were thought to have joined the German forces. Others joined the partisans, but the partisans were mostly interested in their weapons, equipment, and coats and resented the Italians for the way they had treated them when they ruled the country. As many as a hundred Italians a day would perish in the harsh winter ahead.

George came out of the hotel along with four other medics, including Wolf, and told Hayes and the others in his group to follow him. They had only walked a short distance down the road before they arrived at an Albanian bar with a handful of local men perched at tables and nursing their drinks. George introduced them to the bar's owner, an English-speaking man who would host Wolf's group of medics that night.

As the Americans seated themselves, the bar owner asked if they wanted some schnapps. Hayes rarely drank, but the others wanted to try it. The man brought out four glasses and poured about an ounce of clear liquid in each. The three men downed their drinks, one at a time, until only Hayes's was left. They motioned for him to take it until he finally picked up the glass and swallowed. Before he knew it, his throat burned as if it was on fire, and the top of his head felt like it was going to explode.

The other men laughed as Hayes tried to regain his composure. They had just had their first sip of raki, a potent and treasured Albanian spirit made from distilled fruit.

Hayes, Owen, Abbott, and Cruise followed George to his home after they parted ways with the bar owner and his charges for the night. The men walked along the hilly streets of Berat with a cool wind escorting them, and George warned them that they would need much warmer clothes for the quickly approaching Albanian winter. He said he would find some for them and suggested they stay at his house until spring. The men exchanged surprised glances, and one of them quickly spoke up. The medic explained that though it was a generous offer, they had no intention of remaining in Albania through the winter and hoped the partisans would lead them to the coast. That wasn't possible, George said, because the partisans didn't control the coastal areas. The news startled the men, and it reignited their concerns about how much they could trust the partisans.

When they arrived at George's home, they were surprised to find it decorated with couches, handwoven rugs, and pictures. He even had electricity, which they had not yet seen in an Albanian home. George's teenage son brought out a pot of tea and cups, and they sat around a table enjoying the warmth of the drink while George told them about starting his own diner in America in the 1930s. He'd come back in 1939 to get his wife and children after he'd found some success, but then the Italians had invaded, and he and his family found themselves trapped.

The men talked for hours until George's son cleared the dishes, and George took them back to the hotel where they were served a dinner of liver and vegetables, the only selection offered. Hayes's lifelong aversion to liver was tempered by his hunger, and he managed to eat several bites of it along with everything else on his plate.

When they returned to George's house that night, Hayes and Cruise were given a room to share. Though George apologized for having only one bed to offer, the men had come to appreciate every small luxury, including the fresh water they were given to refill their canteens and the towels they'd used for washing in a small basin of water. While Cruise slept in the bed, Hayes took off his uniform for the first time since they'd crash-landed and slept soundly on the floor on a soft mattress with clean white sheets and a blanket.

They were so grateful for George's hospitality that when he offered them tea the next morning and apologized for not having sugar, an expensive and scarce item few in Albania could afford, they offered him the box of sugar cubes Abbott had taken from the plane. After their tea and a small breakfast, George escorted the men through town to meet the other Americans. Their path took them along the busy main street, where locals bought and sold fruits and vegetables and a butcher used an ax to chop off pieces of meat from a carcass hanging from a tree limb.

When they finally arrived at the meeting place, a former school, they were led to a large room on the second floor. Stefa stood in front giving orders to several men while dictating to one who typed. Jens and Lytle were also there. The night before, Stefa had taken the two nurses to his home to meet his family, including his wife, his children, and his parents. The women had even played a few rounds of cards with Stefa's mother before being given the chance to bathe and to sleep in a bed for the first time since their arrival.

As the rest of the Americans filed in to sit in wooden folding chairs, they waited anxiously to hear about plans for their escape. Outside the room a group of men bellowed out partisan songs, and when they finished their performance, Stefa and another partisan leader named Gjin Marku began an hour-long speech about Albania's troubled history. They talked about the prestigious Albanian Vocational School and how much the partisans desperately needed the Americans and British to send them arms and supplies so they could liberate their people. Though the Americans listened patiently, they kept waiting to hear some reference to how the partisans were going to help them get to the coast, but it never came.

Stefa finished the lecture by teaching the Americans the partisan salute, a clenched right-handed fist touching the right side of the forehead and accompanied by the phrase *Vdekje Fashizmit,* which meant "Death to Fascism." They learned the proper response, which included the same salute followed by the words *Liri Popullit,* or "Freedom to the People." The rival BK, of which the Americans were still unaware, also had a slogan: *Shqipëria Shqiptarëvet,* or "Albania for the Albanians," to which the proper reply was *Vdekje Tradhëtarëvet,* or "Death to the Traitors," meaning the partisans. When the speech finally ended, Thrasher and Baggs asked Stefa what they all wanted to know, but the Americans didn't receive the answer they'd hoped for. Stefa simply replied that he had to "make preparations," a refrain they'd hear from him often. In the meantime, he told them, the Americans would see Berat.

For the next two days, while Shumway recuperated in the hotel, spending some of his time taking pictures of a horse-drawn taxi on the street or scenic views from the rooftop with the little bit of film he had left in his camera, the other Americans were paraded around Berat with Stefa in an old orange Fiat truck. At many of the places they saw — the martyrs' cemetery, the castle towering over the town, a hall where partisans performed a play, and local partisan headquarters — they heard more speeches about the virtues of the partisan movement, which were often feverishly accompanied by the salute they were expected to return. Though they knew Stefa was likely following orders, the Americans were growing impatient with the endless propaganda they heard, but they were helpless to do anything about it.

At night, they were once again parceled out into small groups to various homes or to the hotel. Most were sent to a different house each night. At one of the houses Jens stayed in, her English-speaking host told her that some of the people the Germans had taken away had never come back. Those left behind had hidden or buried any items of value to prevent them from getting into German hands.

On their third night in town, the Americans went back to the hall where they had watched the partisans perform and expected to hear more propaganda. Instead, a man played an accordion for their enjoyment before the partisans showed the Americans an Italian movie.

Though the conditions and the food in Berat were far better than what they'd had in the villages, several of the Americans were starting to suffer from severe diarrhea, or, as many in the military called it, "the GIs." Also of great concern to the Americans was what they had noticed while being driven around town. The photographer who had snapped their pictures as they entered Berat had posted half a dozen photos of the uniformed Americans in the window of his shop on the main street for all who passed by to see.

*　　*　　*

Hayes and Owen awoke early on their fourth morning in Berat to the sound of gunfire. They'd heard it sporadically since they'd arrived in the town, and it was usually a partisan firing off a few rounds for entertainment. But when their host and his teenage son came racing into their room looking worried, the two medics knew there was trouble. The man said something to his son in Albanian, and the teenager dashed out of the room. Then the man turned to the Americans and said, "It is not good. Get your clothes on."

Hayes and Owen rushed to put on their uniforms, which they'd taken off the night before when they were given clean bedding. As Hayes laced up his shoes, the son returned and spoke to his father again in Albanian. Hayes had heard the sound of the front door opening and closing and figured the teenager had gone out into the street to see what was happening. The man told them they must hurry because the Germans had already entered Berat. It was not only the Germans but also the BK who were attacking the town, though the Americans still did not know of the BK. As the man spoke, Hayes heard artillery shells explode nearby. The two Americans tried to thank their host for letting them stay in his home, but he motioned for them to quickly get on their way.

The medics darted to the gate in front of the house as the sun came up and watched as crowds of panicked people ran toward the main street. Despite their own worries, the men decided they had to go back to George's house to get their field jackets, medical bags, and musette bags, all of which were too valuable for them to leave behind. They had kept their belongings at George's house at his suggestion rather than taking them to various homes throughout the town. Though Hayes still had his reservations about leaving anything out of his sight, George had earned his trust.

They pushed through the crowds until they reached George's house. Despite the danger to himself, George stood at his front door with their belongings in his hands. They thanked him quickly and rummaged through their bags until they found their canvas leggings. The leggings, which had straps that went around the bottom of their shoes to keep them in place, were intended to keep pants from getting dirty and caught on brush, and to keep stones and snow out of shoes. The two men were putting them on when some of the other medics came running by. One shouted, "You don't have time for that. Get going!" But Hayes and Owen were determined. When they finished, Owen said, "You ready? Let's haul ass!" and the two took off running as fast as they could.

As they neared the edge of town, they spotted Stefa yelling for everyone to get into the same orange truck that had been used earlier to escort them around town. Medics, nurses, and partisans continued to pile in as Hayes and Owen joined them. Shumway, the injured crew chief, was in the back along with Thrasher and Baggs, who were helping some of the nurses climb on board. When the attack had started, Baggs had told Shumway at the hotel that they didn't have time to find him a horse; he would have to do the best he could, so Shumway had hobbled alongside Baggs until they reached the truck.

The machine gun Baggs had carried was now gone. The pilots had decided the whole group might be safer if they were all unarmed. When the partisans had sent Gina home sometime during the last day or two, the pilots had given him the gun and several clips of ammunition as a thank-you. Hayes had hoped to thank Gina for all he had done for them, but he was gone before he could say good-bye.

When the truck was completely full, the driver cranked the engine and sped away, barreling down the exposed and uneven road with each bump jolting the passengers. It had traveled about a mile when those on board heard the engines of nearby planes followed by the sound of bombs bursting. The Germans were attacking Berat from the air as well as the ground. A German Messerschmitt Bf109 flew past them, turned around, and headed right for them. The truck driver stopped, and everyone jumped out and scattered as the plane started strafing the road. Jens landed in a puddle of mud, while Hayes dove to the ground and soon heard another Messerschmitt approaching. When he looked up, the plane seemed to be diving straight for him. He kept waiting for it to veer off, but it continued to come. He pressed his face into the ground and waited for the worst to happen, but suddenly the pilot pulled up and eventually the sound of both planes drifted away. When he looked up again, they were gone.

People climbed back into the truck as fast as they could, and they were soon moving, but they hadn't traveled far before the planes returned. The truck came to a screeching halt, and those on board scrambled once again to get out. As Hayes jumped off, the butt of a partisan's rifle smashed into the back of his head, momentarily disorienting him. When he recovered, he was furious at the partisan until he looked at the man and saw the fear in his face and realized the partisan was even more scared than he was.

Hayes started running west until he reached a bank rising almost six feet above a stream. He jumped down and over the water. Owen and Zeiber, the medic from Reading, Pennsylvania, were right behind him. The three men, out of breath from running, crouched behind the bank. Though they couldn't see what was happening, they could hear the planes flying up and down the road in strafing runs.

When it sounded as if the airplanes were gone, Hayes raised himself above the edge of the bank and looked toward the road. One plane remained. It was a Fieseler Fi-156 Storch, a German observation plane that could travel as fast as 110 miles per hour and had a stalling speed of 31 miles per hour, which gave it the appearance of hovering in the air. Hayes also saw that the truck had been strafed repeatedly and all but destroyed. There was no going back.

While Hayes scouted the road, Zeiber yelled he was going back to find the others and took off. Hayes and Owen decided to follow the path of the river leading away from Berat while they kept a lookout for their party. It wasn't long before they found Kopsco, the nurse from Louisiana who had also taken cover behind the bank and was as shaken as they were. As they followed the river they ran into more from their group including the pilots, nurses Jens and Rutkowksi, Ebers, the medic from Steeleville, Illinois, and a couple others, bringing the group to a total of ten. Also with them was Qani Siqeca, a twenty-three-year-old partisan with a slight build whom they'd met on their second day in Berat and who had performed in the partisan play. Fortunately Qani, whom the Americans mistakenly called Johnny, spoke some English from his days at the Albanian Vocational School. Stefa and the other twenty Americans were nowhere in sight.

The group returned to the road and saw that it was covered with German trucks and at least one armored tank. Qani thought it would be best to head for the mountains to the east of them.

They waited behind the bank until the trucks left the area before making a quick dash across the road and marching toward higher elevations.

After walking for about an hour, watching for any sound or movement in the trees and holding on to the hope that they would find the rest of their party, they came upon a small village of just three houses. Qani explained to the village men who they were and asked if they had any food to share. Though the villagers initially told him they had nothing to give, Qani continued asking until they eventually offered two yellow quinces, the only food the group had all day. The tart fruit was cut into pieces and divided among the entire party who, though still hungry, understood the sacrifice even such a small gift of food meant to the poor village.

They soon left and continued to put as much distance as they could between themselves and the Germans before nightfall. As sunset neared, they stopped at the village of Drenovë, where Qani arranged for them to stay. The two-story house they were taken to was built into the side of a hill, and the first floor functioned as a stable. After being led upstairs to a room, a man prepared a fire for them and brought cornbread. The group would eat anything to quell their hunger, and some of them stuffed extra pieces in their pockets for later. When the villager left them alone, the frightened men and women huddled by the fire trying to warm themselves and to figure out a plan.

One voice followed another as they discussed whether the Germans had seen the photos of them posted in the shop window or recognized them as Americans in the attack. If they had, they wondered if the Germans would follow them into the mountains. The threat from the Germans and the idea of being captured now seemed greater than at any other time since they'd been in Albania.

The shaken Americans also couldn't help but wonder what had happened to the others. Had they been on the truck when the Germans strafed it or were they wandering alone in the mountains? Had they been caught and were now at the mercy of the Germans? This was their eighth day in Albania, and it felt as if any luck they'd had before had run out.

One of the nurses said that she'd been told at Bowman Field to give the Germans only her name, rank, and serial number if captured, while Thrasher argued they should stay where they were and should destroy anything that could identify them in case they were caught. He and Baggs started going through their wallets and tossing anything that could identify them into the fire. Jens agreed and also threw a picture with Stefa's name and address written on the back into the flames in an effort to protect him. If he were caught helping them, he would surely be killed. Hayes, Owen, and some of the other medics, however, refused to consider that getting caught was an option. Hayes voiced his objection, and a few of the medics signaled to one another to have a private discussion near the home's crude toilet. They talked and decided that even if the others remained, they were going to leave the village in the morning. Hayes delivered the news, and after a few moments of silence, Thrasher agreed they would all leave together.

CHAPTER 7

Suspicions

The Americans had been missing for more than a week, but hopes of finding them remained alive. An officer from the flight crew's 61st Troop Carrier Squadron had sent a memo earlier in the week to the commanding officer of the 314th Troop Carrier Group suggesting that it alert the Navy as well as all pilots in the area to be on the lookout for the plane and that resistance fighters in Greece be notified. He wrote, "We feel that the number of highly trained personnel involved would justify the action."

Some in the 807th in Catania attended church services to pray for the missing, while they continued to evacuate patients. The strain on the squadron's personnel was mounting as those on duty were overworked and weighed down by thoughts of their lost friends. The flight surgeons helped fill the gaps, but morale was low. "The building housing the enlisted men is like a morgue at present and the villa housing the nurses doesn't have the drawing power of Officers as usual," wrote one member of the 807th.

On November 15, the same day the party fled Berat, Mc-
Knight, the 807th's commanding officer, reported the twenty-six
nurses and medics as officially missing and signed the reports to
the commanding general of the Twelfth Air Force. The papers
included the family members of the men and women who should
be notified of their status.

Knowing that the Germans were somewhere in the area, the
Americans' Albanian host at Drenovë was anxious for them to
leave the next morning, and he rushed them out without offering
any more food. Hayes pulled out the piece of cornbread he'd
pocketed the night before and ate it as they walked along the trail
following Qani's lead. The party occasionally passed small groups
of partisans, who saluted them, and they responded in kind, as
was expected, but their minds were on their missing friends and
their own safety.

About two hours later, as they climbed higher into the mountains, they arrived at a large village of roughly thirty houses. The
group was moving slowly that morning, and medics Hayes, Owen,
and Ebers soon found themselves ahead of the others and noticed
several partisans setting up a machine gun. The Americans had
only picked up a few words of Albanian, so they tried to ask the
men in English if the Germans were close by, but the Albanians
were intent on their task and no one answered them. The medics
continued on and, before they had left the village, they saw a
group of at least eighty Italians, including a lieutenant colonel,
standing on a side street looking as lost as they were. The medics
eyed the large group of soldiers but kept moving.

A few moments later, gunfire broke out from several directions. Qani, Jens, and the others who were still behind Hayes,

Owen, and Ebers heard the volley and dropped to the ground as bullets flew past them. Baggs told the group to crawl toward a small stone building he could see near the hill leading out of town. A few in the group tried to stand, but more shots whizzed by, and they quickly retreated to the ground and continued to crawl. Upon reaching the house, they leaned against its outside walls for protection until they found a door and hid inside.

Hayes, Owen, and Ebers heard the shots, too, and soon realized they were coming from two places: from behind them in the village they were in, as well as a village on the other side of a ravine ahead of them. They were caught in the crossfire and had to get out of the way fast. The main road going through the village was lined on either side with stone retaining walls that had brief openings for steps, and the men ducked into these openings as they looked for more cover. Going back would be too dangerous; the partisans in the village didn't know them and could easily fire.

Hayes spotted a stone building about five hundred feet behind him and downhill, as well as a boulder about halfway between him and the building. He yelled to Owen and Ebers that he was going to make a run for the boulder and then the house. He had only made it a few feet down the mountainside before gunfire from the other side of the ravine exploded around him. Hayes dove and slid down the rest of the slope, while his medical and musette bags slapped against his body. Puffs of dirt from bullets hitting the ground followed him until he finally reached the boulder. Out of breath, he waved to Owen and Ebers to let them know he was okay.

The other two medics soon followed. Owen went first and took Hayes's approach of rolling and sliding, while Ebers crouched down and ran as fast as he could. Bullets followed both men until they were safely behind the boulder. After catching their breath, they all made another separate dash under fire to the building, where they barged in the door and found the rest of their small party. Someone said, "Here they are!" while another asked, "Where have you been?"

With only one small window, the building was dim despite it being early afternoon. In addition to the Americans and Qani, Hayes noticed one partisan lying on the floor and covered with a blanket. He'd been brought in earlier by other partisans after being shot and was still but conscious. Rutkowski told Hayes she didn't think the man would make it through the day. There wasn't much they could do for him except try to make him as comfortable as possible.

The group was anxious to know what was happening outside, and Qani explained that it wasn't the Germans in a shoot-out with the partisans; it was the BK in a neighboring village. Qani warned them to avoid the BK at all costs, as he suspected its members would turn them over to the Germans. It was the first time the Americans had heard of the rival group, and they were beginning to realize they were in as much danger from the country's internal battle as they were from the Germans.

The afternoon wore on and sporadic shots continued to pierce the air as the party remained trapped in the small building. They had hoped they could wait for the battle to end, but it didn't look as if it was going to stop anytime soon. Qani finally decided he had to do something to get them out while there was still some light. He went to talk to four partisans firing at the other village, who were camped about fifteen feet behind the stone building and down the mountainside. When he returned, he told the Americans that the partisans had agreed to barrage the BK with as much gunfire as they could an hour before sundown to provide enough distraction for Qani to lead the Americans away from the village and farther south. The gunfire exploded as planned, and the group scurried out of the building. With no way to help him, the men and women had to leave behind the dying man they had been unable to help. They hurried past the shooting partisans and made their way down the mountain.

As the afternoon light quickly faded, they noticed that the Italian soldiers they'd seen earlier in the day were following them, likely imagining that Qani and the Americans would lead them to food and shelter. The Americans and Qani weren't interested in having any company, as they already had a large enough party, and they started climbing the next mountain with hopes of losing the Italians. A steady rain soon turned the trail into a slippery and muddy mess. Shivering from the damp clothes that clung to their bodies, the men and women were forced to hold on to the belt of the person in front of them to stay together as the blackness of the night enveloped everything around them.

The rain finally let up after several hours, and when they stopped for a moment, someone shouted, "Look back there!" They turned and saw the lights of Berat glimmering in the distance. The town appeared much closer than some expected, considering how much had happened to them in the day and a half since the attack that had scattered the group.

They could still hear the Italians behind them, and the party continued to ascend the mountain as fast as they could until they reached a village called Kapitonë and found an empty stone barn. It was close to midnight, and the temperature had plummeted. Exhausted from the day's events, the men and women fell asleep on piles of hay covering a cement floor. Most of the nurses had thicker

thicker field coats, and the pilots' leather jackets helped ward off the cold, but they were still wet. Hayes's piece of silk parachute he wore around his neck as a scarf and his knit cap provided some warmth, but he was grateful to Owen, who shared the blanket he'd pulled from the plane as the cold pierced his field jacket.

They'd only been asleep for a few hours before Qani woke them and said they had to go. He was certain the Italian soldiers had wandered off, and he wanted to leave the area right away. Though the men and women wanted nothing more than to sleep, the idea of finding their friends and getting home kept them going as they started a march that would last most of the next day.

At every village they passed through, they continued to prod Qani to ask if anyone had seen or heard of any Americans in the area. The answer was always no. Occasionally their walking was interrupted with the curious sounds of someone yelling from a far-off mountain, which would then be repeated by another voice. Qani explained that this was the Albanian system for relaying news, a mountain telegraph of sorts that spread important infor-mation quickly over vast areas of land that would take days to transmit by foot. Since the Germans were as likely as the Alba-nians to hear anything they yelled, it made it useless to the Ameri-cans in finding the rest of their party.

As night neared and they looked for a place to sleep, the first vil-lage council Qani asked refused to let them stay, but he soon found another willing to house them for a single evening, the village of Bargullas. The group knew they were fortunate to have Qani with them. He was not only arranging for food and shelter, he was teach-ing them more Albanian words for necessities like fire and wood that could come in handy if they too were somehow separated.

The party stayed in a one-room house with their hosts, who gave them what the Americans affectionately called "onion strudel." Aside from the extra piece of cornbread some had stashed in their pockets and eaten later, this dish was their first food in two days. They ate it quickly, marveling at how good the flaky dough and chopped onions tasted, given their hunger. When they went to sleep that night with a fire and quilts to warm them, they could only hope the twenty missing members of their party along with their guide, Stefa, had met with as much good fortune.

The following day Qani and the ten men and women traveled through the mountains looking for water to refill their canteens. The only food they'd had was a handful of walnuts they bought from a villager and shared among them. The constant begging for food and shelter as they went from one village to the next added to their growing sense of helplessness and frustration, and they were desperate for some control. When one villager offered to sell Thrasher a few figs for an exorbitant price, Thrasher refused, despite having enough Albanian money. Thrasher was willing to pay for the figs but he refused to be taken advantage of. It seemed that word had spread that the Americans had money, which also put them at greater risk of being attacked and robbed.

That afternoon, their worries eased a bit when the news they'd been hoping for finally came. An old man in one of the villages told Qani that he'd heard about some Americans in Dobrushë, a village about three hours away. It was the first lead they'd had. They set out immediately, trying to keep their enthusiasm measured in case the information was wrong or the other Americans had already moved on.

With their hopes pushing them forward, they made good

time, and within a few hours they had reached the top of a ridge and could see a village of about forty or so houses in the distance. They continued down the mountain, and as they got closer they saw some of their missing party, who spotted them in turn. The other nurses, medics, and Stefa ran toward them. With cheers, hugs, and handshakes, they reunited as if they were all old friends. Those in Qani's group also marveled at Shumway's recovery. He was now able to walk on his own, though with a very pronounced limp.

Their celebration, however, was short-lived. They took a head count and realized there were only twenty-seven Americans. As questions and comments flew through the panicked group, they determined that three nurses—Lytle, Maness, and Porter—had not been seen since the night before the attack in Berat. In the chaos of that morning, no one had noticed they weren't there, though they couldn't have done much if they had.

Determined to try to help the three women, they explored the idea of one of them going back to Berat to see what could be learned while the others remained in the village. Stefa argued it wasn't possible. His party had been camped at the village for the past few days, and the village was running out of food. They had to move on. Another worry was that the Germans were sure to have noticed the pictures in the shop window and would recognize anyone who went back. Their fears had been fueled by rumors they'd heard that the Germans were looking for them. When Stefa suggested that he send a partisan to Berat who would later catch up with the group as they made their way to the coast, the Americans agreed it was their best hope.

Though Stefa had gotten them out of Berat, the Americans' suspicions about his willingness to help them had grown over the past few days. Those who had traveled with him immediately after the attack were frustrated that he seemed more interested in showing the villagers that Americans were in Albania than in helping them find the rest of their party. Stefa told them that he wished he could show all the people of Albania that they had Americans with them so the people would join the partisans' fight. Despite his constant reassurances that he knew where the others were and that they would be reunited shortly, Qani's group had been the ones to find them.

Those who had been with Qani had their own suspicions about Stefa. An older man in one of the villages had tried to tell Jens something as he shook his finger back and forth. When Jens asked Qani what he was trying to say, he told her the man thought Stefa was a friend of the Germans and would turn them in. Jens found it hard to believe, but it seemed anything was possible in war, and they would have to stay on guard. Stefa was still their best hope of finding a way out, and she was grateful for the kindness he and his family had shown her and Lytle in Berat.

Stefa also suggested that they contact some of the British working with the partisans, who could alert the American military and possibly help evacuate them. It took a few moments for the Americans to fully understand what he was saying. He had never mentioned that British officers were operating in Albania. They had only heard that perhaps a British pilot was hiding in the woods somewhere. Had any of the partisans told them about the British, the Americans would have searched until they found them.

The British had first sent in a handful of highly trained men who worked for Special Operations Executive (SOE), a clandestine organization also called Churchill's "secret army," in April 1943 to help the main resistance groups fight the Italians. Britain's Prime Minister Winston Churchill had approved the formation of SOE shortly after Germany invaded France in 1940 and ordered it to "set Europe ablaze!" SOE's mission was to carry out sabotage and subversion and aid resistance groups behind enemy lines. In addition to its London headquarters, SOE had set up other offices around the world, including a section in Cairo and, by late 1943, one in Bari. To the growing frustration of the British sent into Albania to work with the resistance groups, however, the partisans and BK often seemed more interested in killing one another than anything else.

In early November, months after the Germans had invaded, Churchill addressed the situation in Albania in the House of Commons, and, for the first time, admitted that British officers were operating in the country. "Thousands of Albanian guerrillas are now fighting in their mountains for the freedom and independence of their country.... The Germans are employing the usual methods by which they seek to subdue all warlike peoples; already they have bombed Albanian villages and killed Albanian women and children, but the Albanian guerrillas continue to harass the enemy and attack his communications.... The British liaison officers who are with these guerillas have paid high tribute to their fighting qualities."

These British officers, as well as British noncommissioned officers, or noncoms, also working in the country, often paid a high price for their efforts. The day before the Americans crash-landed, several SOE personnel came under attack by German machine guns as part of an assault on the partisans. As the British crossed a riverbed trying to get away, the mission's wireless operator was shot in the head and torso. A sergeant who had volunteered to parachute into Albania after growing bored as a Royal Air Force machine gunner grabbed him and dragged him to cover, but he was already dead. The group's commanding officer sent two men away to report what had happened, while he, the sergeant, and a corporal remained in the area. That evening, the Germans ambushed them. Though the commanding officer and sergeant got away, the Germans captured the corporal. They took one of his weapons, but he managed to keep a second pistol hidden in his sock, and he eventually escaped by shooting one of his guards and pushing another over a cliff. When a British officer finally found the corporal weeks later with the partisans, he was ill from malnutrition and exposure and died shortly afterward of pneumonia.

Filled with a mixture of frustration and excitement, the Americans decided the best course of action was to send a messenger to find a British officer and bring a note from them saying who and where they were. Stefa immediately dispatched a man with the note signed by Thrasher, but they all knew it could take days or weeks before the messenger returned with news.

With their plans in place, the Americans learned that the villagers would not only let them stay one more night, they would kill a sheep for a meal in honor of the party being reunited. While the mutton was being prepared, the Americans were led to a house and taken inside to a well-kept room with wooden floors and white plastered walls. Their host indicated they should sit on the floor by the fire in a semicircle. He briefly left the room, and when he came back a few minutes later, he carried a bottle of raki and a shot glass and moved to one end of the seated party.

He filled the shot glass, swirled the raki around for a few seconds, and then threw the liquid into the fire, where it burned in a blue flash. He refilled the glass and offered it to the first person in line and then repeated the ceremony for each person in the group before setting the glass and the bottle on the floor for those who wanted more. Though most of the men and women continued to dislike the strong drink, they took a sip as custom dictated.

Baggs found another use for raki a few days later when he poured some in his Zippo lighter after it ran out of lighter fluid. He found that it worked just as well. Several in the group smoked and had run out of tobacco within a few days of landing. To their relief, villagers had given them rolls of dried tobacco on a couple of occasions. The tobacco was sliced into shreds with a pocket-knife, shared with those who wanted some, and rolled with paper from books the party had brought with them.

When the mutton was ready, the party was divided into three groups and taken to separate houses, where they ate. Despite the villagers' generosity, it was a hollow celebration for the Americans, whose thoughts were with the missing nurses and their own futures.

Those who had been in Qani's group spent their first night in Dobrushë and soon learned what the other party already knew: some of the blankets offered to them to ward off the cold night air were infested with fleas and lice. Hayes still had the louse powder he'd been given while on board the *Santa Elena,* and he started using it diligently. Many in the group, however, had left behind their medical and musette bags in the chaos of the attack on Berat and would have to do without. Watson was embarrassed by the lice that ran "foot races" across her middle anytime she sat by a fire to warm up, and though she constantly wanted to scratch, she didn't want to offend her hosts. The loss of the bags also meant they now had to function with even fewer supplies, including iodine ampoules to sterilize water, cigarettes, and the books whose pages they'd also used for toilet paper.

After they had crossed two mountain ridges that day, Stefa told them that they would reach the coast in two to three days, which was incentive enough for them to keep going. Stefa also told the party that the walking would continue to be difficult because they still had to cross six more mountain ridges, but the route was necessary to avoid territory controlled by the rival BK.

Owen had announced that morning that when they finally got to a place where he could see the Adriatic, he was going to lie down and roll all the way to the water. They were all weary from the constant walking as well as the perpetual search for food and water, and now they were getting into higher mountains and colder temperatures. Since they'd crashed, most of them had been unable to bathe, aside from splashing some water on their faces and arms from mountain streams or an occasional basin, and they were all filthy and now battling fleas, lice, and the GIs.

The men had grown patchy beards, and many of the group members' shoes were starting to show wear and tear, particularly the nurses', which were made of lighter leather than the men's. The galoshes that some of the nurses had on over their shoes had helped protect them, but they wouldn't last much longer. Hayes was fortunate enough to have on a brand-new pair of shoes, and Shumway wore a pair of fleece-lined winter flying boots over his regular pair, which protected them. If the Americans didn't find their way out of Albania soon, however, some in their party would be walking over the rugged terrain with shoes full of holes.

Stefa, Qani, and other partisans continued to lead them up steep trails that left their muscles aching and their spirits diminished, but despite the difficult trek, the nurses kept up with the men. To the group's great concern, they also seemed to be heading eastward, rather than west toward the coast and their hopes of escape, but Stefa assured them they were on the right path.

When they arrived at the village of Vërzhezhë that night, the exhausted men and women were separated into groups of five or six. A nurse in one group was so happy to have clean bedding after a small meal of bread and raki that she decided to slip under the linens and take off her filthy uniform despite being in mixed company. The rest soon followed, leaving behind another formality of their former lives that no longer seemed to matter.

They continued the difficult walk the next day, as they tried to push away thoughts of their hunger as much as they could. A few in the party were so hungry, they ate some red berries from bushes along the trail without worrying they might be poisonous and stopped only when Stefa told them the berries would add to their troubles with the GIs. They made their way around the side of a mountain to avoid nearby BK territory, and in the afternoon they stopped at a village to eat.

Hayes and Abbott were assigned with a few others to a home where they were served cornbread covered with the same sweet liquid they'd had in another village and liked so much. It made the dry bread much tastier, and the medics wanted to add more. Their hosts didn't speak any English, so Abbott grabbed off a nail on the wall the tin cup that the woman had used to pour the liquid over the cornbread, and he pretended to do so. The woman then understood what he was asking for, refilled the cup, and gave them more as the medics thanked her repeatedly in Albanian.

When the group gathered together once again, Stefa told them he was ashamed because the medics had asked for more food—something that was never done in Albania. The men took what Stefa said seriously and didn't do it again.

As the party started on the trail again, the weather turned to rain and they had to cross a crude bridge, roughly thirty feet long and made out of tree trunks that connected one cliff to another. The bridge lacked any railing and traversed a rushing river that quickly descended into a steep waterfall. Their worn shoes, particularly the nurses', made the journey even more dangerous. Had any of them lost their footing on the slick, wet wood, they would have met with certain disaster.

The afternoon was occasionally interrupted by the sound of gunfire, though no one knew where it was coming from. They also heard various voices repeating what others yelled across the mountains. Before they knew it, one of the partisans in their group was yelling, too. Stefa told the men and women that the message said the Americans had invaded Albania. Excited by the prospect, the party pressed him for more information in hopes that if the Americans had invaded, the group could find a way out. Stefa knew nothing more, but he offered to send a partisan to see what he could learn.

The men and women were parceled out to various homes in small groups that night in a village called Leshnjë, and Hayes, Owen, and Wolf found themselves in a small house with no windows and a door made out of rough planks. They were taken to a room with a dirt floor, a fire pit with a small flame, a few rugs, and a hole in the roof that allowed the smoke to escape. Their host brought out a bottle of raki, and they all took a sip to be polite. As the hours passed, their host brought another man into the room, and the two men continued to make toasts and drink more raki. They served the Americans onions and bread, and when the men were busy making more toasts, the three medics slipped extra food into their pockets.

On their fourteenth day in Albania, the Americans awoke to a light dusting of snow and renewed concerns that the winding path they were on seemed to be taking them away from the coast. As they trudged onward, the snow melted and the trail became muddy. By midafternoon they walked up another mountainside and into the next village as it started to rain.

It was the third week of November, and the weather was growing as bitter as they felt. A heavy rain continued for the next three days, and the villagers of Turbëhovë agreed to let them stay until the weather improved. To pass the long hours in the various homes they were scattered among, the men and women played cards, swapped stories, thought of their families, and wished they were someplace else. Cruise told some of the other medics about showing one villager a photo of his father that he kept in his wallet. When the man asked his father's age, Cruise told him he was in his sixties, but the man refused to believe him, because no one he knew lived that long. Owen, meanwhile, kept busy by repeatedly trying to trade a tarp he had from the plane's survival kit for his host's coat, a short, gray jacket made out of wool, but the host refused.

Despite being bored and miserable, the Americans thanked their hosts in Albanian as often as they could. They knew their presence was taking a severe toll on the village's food supply and putting their lives in danger from the Germans.

*   *   *

While the party camped in the village, highly trained German soldiers from the 100th Jäger Division, whose name means "hunter" in German, found what was left of the American plane. Because the pilots had burned the C-53D and nearby villagers had salvaged anything they could from it, the only item the soldiers were able to retrieve was a damaged radio.

CHAPTER 8

Albanian Curse

After three nights in Turbëhovë, the heavy rain turned into a mist, and the party headed out. They covered several mountain ridges that gray day but didn't see another village until they came across one as the sun peeked through the clouds in the late afternoon. The village council of Krushovë granted them permission to stay, and they were divided up into parties of three or four to spend another night wondering if they'd ever get back to Allied lines.

When the Americans awoke the next morning, it was Thanksgiving, and though they were miserable and exhausted, they were grateful to still be alive. Thoughts of their families and what they'd possibly been told by the AAF had started to run through their minds as they sometimes walked more than ten miles a day, and the days had turned into weeks. For Hayes and some of the others, the idea of their parents suffering as they wondered what had happened to them was one of the most difficult challenges they faced.

That morning, rather than meeting somewhere outside as they had at other villages, guides brought them all to a stone building. As they filed into a large room, a bearded man wearing a long, black robe and black hat sat in a large wooden chair with a high back and arms that resembled a throne. Through Stefa, he explained that he was a Muslim imam who had been to the holy city of Mecca and required their respect. The pilgrimage to Mecca, or hajj, is one of the five pillars of Islam and is required of all adult Muslims at least once in their lifetime if they are physically and financially able. The meeting with the imam was short, and the Americans were unclear as to the purpose of it, but they had grown to accept that there was much about this country they didn't understand.

They were soon back on the trail, which led them down the mountainside. When they reached the bottom about four hours later, the sound of someone running behind them caught their attention. It was a man from the village. As he spoke to Stefa for several minutes in Albanian, the Americans knew from his tone of voice that something was wrong. Stefa turned to the group with a stern look on his round face and explained that someone had taken a sacred stone from a shelf in the imam's room and was to return it immediately. An awkward silence filled the air for several tense moments. Then, to the surprise of the group, Eldridge, a ruddy twenty-four-year-old medic from Kentucky, sheepishly pulled a flat stone out of his pocket. It was about three inches wide with a sharp edge. He replied that he had thought it was just a rock. The man who had come looking for the stone snatched it from Eldridge and spoke harshly to him in Albanian.

Stefa told Eldridge the man said he had sinned and placed a curse on him, but Eldridge simply shrugged his shoulders. Had it been a partisan who had taken the stone, violating the partisans' policy on stealing, he most likely would have been shot.

With the rock returned, they moved on to the next village, Faqekuq, where they spent another long night. When they gathered the next morning, Qani was nowhere to be seen. Stefa explained that the partisans in Berat needed him more than they did, and he'd been sent home. It was a disappointment to those who'd been with Qani since the attack on Berat and had taken comfort in his presence and considered him a trustworthy friend.

The group continued once again in an easterly direction rather than heading west toward the coast, but no matter how many times the Americans questioned the route, Stefa assured them they were headed the right way. As they slowly made their way up another imposing mountain, Mount Ostrovicë, the sky grew darker and rain soaked their uniforms. The ground was slippery, and before long the rain turned into a light snow.

Within the hour, as they ascended to higher elevations, the snow grew heavier until they found themselves in the middle of a raging blizzard. Huge gusts of wind blasted every inch of their wet clothes as they stuffed freezing hands into their pockets and kept their heads down to block the cold air. The wind was so strong, it blew Cruise's hat off his head. Though all of their feet soon felt like blocks of ice and their bodies shivered, they knew they had to keep going. Their uniforms offered little protection from the extreme conditions, but some were better off than others. Shumway, who was still limping from his injury, wore a leather flying jacket, but underneath he had on just a thin summer flying suit; and three of the nurses, Watson, Schwant, and Nelson, were without field coats. The snow was coming down so fast they could barely see the person in front of them, but they had to try to stay together to avoid losing one another in the blinding white storm or stepping too far off the narrow trail and facing disaster. "Some of the girls were sleepy and insisted on lying down in the snow," Rutkowski later said. "The rest of us slapped their faces and dragged them along. I wiggled my face muscles up and down to keep from freezing."

The trail was soon covered with a couple feet of fresh snow, and the markers leading the way could no longer be seen. The partisans in the front of the single-file line unexpectedly stopped and, to the surprise of those who could hear them, started singing sorrowful partisan songs. It was too dangerous to keep moving, and the partisans were waiting for the storm to die down so they could once again pick up the trail.

At some point along the way, Dawson, the nurse from Pennsylvania whom the other nurses called "Tooie," lost her footing and suddenly started to slide down the mountainside. Hornsby, the medic from the 802nd, was closest to her and instinctively grabbed her hand. His grasp stopped her from sliding any farther, and he was able to pull the shaken nurse back onto the trail. There was no question in the mind of anyone who saw it that the young Kentuckian had saved Dawson's life, but there was little time to celebrate. They knew they had to get off the mountain as quickly as possible.

By early afternoon, after some four hours of trudging uphill through the relentless wind and snow, the men and women reached the summit of the trail and headed down the mountain, their bodies numb with cold. The snow turned into rain, and that, too, stopped within the next hour. It took roughly three more hours, however, of walking in cold, wet clothes before they reached the next village.

When Stefa explained to the village council of Çeremicë who they were and where they had come from, the villagers stared in awe. They couldn't believe the party had taken the mountain trail at the end of November when others had died trying to cross it in warmer months. As word spread through the village, more people crowded around to see those who had accomplished such a daring, and foolish, feat.

Though Stefa didn't tell the Americans until later, some of the villagers had argued against the Americans staying. They had watched the Americans come down the mountain and toward the village and had seen a medic walk side by side with one of the nurses. Women and men were prohibited from socializing in many of Albania's Muslim villages, including this one. Ultimately, however, and to the good fortune of the Americans, the village council decided to let them stay in honor of their having survived such a dangerous journey.

It was during their two-day stay in Çeremicë that the messenger Stefa had sent to look for the British returned with a note from a British officer. The note instructed the party to meet him in the nearby village of Lavdar, where arrangements would be made to escort them to the coast for evacuation. It was the best news the Americans could have hoped for. They still had no information about the three missing nurses, but escaping once again seemed possible — for those who were told of the note. Not everyone knew right away. Because the party was often spread out among several houses, and the officers, which included the pilots and nurses, spent the most time together, they often knew details long before the enlisted men, who had learned to pick up information wherever they could rather than wait for it to be shared.

As soon as the British officer received the note from the partisans, he informed SOE headquarters in Cairo, who then relayed the information to American officials that the party was safe and in contact with the British. The Office of Strategic Services (OSS)—America's first national intelligence agency and a counterpart to SOE—was then informed, including those working at the new OSS base station in Bari. On November 27, twenty-three-year-old David Brodie, a lieutenant in the U.S. Army Signal Corps in charge of OSS Communications at Bari, received word. Brodie had sent a wireless operator over to Albania just ten days before, and his men were ready to help in whatever way they could.

British Brig. Edmund Davies, one of the senior SOE officers in Albania, had been at his makeshift headquarters in Bizë, east of the capital of Tiranë and farther north than the Americans, on November 28 when his Albanian interpreter informed him that he had heard "an American aircraft containing many doctors and nurses to help the partisans had landed the day before at Berat." The tough yet well-liked Davies, a balding and stout forty-three-year-old who had spent most of his career with the Royal Ulster Rifles and had twice been awarded the Military Cross for gallantry in the field, had laughed and told him it was "a Balkan rumour as usual—that there was nothing to it." Though he'd only been in the country since October, Davies had quickly learned that false rumors were rife in Albania. But the next time he and his men heard from SOE headquarters in Cairo, they received "a top priority signal" that informed him a plane of

Americans, including thirteen nurses, had crash-landed. He was to "take all steps to rescue the downed Americans and get them to Italy by sea as soon as possible."

A day later, a copy of a radiogram received from the Air Service Command at Bari was sent to Eisenhower's chief of staff at Allied Force Headquarters (AFHQ) in Algiers recommending that Eisenhower and other senior officials be notified that the Americans were believed to be in Albania and attempting to reach the coast. That same day, newspapers across the United States ran a front-page wire story from AFHQ in Algiers that a transport plane carrying thirteen nurses had been missing since November 8. The story was brief and offered only a few details: The last word from the plane was thought to have come while it was over the Adriatic, the nurses were part of an air evacuation unit, and next of kin had been notified.

The families of the lost personnel had received devastating telegrams issued by the War Department over the previous few days. Beginning with the infamous words "Regret to inform," the terse message sent to each family by Gen. James A. Ulio, the Army's chief administrative officer, offered little solace or hope regarding the young women and men. It indicated that they had been missing in the North African area for three weeks, and that the families would be promptly notified if "further details or other information are received."

Nolan McKenzie, Watson's husband of just a few months, was at a flight training school in Oklahoma when he received a telegram from Watson's father alerting him to the heartbreaking news. McKenzie immediately wrote a letter to Watson's parents. "I don't know what to say. I'm so grief stricken that nothing now seems to matter except the thin thread of hope that always exists when the word is 'missing.'" His mother also wrote to Watson's parents, whom she had not yet met. "Your grief is mine too. All the tears I shed do no good. I am trying to get hold of myself and be brave....I am worried and fear for Nolan. When he heard my voice, he went to pieces and could not talk. I fear he might lose control of his plane. Then our grief will be doubled....Let's keep praying and hoping yet our darling will be safe. Altho' I prefer death rather than know she must suffer as a prisoner."

For weeks, Hayes's mother had been experiencing nightmares and premonitions that something had happened to her oldest son. Her deepest fears were confirmed when the call from the telegraph office came to the Hayeses' Cape Cod–style home in Indianola. She and her husband were in such shock they sent their sixteen-year-old son, Karl, who had just received his driver's license, to pick up a copy of the telegram at the Western Union office in the train station. When he returned to the house, the shaking boy handed the telegram to his parents, who read it over and over, as if in doing so the message might somehow change.

For the parents of Adams, from Niles, Michigan, whose brother was a Japanese POW, and of Schwant from Winner, South Dakota, whose brother was missing, this was their second horrific telegram in a matter of months.

As the weary party of American men and women left Çeremicë, Stefa stopped them and warned them all to be more careful of their behavior in the Muslim villages or risk their chances of finding shelter and food. It was then that Thrasher told Hayes and some of the other enlisted men that they were going to head northeast in hopes of finding a British soldier, though he didn't mention the note they had received. He went on to say that if they were unsuccessful, they would split into smaller groups. Finding food and shelter for such a large party was proving too difficult to continue.

Stefa led them through bouts of rain and fog, and they spent the night in the village of Lekas. The trail, which had been steep and rugged since they fled Berat, had finally become smoother and more level, which made it easier for those whose shoes, particularly the nurses, now had gaping holes.

They continued heading east, spurred on by the news of the British soldier, but the GIs, blisters, lice, hunger, and general exhaustion suffered by so many of them was slowing them down.

On the last day of November, after twenty-two grueling days in Albania, they found the British soldier. As they approached the mountain village of Lavdar, they could barely believe it when they saw a fair-haired young man with a boyish face and blue eyes in full British uniform. He was engaged in conversation with the locals, and as he came over to greet them, he was surrounded by the men and women who all wanted to shake his hand. After introducing himself, twenty-three-year-old Capt. Victor Smith escorted the party out of the cold and into a one-room building with a blazing fire.

As an SOE officer, Smith had completed specific training before he'd been dropped into Albania by parachute less than a month before. Like other SOE personnel, he had been instructed in numerous spycraft techniques, including "silent killing" as well as operating traditional arms and explosives.

SOE personnel, who came from a variety of backgrounds, attended paramilitary schools, mainly in the Scottish Highlands. In addition to preparing them physically for the field, the schools taught them skills such as map reading, weapons handling, raid tactics, and demolition training. They were then sent to the Royal

Air Force base in Ringway, Manchester, in northern England, to learn parachuting and complete at least two jumps. They ended their training at finishing schools on the Beaulieu Estate in New Forest in southern England, which covered everything from how to maintain a cover story to proper communication in the field, and even honed their skills in lock picking, the use of secret inks, and disseminating effective propaganda.

The majority of the British officers in Albania received the same type of training but at SOE schools in the Middle East, including a requisitioned monastery in the British Mandate for Palestine on the slopes of Mount Carmel, and a jump school at a Royal Air Force station at Ramat David near Nazareth. Though the basic coursework remained the same, there were some specialty courses offered, such as skiing and climbing and mule management at a mountain warfare school in Lebanon. One officer found that the mule management class was "just about the most useful course of the lot." They had to be prepared for almost anything, and they trained accordingly.

Though SOE officers often entered enemy territory in disguise, the men in Albania wore uniforms that could withstand the harsh conditions of the mountain caves from which they operated. Some added local touches, including curly-toed slippers or fezzes, but battle dress was standard. Given that they worked in uniform rather than undercover, the men working in Albania were often referred to as British Liaison Officers (BLOs).

SOE had sent its first mission into Albania in April 1943 with the goal of organizing the Albanian resistance and destroying Albania's oil fields and chrome mines. By then, Churchill and his advisors believed that encouraging resistance in the Balkans would help divert enemy troops from other fronts and assist the

Allies in any future attacks on German forces in Italy and the Balkans. With the go-ahead to move in, a group of four men had parachuted into northern Greece in the dark hours of an April night and eventually made their way on foot over the Albanian border. Had any of them been captured by German troops, they stood a good chance of being executed following Hitler's Commando Order of October 18, 1942, which demanded that Allied men caught behind enemy lines be killed before being given a trial — a policy that violated international law. It stated that "all men operating against German troops in so-called Commando raids in Europe or in Africa, are to be annihilated to the last man. This is to be carried out whether they be soldiers in uniform, or saboteurs, with or without arms; and whether fighting or seeking to escape."

By mid-August 1943, SOE had trained some eight hundred Albanian men of the First Partisan Brigade and outfitted them with weapons to help them wage war against the Italians. By October, after the German invasion, twenty-four British special operations men worked in the country and were organized into seven small missions — all of which faced constant danger. Of the first fifty men sent into Albania, sixteen of them were eventually captured or killed. In comparison to the other Balkan countries of Greece and Yugoslavia, however, the number of personnel sent into the country was small. More than one hundred SOE men were stationed in Yugoslavia and nearly two hundred in Greece.

When the Americans arrived in Lavdar and met Smith, they knew nothing of SOE. They only knew that Smith was a captain in the Lancashire Fusiliers, a British infantry regiment. They told him about their long and tortuous route through the mountains and the three nurses who were missing. When they finished,

Smith turned to Stefa and asked, "Why did you bring these people all the way here?" Lavdar was so far east that they were now close to Korçë, a town only about twenty miles from the border with Greece and heavily occupied by German troops. It was almost as far as they could possibly be from their intended destination on the western coast and far too close to the enemy for comfort. Stefa's response was calm and vague. He explained that he needed to avoid the territory controlled by the BK and was looking for villages that could feed and shelter the large party. The Americans stood speechless as Smith reminded Stefa that there were other British near Berat, and if the partisans had contacted them, it was likely that the Americans could have been evacuated within a few days.

The Americans simmered with frustration and confusion at the unnecessary suffering and risk of capture they had experienced since they'd been on the run with Stefa over the past two weeks. Three of the nurses were still missing, and the party wondered if they had been captured or were dead. They weren't sure what to think. They'd never heard from the messenger Stefa had said he would send to Berat, and now they were hearing that so many of their troubles could have been avoided if the partisans had taken them to the nearby British immediately. Though Stefa had kept them out of German hands and secured food and shelter for them, he had dragged them across the country while putting his own life in danger. Had he done all of that to encourage the people to support the partisans? Was he under orders to do so?

Smith made a list of their names and told the Americans that his team would send a message to the U.S. military alerting them that the group had been located. As the Americans continued to give Smith details of their journey, they explained they'd had little to eat for the past several weeks and showed him the condition of their shoes. He assured them that his mission, or team, at a nearby village called Krushovë would provide them with food and would try to find some replacement shoes. He had already arranged for the party to stay in Lavdar while he went back to his headquarters to make arrangements for them to join him.

After the group followed Smith into the main part of the village to say goodbye, Smith handed several local maps to Baggs, who often took the lead within the party despite not being the senior officer. Baggs looked around for something to put them in and decided that Hayes's medical kit could serve as a map case. He asked Hayes to give it to him. Hayes had no choice but to hand Baggs the kit, but he was hesitant because he still had the K rations he'd taken from the plane, which he planned only to reveal to the others or use if it seemed like it was a matter of life or death. When he opened the kit and transferred the K rations to his musette bag, he felt the disapproving eyes of the entire group watching him, but no one said a word.

As soon as Hayes, Owen, Abbott, and Wolf, the four medics who'd become so close during their training at Bowman, arrived at the house they'd been assigned to for the night, the other men demanded that Hayes share the K rations. They argued that Smith had assured them the British would give them food so there was no reason to save them. Hayes refused and said they were to be used only if someone was in dire need, but the men told him either he could share them or they would take them. Hayes quickly decided it would be better to share, and they opened two of the rations. They were all so hungry that, for the first time, the K rations tasted fairly good to the malnourished men.

That night, a few of the nurses, including Jens, were assigned a home where they took baths in a shallow, wooden tub the family placed in front of a fire, ate a meal of mutton, and were treated to a bed with a feather mattress. With food in their stomachs and a warm place to sleep, however, all Jens could think of were her three missing friends, nurses Lytle, Maness, and Porter, and what could have happened to them.

CHAPTER 9

Secret Agents

W hen Smith returned to Lavdar, the party met him in the center of the village. Several inches of snow had fallen the previous night, and it was still coming down when they left for Smith's headquarters at Krushovë, where they would stay for the next few days.

They walked for roughly six hours into higher elevations as the snow continued to pile up, and several in their party, including Eldridge, who had taken the rock from the imam, struggled to continue as exhaustion, illness, and sore feet made each step of the strenuous walk that much harder. Many were cold, particularly the three nurses who didn't have coats and the medics wearing just field jackets. A few in the party rode mules while others tried to keep their minds off the walk with talk of when they would finally escape. Jens even bet Wolf a dollar they'd be home by Christmas. Wolf took that bet, saying he couldn't lose; he'd either have an extra dollar, or they'd be back behind Allied lines.

As they continued on, they passed three Italian soldiers, who looked even colder and more miserable than they and who were huddled by the remains of a demolished building. It was a desperate and haunting scene of men barely clinging to life. Portions of two walls provided some cover from the wind, but without food or proper shelter, the Americans knew the Italians would most likely not survive for more than a few days.

By the time the party arrived in Krushovë, they were trudging through knee-deep snow. Smith assigned the enlisted men to two homes, and the ten nurses shared a single room, while Thrasher, Baggs, and Stefa were housed together. As they had so many times over the past few weeks, the enlisted men slept on hard floors without blankets. This time, however, the villagers had blankets to offer, but they refused to share them because they had heard the Americans were infested with lice. The hardy insects that raced across their bodies throughout the day and night and made them constantly itch had remained the Americans' constant companions while they continued the fight against hunger and the GIs.

With so many difficulties weighing on them, the nurses and medics were now battling each other as well. "Some individuals grated on one another's nerves in close quarters," Jens wrote. "A few were almost blood enemies from earlier arguments over things that would not have mattered back in Sicily." One argument in Albania left Adams, the medic from Niles, Michigan, whose brother was a prisoner of war, with a black eye.

While the enlisted men adjusted to their quarters, Smith introduced the nurses to twenty-nine-year-old Alan Palmer, a major in the Royal Berkshire Yeomanry and leader of the small mission at Krushovë. Palmer had parachuted into Albania in October along with Smith and several other men; and, like many SOE officers, Palmer had come from a background of privilege and prestige. His great-grandfather was one of the founders of the world-famous British biscuit company Huntley & Palmers, and he had attended the exclusive Harrow public school followed by Oxford University. Palmer told the delighted nurses that through the mission's SOE wireless operator and their headquarters in Cairo, they had successfully alerted the American military that the party was now with them.

On December 2, on the group's twenty-fifth day in Albania, the War Department announced to the media that the group had been found and was safe. The premature announcement, which was meant to reassure the public, offered no other details, but by then an American rescue plan was already well under way. Twenty-four-year-old Lloyd G. Smith was being sent into Albania to find the Americans and get them out. A stocky and rugged captain in the Army Ordnance Corps, Smith was on detached service with America's OSS, the precursor to the Central Intelligence Agency.

In 1943, OSS was still a relatively new organization. It had gotten its start in July 1941 when President Roosevelt created the civilian office of the Coordinator of Information (COI) and placed former World War I hero and renowned New York lawyer William "Wild Bill" Donovan in charge. In June 1942, six months after the attack on Pearl Harbor, Roosevelt reorganized and expanded COI into OSS, which charged civilian and military personnel with gathering and analyzing strategic information, engaging in psychological warfare, and helping to organize resistance movements and carry out sabotage.

To determine how to train the male and female recruits of

OSS, Donovan, who had visited SOE training schools at country estates in Britain, had his senior officers inspect Camp X, on 275 acres of Canadian farmland outside of Toronto. At least a dozen OSS instructors and several dozen recruits would be trained at the secret camp. SOE also assisted OSS by providing training manuals and materials, including the use of Axis weapons to study. Eventually, however, OSS training distinguished itself from SOE training by focusing less on strict military discipline and formalities between officers and enlisted men and more on self-reliance and initiative. Donovan said, "I'd rather have a young lieutenant with guts enough to disobey an order than a colonel too regimented to think and act for himself."

Given that the agencies' missions were similar, OSS and SOE had to determine how they would work together in the various theaters of war. In June 1942, Donovan met with Sir Charles Hambro, SOE's executive director, in London where they carved the world into zones that would be controlled by one or the other or shared by both. They agreed that the Middle East section, which controlled Albania and other nearby countries, would be run predominantly by the British. It took more than a year of further discussions, however, before the specifics of the agreement were determined.

By March 1943, OSS had established a Cairo office, but it wasn't until July 1943 that OSS and SOE finally determined that American officers would be sent into the Balkans. Any OSS missions in Yugoslavia, Greece, and Albania, however, had to be coordinated by SOE Cairo and would share a cipher with SOE. To help ready men for the field, OSS officers would be given access to British training facilities in the Middle East.

It wasn't until mid-November, just weeks before Lloyd Smith

arrived, that Americans were sent into Albania, and Harry Fultz, the former principal of the Albanian Vocational School, was placed in charge of the new OSS Albania desk at headquarters in Bari. Despite the agreement, suspicions and tensions between OSS and SOE units in Albania remained high in 1943 and information was not always readily shared. When one SOE officer learned an OSS team had arrived on the coast, he replied, "They are not under our jurisdiction and we wish to have nothing to do with them. They can only be a public menace."

OSS officer Lloyd Smith, who had grown up mostly in State College, Pennsylvania, joined the Army in 1940 after deciding during Christmas vacation of his senior year at Penn State that he no longer wanted to pursue a career as an agronomist. He was sent to Wheeler Field, where he was assigned to the 696th Ordnance Company, Aviation (Pursuit), and took a two-month small-arms program before earning several promotions. On December 7, 1941, he was on temporary duty at Bellows Field on the southeast coast of Oahu providing Ordnance service to AAF squadrons when the Japanese attacked.

With the country at war, Smith went to Officer Candidate School at Aberdeen Proving Ground in Maryland, where he was commissioned a second lieutenant in April 1942. He was placed in charge of machine-gun instruction at the Ordnance training school, and in July he was made commander of a small-arms company of an Ordnance maintenance battalion and was sent to Egypt.

He'd been stationed in Egypt for almost a year and been promoted to captain when he was recruited by OSS in Cairo in early September 1943. An OSS recruiter promised Smith the excitement he craved, particularly because his brother Clayton was headed overseas to serve as a pilot on a B-26 bomber. Smith later wrote, "Unless I did something more exciting than Ordnance, I would have trouble living with him when we got back home after the war." Within ten days, he had started a two-month paramilitary course with the British 11th Commando Regiment at Ramat David.

When he completed his training, he was ordered to travel to the OSS base in Bari and then to Sicily, where he would determine which weapons and ammunition in an enemy supply dump could still be used. He would then bring the weapons and ammunition to partisans in Yugoslavia, where he would observe the weapons in action. Accompanying Smith on the trip to Bari was Hollywood actor and OSS officer Sterling Hayden. Hayden had run away to sea at the age of seventeen and sailed around the world several times before signing with Paramount in 1940, where he was dubbed "The Most Beautiful Man in the Movies." He joined the Marine Corps in 1942 with hopes of being stationed overseas and was commissioned a second lieutenant. When he learned he would be assigned to the States for two years, he volunteered for OSS using the name John Hamilton. Because of his experience with boats, Hayden was on his way to work on seaborne operations run out of Bari.

The two men traveled from Cairo to Alexandria in a three-quarter-ton weapons carrier before boarding a Liberty ship headed to the port of Taranto in Italy. When they finally arrived, Hayden was ordered to stay on board to look after several OSS vehicles, while Smith took a boat to shore and hitchhiked to Bari, roughly sixty miles away.

Smith arrived at OSS headquarters in Bari in the afternoon

and reported to the commanding officer, Maj. Robert Koch. Koch told him to get a room at a local hotel and either come back that evening or the following morning, depending on what he preferred. With nothing else to occupy his time, Smith returned at six that night, upon which Koch said, "We have a priority job. How would you like to volunteer to go to Albania?" Though Smith knew little of the terrain or the language, he agreed to the mission to find the Americans and bring them to the coast for a sea evacuation with just a three-hour briefing under his belt.

Smith received his orders on November 30, and by the evening of December 2, he had already made two attempts to cross the Adriatic by boat from Brindisi, another port city southeast of Bari. When his second attempt had been canceled that day because of the discovery of German mines in Brindisi's port, he decided to go back to the OSS office in Bari to wait until the area was cleared; he had just arrived when the Germans unleashed a massive air attack on the harbor only three blocks away.

Dubbed "the second Pearl Harbor," the nighttime assault on the crowded port under British jurisdiction was entirely unexpected. In fact, British Air Vice Marshal Sir Arthur Coningham had held a press conference that afternoon telling reporters that the Luftwaffe had been defeated in Italy. "I would regard it as a personal affront and insult if the Luftwaffe would attempt any significant action in this area." At seven thirty p.m., however, 105 German Junkers Ju 88s began their attack on the well-lit port where crews planned to unload cargo into the night. By the end of it, the Germans had sunk seventeen Allied ships and damaged several more. The deadly strike also killed at least one thousand people, including civilians, and left countless injured—in part because of an Allied secret. The SS *John Harvey* was delivering poison gas to Italy in the event that it was necessary to strike back against the Germans. Roosevelt had condemned the use of chemical warfare, but he had made it clear that the United States would retaliate in kind if attacked first by the enemy. When the SS *John Harvey* exploded in the harbor, it was carrying about one hundred tons of mustard gas. All those on board, most of whom never knew about the lethal cargo, were killed, and the deadly poison spread through the air.

Doctors treating casualties immediately after the attack were unaware that patients had been exposed to a chemical agent. It wasn't until local hospitals were flooded with people suffering from skin lesions, irritated eyes, and difficulty breathing that they began to suspect what had happened. Neither the British nor the American military revealed to the public the role poison gas had played. As a result, some of the affected civilians never knew they'd been exposed and suffered without receiving help. Despite the secrecy, American-born Mildred Gillars, dubbed "Axis Sally" for infamously broadcasting Nazi propaganda, learned of it and taunted the Allies on the air for gassing themselves.

After witnessing the massive attack just a few blocks away and unaware that a chemical weapon had been unleashed, Smith focused on preparing for his mission to find the missing Americans.

Those in the 807th who were evacuating patients from Bari also found themselves in the middle of the attack. Commanding officer McKnight, flight surgeons Voigt and Simpson, and some of the nurses were watching a movie at a local theater when they felt the building shake. They soon heard a loud crash, the power went out, and suddenly everything around them was covered with shattered glass and plaster. The roof of the theater's bar had been hit and destroyed. When the attack was over, the rattled but unharmed medical personnel walked back to their hotel and saw that the three tall buildings next to it had also been demolished in the raid. The wall in the nurses' room was "caved in, and the window frames were lying helter-skelter over the beds. Had any of the nurses been in their room during the raid, they most surely would have been seriously injured if not killed." With the area in ruins, the team decided to stay in the schoolhouse outside the city that functioned as their holding unit for patients waiting to be evacuated. As they drove past the harbor and saw numerous ships burning, they felt lucky to have survived unscathed.

Explosions continued throughout the night as one magazine after another exploded. Even when the members of the 807th boarded the plane the next day after hearing rumors about mustard gas, they could still hear and feel more explosions.

With word from the British that the Americans were still alive, the War Department sent new telegrams over the next few days alerting the family members that the lost personnel had been found. Though the telegrams offered welcome news, they provided little information except to say that the missing were "now safe and accounted for" and that the found men and women would be in touch with their family members soon to offer more information. Jens's parents received their telegram at their farmhouse in Stanwood, Michigan, on December 3 — her twenty-ninth birthday. Watson's parents received their telegram on December 5 and immediately sent word to her new husband, who wrote them back expressing his happiness. "It is certainly the best piece of news I have ever received. I'm so happy and so thankful, although still weak from the whole thing." Watson's parents and husband, however, like the other families of the missing, would not hear anything more for weeks and would be left to wonder if something had happened to their loved ones to prevent them from contacting them.

The American party spent several days in Krushovë. The medics in Hayes's group of enlisted men lived on cans of oily sardines supplied by the British and dark bread given to them by the villagers. Hayes's host also brought them an armload of straw and showed them how to make tea by putting the dried grass in water and heating it by the fire. They sipped it from a tin can someone had with them, since they'd all either lost their canteen cups or thrown them out when they'd started to corrode. The fare was far from what they had hoped for, but it was at least a change from the cornbread they'd lived on for so long.

The men and women all had time on their hands as they waited for the British to alert them to their plans for getting them out. In the meantime, the British found a couple pairs of shoes for the nurses who needed them the most, including Watson, whose soles were almost completely gone. The hobnails in the shoes, however, made them "heavy as lead." As men's shoes, they were also far too large for the women, who had to don several pairs of woolen socks, also supplied by the British, in order to walk in them. The rest had to carry on with the gear they had, though the British gave Thrasher gold sovereigns so the group could buy food and other items as they made their way to the coast. Thrasher handed out some of those coins to at least a few of the nurses. Jens was given one that was dated 1913, which depicted George V's profile on one side and Saint George on horseback slaying a mythical dragon on the other.

Though the British had dropped more than twenty tons of materials into Albania by the fall of that year, most of it had gone to supplying the partisans, including uniforms, weapons, and the British gold sovereigns used to finance the missions. Gold sovereigns hadn't been widely used in daily circulation in Britain since World War I broke out and the government started issuing treasury notes, but the sovereigns could still buy whatever the men might need.

Twenty-six-year-old Maj. David Smiley, who was second in command of the first group of British sent into Albania, reported that his mission received over thirty thousand sovereigns by parachute. "Some of the bags in which they came bore the Bank of England seal and certificates stating that they had been checked over forty years ago—the dates were stamped on them—and most of the coins bore the head of Queen Victoria." While the gold helped them buy supplies and assistance, the British also knew the dangers that came with it. The night Smiley was to receive his first supply drop, the local commissar hired two men to work as Smiley's bodyguards. Smiley gave one of the men two hundred sovereigns to pay his band of partisans, but before the night was over, the other bodyguard had shot and killed the man for the money and fled.

Delivering supplies to the men often proved difficult because of bad weather, last-minute cancellations, and poor communications. SOE personnel in the field often stood outside for hours in freezing temperatures waiting for the sound of the planes before lighting signal fires. If the sortie was canceled because of dangerous weather conditions or other problems, the mission wasn't alerted until much later, because the Royal Air Force in Derna, Libya, first had to get word to SOE headquarters in Cairo, which then notified those in

Albania. Often supplies landed so far from drop zones that desperate locals were able to reach them before the British.

One of these supply drops was attempted while the Americans were in Krushovë. Included in the drop were extras like peanut butter, soap, and feminine products specifically sent for the American party. The supplies, however, never reached the mission. Locals ransacked the container before SOE officers could retrieve it.

The feminine products for the most part were no longer needed. For the first few weeks in Albania, the nurses who had their periods made do using gauze from medical kits and other makeshift supplies, but by now most had stopped menstruating because of the stress on their bodies.

Early on the Americans' fifth day at the British mission in Krushovë and nearly a month after crash-landing in Albania, Major Palmer asked the whole party to gather in front of his headquarters, where he introduced Lt. Gavan Duffy and Sgt. Herbert Bell to those who had not yet met them over the past several days. Duffy, whose dark hair, slight build, and Clark Gable mustache gave him a distinguished appearance and made him look older than his twenty-four years, was with the Royal Engineers and had been a builder for three years before enlisting in the British Army in November 1939. Bell, a quiet, baby-faced young man with blond hair from North London, also twenty-four years old, was with the Royal Corps of Signals and had been trained as a wireless operator. Though both men were working for SOE like the others at Krushovë, no mention was made of that to the Americans.

Originally from Leeds in West Yorkshire, England, Duffy was

a demolitions expert who had been working in the Middle East since 1940. He was also part of the first SOE mission, a team of four men sent into Albania in April 1943 by parachuting into Greece and pushing north on foot. Along with Duffy, the men included Lt. Col. Neil "Billy" McLean; Smiley, whose bodyguard had been murdered for gold sovereigns; and a wireless operator named Willie Williamson. The men knew very little about the country, though Margaret "Fanny" Hasluck, a widowed anthropologist in her fifties who wore her gray hair swept into a bun, had briefed at least some of them on Albania's customs and language. At the time she was the sole member of SOE's Albania desk in Cairo and had lived in Albania for sixteen years before the Italians expelled her in 1939 as a suspected spy. She referred to the men sent into Albania as "her boys," and they called her Fanny, a witty reference to the much younger women in the SOE office who were part of the First Aid Nursing Yeomanry (FANY) and who decoded messages from the field.

One of Hasluck's boys who was sent in later was British actor Anthony Quayle, who would go on to star in movies like *The Guns of Navarone* and *Lawrence of Arabia* and who would encounter the Americans along their journey. Of Hasluck he wrote, "She was an enthusiast, but gave us little instruction in the kind of questions we were most likely to need — questions such as: 'How deep is the river? Can the mules get across? Where [is] the enemy?'" She did, however, have them translate and memorize fairy tales she'd learned while in Albania. One story told of an old couple who had adopted a mouse as their son and found that he had fallen into a pot on the stove. Though Quayle thought the exercise was useless at the time, he would later blurt out a few lines, the only Albanian words he could remember, during a tense moment with the commandant of the Fifth Partisan Brigade in which the man started to "loosen his revolver from its holster." The absurdity of Quayle's words at that moment eased the tension, and Quayle credited the lines with saving his life.

Duffy's team had also taken an escape course from Jasper Maskelyne, a famous British magician. One SOE officer who was sent into Albania in December 1943 recalled Maskelyne hiding "all sorts of items on his person" and asking his students to find them. When they finished, he would then "produce about twenty things [they'd] failed to find." The men also had "magnetic fly-buttons, mini-compasses concealed in buttons, pencil clips that pointed north when balanced on the tip of the pencil, files, silk maps, and money" sewn into their clothes along with gold sovereigns.

When they had completed their training, the men traveled from Cairo to a desolate camp in Derna, Libya, where they anxiously awaited their departure into the Balkans. The delivery of men into the field was often delayed because of bad weather, lack of available aircraft, or problems with the drop zones. Trouble with the planes themselves also plagued the missions, and several men were killed on their flights into Albania. When one SOE mission was sent in early December, their plane caught on fire while in the air over Greece and crashed. All five of the men, along with the flight crew, were killed.

The day before their departure, Duffy and the other men learned their Albanian interpreter had refused to go with them for reasons not entirely clear and had been arrested to prevent the mission from being compromised. Though rattled by the change in plans and the lack of an interpreter, the men boarded a Halifax bomber the following night wearing battle dress, flight suits, padded overalls, and parachute harnesses and feeling like "trussed chickens." While some slept, Smiley was so anxious that he read the latest issues of *Horse & Hound* and *Tatler* from cover to cover, including the advertisements.

The plane flew for some four hours before the pilot saw the sign on the ground that it was safe to jump: nine signal fires made into a V. "We sat round the hole with our legs dangling through. It was all rather unreal and ghostlike. The landscape below us was grey and white and green with the dark shadows thrown up by the clouds from the full moon. Suddenly the red light went out and a green light flashed on. I jumped immediately," recalled twenty-four-year-old McLean, the leader of the mission. Smiley wrote, "We dropped from two or three thousand feet. My first reaction was relief as my parachute billowed opened. Our descent took barely a couple of minutes, the noise of the Halifax engines fading as their aircraft gradually disappeared from view up the valley, below the tops of the snow-covered mountains, then came a silence broken only by the whistling of the wind in my rigging lines.... As we neared the ground I heard the jingling of the bells of the goats or sheep in their herds, then shouts, followed by a heavy thud as I hit the Epirote mountains of Greece."

The men were lucky, as all four landed safely, though Smiley tore a leg muscle when he hit a dry riverbed only some fifteen feet from one of the signal fires. Their plane circled the area and dropped supplies until the new arrivals used a torch to signal the pilot that they were safe. With that, the plane headed back to the base.

One SOE officer who had tried to parachute into Macedonia, a spot McLean had first considered, just two nights before, had disappeared. It was later learned by SOE that he had been captured by Bulgarian troops.

CHAPTER 10

Rumors

As the Americans huddled together outside one of the small village houses in Krushovë, Palmer explained that Duffy and Bell, the wireless operator who had also dropped into the Balkans in April, would lead them to the west coast where SOE personnel had successfully evacuated others by boat. SOE knew that OSS was sending an American captain to help get the party out and would meet them along the way. Some of the Americans were also aware of the American captain, but not all of them knew, including Hayes.

Duffy, who the Americans would soon learn was all business, and Bell, whom the Americans dubbed "Blondie," were both due for a respite from being in the field for some eight months and would leave Albania with the party when they were rescued. The two had seen their fair share of action and had adjusted as much as possible to the hardscrabble life, though it wasn't easy for any SOE men in Albania. Duffy viewed himself as "a kind of guinea pig set up by the Communist dictators in that country, being exploited to test how far they could go." Smiley later wrote of the toll the environment took on the men's mental state. "Under these conditions we were, to a certain extent, living on our nerves, and, as a result of the heavy mental strain, nightmares were not uncommon." Smiley and McLean had recommended to Brig. Davies when they left a few weeks earlier that men only serve in the field in Albania for six months before being given "time to rest and refit." They were certain some would never want to come back.

The British officers estimated it would take the party fourteen days to get to the coast, which would put them behind Allied lines a few days before Christmas. It looked like Jens was going to win her bet with Wolf. To the bitter disappointment of the anxious Americans, however, they would not get started until the following day. The Germans had just destroyed a village they would travel through, and the British wanted to be certain the Germans were long gone when they arrived.

While the men and women spent their final night in Krushovë, Lloyd Smith, the young American OSS officer, headed from Brindisi, Italy, to the coast of Albania in a British Motor Fishing Vessel under the cover of dark and wearing the uniform of a captain in the AAF to help support his cover story as a downed pilot if the Germans captured him. The treatment of a prisoner of war was far better than that of a spy, particularly with Hitler's Commando Order in place.

In charge of Smith's boat was Lt. Jack H. Taylor, a former dentist from California with the United States Navy Reserve who also served as Chief of OSS Maritime Unit in Bari. Taylor was not only secretly delivering Smith into the Nazi-occupied country, he was also bringing desperately needed supplies, some of which eventually landed in the hands of the Americans. Between December and January, he and his crew maneuvered through Nazi-infested waters to deliver seven sorties, each carrying ten tons of supplies, to the Allied men working in Albania.

Rough seas had forced Smith's boat to turn around during two previous attempts, and on one evening the crew had hastened their retreat when they spotted German patrol boats. Tonight, however, around eleven p.m., the captain was able to safely anchor a half mile off the Albanian coast, and the crew rowed Smith and supplies to the narrow shore.

With the black shadows of mountains looming over him, Smith hiked some eight hundred feet up a switchback trail to reach Seaview, a series of caves overlooking the Adriatic that had been established by SOE as a secret base camp just weeks earlier. Seaview allowed SOE and OSS to infiltrate and evacuate personnel, deliver weapons and supplies into the country, and pass on intelligence material. Because the Germans had occupied much of the Albanian coast through October, it was only in early November that an SOE officer was able to establish the camp, which he picked for its location in the Kanalit mountain range. The mountains ran adjacent to the coastline and created a barrier between the sea and the main road, which offered significant protection from the Germans. The main difficulty with the camp's location, however, was that it sat in the middle of BK territory. Because the BK was no longer fighting the Germans, the British would only give arms to the partisans, the BK's rivals. The BK, however, had no intention of letting the British supply the partisans with weapons to use against them, "so they lay there uselessly until in the end the base was betrayed to the Germans, who stepped in and took the lot."

Filled with lice and black scorpions, Seaview became the temporary home of several SOE personnel, an officer with MI6— Britain's secret intelligence service—as well as two Americans, twenty-eight-year-old civilian Dale McAdoo and twenty-one-year-old Corporal Don Orahood, and their Albanian guide and interpreter Ismail Karapiçi. McAdoo had volunteered for OSS's first mission in the country after previously heading OSS Albania in Cairo and was operating under the cover name of Maj. S. S. Kendall. Born in New York, he had a master's degree from Harvard and spoke Italian and French fluently. Orahood, a Chicagoan who stood over six feet four inches tall with blue eyes and blond hair, had been an amateur radio operator before the war and joined OSS in December 1942. While in Cairo he had expressed interest in fieldwork, and when he was transferred to the OSS office in Bari and OSS needed a wireless operator to go into Albania, he was chosen. Like Smith, McAdoo and Orahood had arrived at Seaview by boat. Referring to the easy docking, McAdoo recalled, "The landing was duck soup, except that we had all vomited ourselves to a mere shadow just before arriving."

McAdoo and Orahood spent their time in Albania working at or near Seaview to establish a critical intelligence system that relayed information to and from the Bari base station. With the help of Karapiçi, as well as two other Albanians, they established an intelligence network along the coast. Karapiçi, a partisan from Vlorë, had been imprisoned in Italy for five years, accused of plotting to kill Mussolini, and had been in a displaced persons' camp when OSS had tapped him for service. McAdoo considered him "an outstandingly capable worker of great courage and intelligence" and was distraught when Karapiçi was killed just a couple months later.

While traveling with thirty gold sovereigns on a reconnaissance mission with a guide from Dukat hired by McAdoo, Karapiçi had been shot in the back three times, once in the palm of his hand, and then stabbed. He was found naked, his belongings stolen, and the gold long gone. His guide alleged that two unknown men had attacked them, but the village of Dukat found the young man guilty and sentenced him to death. The man's family retaliated by threatening to expose the British mission at Seaview to the Germans if he was not released, and the village was forced to let him go. McAdoo blamed himself, because he had hired the guide and given the money to Karapiçi in front of him. In a letter to Fultz, the head of the OSS Albania desk, he wrote of Karapiçi: "Ismail had become a real friend of mine. I am too sick to write anymore.... Is Ismail's fate the fate of any man who tries to be honest in this God-forsaken, savage country?"

With little knowledge of Albania's culture or terrain, newly arrived Smith settled into the barren camp at Seaview with these other men and waited for information about the location of the American party to come over the wireless from Bari and Cairo.

Lt. Duffy, Sgt. Bell, and the American party met the next morning to begin their journey to the coast. It was December 7, the second anniversary of the attack on Pearl Harbor and America's entry into the war and nearly a month since the party crashlanded. Several partisans joined them, including Stefa. To make sure the Americans understood what they would face over the next two weeks, Duffy explained in his thick Yorkshire accent that they would walk five to six hours a day and possibly more as

they got closer to the coast. They would also face meager lodg-
ings, little food, and a constant threat from the Germans. The
grim news, however, was nothing new to the Americans who,
more than ever, were willing to do whatever it took to find a
way out.

Going with them were two mules that would carry Bell's wireless set, which included a transceiver, batteries, a gasoline-
powered generator, fuel, and an antenna. It was a Type B Mark 1,
a suitcase set with a canvas cover that had been designed just the
year before at Station IX, a secret SOE research and development
lab at the Frythe, an estate north of London. The inventor, Capt.
John Brown, had been tasked with quickly developing a portable
radio set that would allow communication between Great Britain
and Northern Europe. He first designed the Type A, a lower-
powered set with a frequency range of up to about four hundred
miles, and quickly followed it with the Type B, which was a more
powerful set with wider frequency ranges that could be used for
communicating over longer distances. His next set was a Type B
Mark 1, the kind used by Bell, which was supposed to weigh only
about twenty pounds but with everything in its suitcase it pushed
the scale to forty-two pounds. The inventor, who regarded it as an
"ad hoc, rush job" and considered it too fragile, began designing
the lighter Type B Mark II, but Bell found his set reliable and
relatively easy to transport using the mules.

As their only link to the outside world, the wireless set was
critical to the men in the field. Though they could not use it to
communicate with other SOE operating in Albania for security
reasons, they were in frequent contact with Cairo to inform them
of their supply and ammunition needs, their sabotage efforts, and
information on the enemy, resistance groups, and the weather.

The operators sometimes had difficulty getting messages in and out of the mountainous terrain, however, particularly in the winter months. They also had to be concerned with the Germans using their transmission signals to pinpoint mission headquarters, so they often moved to locations several hours away before sending and receiving messages.

Field operators, like Bell, sent coded messages at designated times and frequencies to operators at the Royal Corps of Signals working from Cairo's Mena House Hotel in the shadow of the Great Pyramid of Giza. By 1943, most SOE operators were coding messages using one-time pads, which required the original message plus a random key that both the field operator and the home operator held. Each key was used for one message and then destroyed, which made it unbreakable if used properly. Once the encrypted messages arrived at the Mena House Hotel, they were sent via teleprinter to coders, often young women officially working as members of FANY at Cairo's SOE headquarters at the Rustum Buildings, called "the Secret Building" by taxi drivers in Cairo. If an operator was unable to get his message through at the designated time, or "sked," for one reason or another, he had to wait until the next appointed time. The process was inefficient, but it invariably saved lives.

Along with Bell's mules were another two mules Duffy had procured so the Americans whose shoes were showing wear could take turns riding them. The mule skinners were coming along to ensure that the animals were returned to them when the British needed fresh ones. Finding mules was never an easy task, and Duffy despised it. "I would prefer running into Germans rather than go through the tortuous hours I spent in haggling for mules," he wrote. "Generally, on the question of mules, the only

The nurses and medics aboard the missing plane were part of the Medical Air Evacuation Transport Squadron (MAETS), an innovative Army Air Forces program that transported more than one million wounded and sick troops during the war. Taken in July 1943, the photo includes the 807th MAETS nurses and enlisted men. *(Courtesy of the Harold Hayes Collection)*

Captain William P. McKnight served as the 807th's commanding officer and helped in search efforts for the missing. *(Courtesy of William P. McKnight, Jr.)*

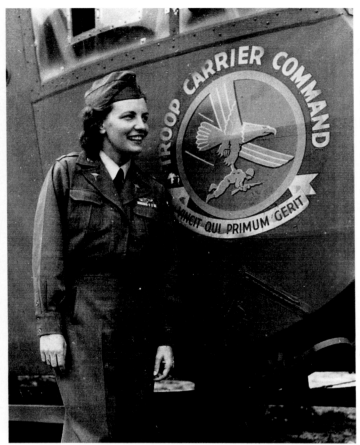

Agnes Jensen, one of thirteen nurses aboard the flight, joined the Army in 1941 in hopes of seeing the world. *(Courtesy of the Agnes Jensen Mangerich Family)*

Twenty-one-year-old Harold Hayes, seen here in 1945, was one of the first medics added to the 807th's roster. *(Courtesy of the Harold Hayes Collection)*

Medics Robert Owen (*left*) and Lawrence Abbott (*right*) became fast friends with Hayes during their air evacuation training at Bowman Field Air Base in Louisville, Kentucky, and were also on board the ill-fated flight. (*Courtesy of the Robert Owen Family*)

A German attack on the Albanian town of Berat almost cost the Americans their lives and left the party scattered. (*Courtesy of the National Archives at College Park, RG 226, Entry 165, box 11, folder 105*)

Kostaq Stefa, shown here with his wife, Eleni, and their dog Rosy in their garden, led the stranded party through the mountains for weeks, finding food and shelter for them and keeping them from the Germans. Stefa was tortured when he returned to his home after helping the Americans and in 1948 was executed for having collaborated with the Allies. *(Courtesy of the Kostaq Stefa Family)*

Sergeant Willis Shumway, the flight's crew chief, who had to be carried from the battered plane, rests his injured knee while overlooking the town of Berat. *(Courtesy of the Willis L. Shumway Family)*

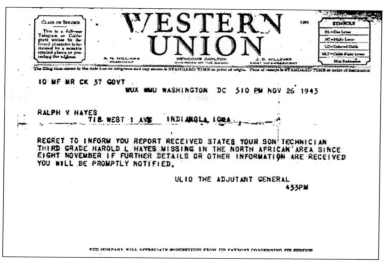

ID MF MR CK 37 GOVT

WUX WMU WASHINGTON DC 510 PM NOV 26 1943

RALPH V HAYES
718 WEST 1 AVE INDIANOLA IOWA

REGRET TO INFORM YOU REPORT RECEIVED STATES YOUR SON TECHNICIAN THIRD GRADE HAROLD L HAYES MISSING IN THE NORTH AFRICAN AREA SINCE EIGHT NOVEMBER IF FURTHER DETAILS OR OTHER INFORMATION ARE RECEIVED YOU WILL BE PROMPTLY NOTIFIED.

ULIO THE ADJUTANT GENERAL
433PM

Telegrams, like the one sent to Hayes's father in Iowa, alerted family members in late November that their loved ones were missing. *(Courtesy of the Harold Hayes Collection)*

In late December, the valley beyond the Albanian town of Gjirokastër became the site of a daring but failed air evacuation. The ill and exhausted party was inconsolable when the arrival of German troops prevented rescue planes from landing. *(Courtesy of the National Archives at College Park, RG 226, Entry 165, box 11, folder 105)*

British Lieutenant Gavan Duffy (*third from right*) of the clandestine Special Operations Executive (SOE), shown here with other British officers and top-ranking partisans, including future Albanian dictator Enver Hoxha (*second from right*), led the party from eastern Albania through the war-ravaged country to the Adriatic coast. (©*Imperial War Museums, HU 64764*)

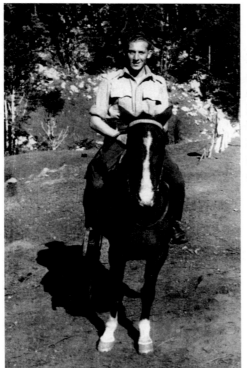

British Sergeant Herbert Bell served as Duffy's wireless operator during the journey and helped provide a critical link between those in the field and SOE headquarters in Cairo. (©*Imperial War Museums, HU 65068*)

The crew of the British motor launch, which rescued most of the Americans after months of being trapped in Albania, braved waters patrolled by the Germans during the nighttime mission. *(The National Archives of the UK: ref. HS5/121)*

McKnight (*left*), the 807th's commanding officer, greeted Gertrude Dawson and the rest of the party at the dock in Bari, Italy, while unseen military photographers snapped pictures of the event. (*15th Air Force [USAAF] photo courtesy of Air Force Historical Research Agency, Roll A6544*)

Some of the nurses—(*left to right*) Lois Watson, Lillian Tacina, Pauleen Kanable, Elna Schwant, Ann Kopsco, and Frances Nelson—showed off oversized men's shoes given to them by the British in Albania when their own fell apart after they walked hundreds of miles. (*15th Air Force [USAAF] photo courtesy of Air Force Historical Research Agency, Roll A6544*)

Duffy poses with nurses Eugenie Rutkowski (*left*) and Ann Kopsco in front of one of the staff cars that transported the Americans from the dock in Bari, Italy, to the 26th General Hospital. *(15th Air Force [USAAF] photo courtesy of Air Force Historical Research Agency, Roll A6544)*

The British crew (*above*) who helped rescue the Americans offered them shots of rum to celebrate their escape during their journey back to Italy. *(15th Air Force [USAAF] photo courtesy of Air Force Historical Research Agency, Roll A6544)*

The flight crew—(*left to right*) copilot James Baggs, pilot Charles Thrasher, radio operator Richard Lebo, and crew chief Willis Shumway, members of the 61st Troop Carrier Squadron—were fortunate to have had their leather flying jackets with them to help battle the brutal weather in Albania's mountains. *(15th Air Force [USAAF] photo courtesy of Air Force Historical Research Agency, Roll A6544)*

Charles Adams (*left, front*), still sporting a black eye, and William Eldridge (*far left*) are among those who enjoyed coffee at the 26th General Hospital in Bari, where the group was confined for several days upon their return. *(15th Air Force [USAAF] photo courtesy of Air Force Historical Research Agency, Roll A6544)*

Duffy, who received a kiss at the hospital from Tacina and Nelson for helping to rescue them, later noted that the nurses "always managed to create an impression, either entering or leaving a village. For years to come I feel sure that certain inhabitants of Albania will never forget the 'Çupke Amerikane' (American girls)." *(15th Air Force [USAAF] photo courtesy of Air Force Historical Research Agency, Roll A6544)*

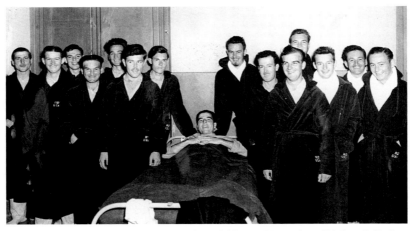

The enlisted men—(*left to right*) Gilbert Hornsby, Richard Lebo, Charles Adams, Robert Cranson, Willis Shumway, Paul Allen, William Eldridge, James Cruise, Robert Owen, Gordon MacKinnon, Raymond Ebers, Harold Hayes, Lawrence Abbott, Charles Zeiber, and John Wolf—stayed together in the hospital before briefly returning to Catania. *(15th Air Force [USAAF] photo courtesy of Air Force Historical Research Agency, Roll A6544)*

The nurses—(*left to right, front row first*) Gertrude Dawson, Elna Schwant, Lois Watson, Lillian Tacina, Ann Kopsco, Ann Markowitz, Frances Nelson, Agnes Jensen, Eugenie Rutkowski, and Pauleen Kanable—were confined to the same ward as the enlisted men while military officials decided what information about their journey to release to the public. (*Courtesy of the National Archives at College Park, 342-FH-3A-13650*)

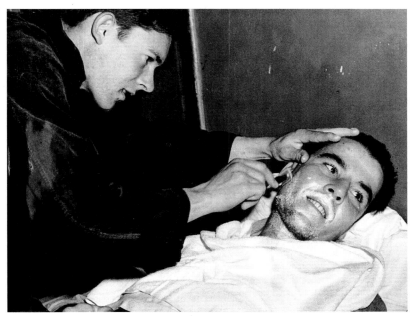

Eldridge, one of several in the party who were ill while stranded in Albania, offered Cruise a hand shaving in the hospital while Cruise recovered from pneumonia. *(15th Air Force [USAAF] photo courtesy of Air Force Historical Research Agency, Roll A6544)*

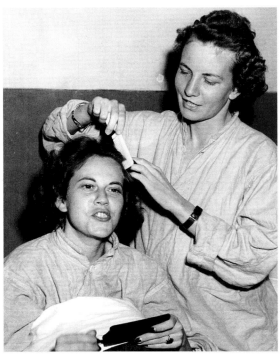

Dawson (*left*) and Jensen passed the time in the hospital waiting for word of when they would be released and allowed to go back to their headquarters in Catania. *(15th Air Force [USAAF] photo courtesy of Air Force Historical Research Agency, Roll A6544)*

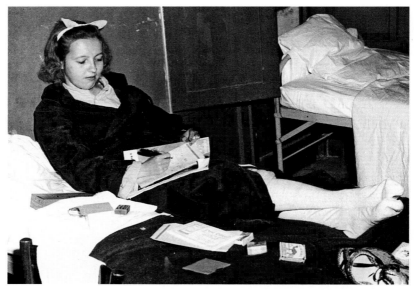

In the hospital, though she and the others were forbidden from discussing details of their time behind enemy lines even with their loved ones, Watson wrote a V-mail letter while enjoying a cigarette. *(15th Air Force [USAAF] photo courtesy of Air Force Historical Research Agency, Roll A6544)*

Lloyd Smith, a twenty-four-year-old captain on detached service with America's clandestine Office of Strategic Services (OSS), helped rescue the main party. Months later, he returned to rescue the remaining three nurses. *(Courtesy of the Agnes Jensen Mangerich Family)*

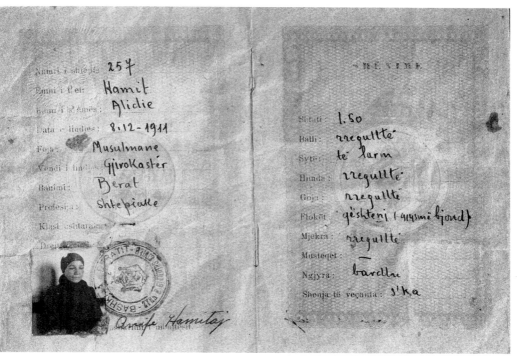

False papers, like this document made for Wilma Lytle, helped the three nurses trapped in Berat eventually escape. *(Courtesy of Carolyn Sue Lytle Lonaker)*

Several Albanian men, including Hodo Meto *(center)* and Tare Shyti *(far left)*, risked their own lives leading the three nurses to OSS officer Lloyd Smith near the coast. *(Courtesy of Carolyn Sue Lytle Lonaker)*

The three nurses, Wilma Lytle, Ann Maness, and Helen Porter (*left to right*), seen here with Sulejman Meço, Tare Shyti, and an unknown man (*left to right*), walked the mountain trail from the coastal road to the caves that served as an Allied base camp. (*Courtesy of Carolyn Sue Lytle Lonaker*)

Jensen (*left*) and Maness, shown here in uniform with a little girl trying on one of their flight jackets, returned to Bowman Field as instructors and sold war bonds, but like the others in their party, they never forgot their harrowing journey and ultimate rescue. (*Courtesy of the Agnes Jensen Mangerich Family*)

answer I used to receive was 'S'ka [Mushka]!' (No mules). I advise anyone visiting Albania that the first word to learn is the counter to 'S'ka.'" Duffy wasn't alone in his frustration with haggling. Many other SOE personnel also complained of bitter negotiating and price gouging. One wireless operator was particularly disgusted when a man tried to charge the mission for having burned the grass at a drop zone with its signal fires.

Though the partisan commandant of the area had earlier asked Duffy to take along a battalion of partisans with the Americans, he had wisely declined. The battalion, which had just arrived from Berat, was led by a man who later deserted the partisans and joined the BK. "After being in Albania, one certainly does acquire an increased sense of intuition and also suspicion," Duffy wrote. He was not only suspicious of the battalions' sudden appearance, he also believed that it had taken the Americans so long to find the British because the partisans "had taken the party on a propaganda and goodwill tour." He wasn't about to let that happen again.

When they left that cold morning, Duffy "looked back and surveyed a seething chain of American army personnel, 27 in all, trudging through snow a foot deep." As they made their way, he rested an MP40 against his shoulder while he held the barrel with one hand. A popular German submachine gun, the MP40 was also called a Schmeisser and was similar to the tommy guns issued to Allied forces, yet it was lighter, which caused some Allied soldiers to ditch their tommy guns for them.

Duffy led the group for a while, then fell back so he could keep track of everyone. "Sometimes he would stand on the side of the trail as we passed by and looked us over," Jens wrote. "We used to . . . say [Duffy] is counting his chickens." Regardless of his position, he always seemed to have his hand clasped on the barrel of the gun and the body of it resting against his shoulder.

Bell had chosen a Sten gun, one of the cheaply and simply made submachine guns the British started to produce to increase their store of weapons when the threat of a German invasion appeared. Though soldiers both revered and hated the gun and gave it a variety of nicknames, including the "Dime-store Tommy," "Stench Gun," "Woolworth's Special," and "Plumber's Nightmare," their low production cost and simple design made them a popular choice for the Allies to give to resistance groups. Their tendency to fire if dropped, however, later cost one SOE officer working in Italy his life. When Bell later sprained his ankle while trying to load one of the mules, Hayes carried his gun to help him, unaware of its notorious reputation for accidentally discharging. Despite the injured ankle, Bell, like Shumway, who was still limping from being hurt in the crash landing, carried on the best he could and never complained.

The snow soon began to melt and the sun warmed them. By late morning, they passed through a village, thought to be Voskopojë, which was known for its domed churches and their priceless vibrant frescoes. Much of the village had just been destroyed by the Germans, and the smell of smoke overpowered them. Many of the buildings had been burned, and the remaining stone rubble was still warm. The only people they saw were women and small children, and Duffy told the Americans that some of the boys and men had fled before the Germans arrived—those who hadn't had been shot. With destruction and death all around them, they hurried through the village and continued walking until they came to their next stop for the night, Gjegjovicë. The enlisted men were all quartered in the same house, and as they tried to sleep, Owen announced it was his twenty-first birthday. "It's a hell of a place to spend your birthday," he said.

Eldridge, the medic who had taken the rock from the imam, had vomited throughout the night and was still sick the next morning. He looked so deathly ill that the others insisted he ride one of the mules until they reached their destination for the day. Some of the enlisted men wondered if the Albanian's curse had affected Eldridge more than he'd let on, but none of them felt well. The cold weather, continued hunger, lice, and the GIs were taking their toll on everyone, and they were tired from the constant walking and the endless search for clean water to refill the few canteens they still had. Those who'd lost their canteens shared with the others. Their only comfort now was a single roll of toilet paper given to them by the British at Krushovë and dubbed "the piano roll," after the roll of paper used on a self-playing piano. They longed for the everyday necessities they had once taken for granted, and many constantly thought of food. Hayes's dreams were now filled with mashed-potato pie and other homemade dishes he craved.

That night Duffy split the group between two villages, Panarit and possibly Manëz, after talking it over with one of the village councils for roughly an hour. Dividing the group would become a frequent routine with Duffy and lessened the burden on each village. Though the enlisted men were as exhausted as the others who were able to settle into their assigned quarters, a partisan guided them for another thirty or so minutes along the trail to the village where they would stay. As they made their way, they passed a group of men walking next to a woman dressed in bright, colorful clothing and makeup and riding a mule. No other woman they had seen in Albania had been dressed so elaborately and they wondered who she was.

They found out the next morning when the party met again. Stefa told them that the gunshots that had repeatedly woken them through the night were in celebration of a wedding, and the men had passed the bride. Most marriages in Albania at the time were arranged, and those who fell in love with someone else often paid a heavy price if they pursued it. Brig. Davies had heard the story of a young couple in love whose families were involved in a blood feud in which only a death could avenge a wrong, whether real or perceived. The couple eloped and ran away to live, but bad weather and a lack of food forced them to return to their village. When they came back, they had hoped to be greeted with happiness. Instead, the fathers each shot their own child. Some women in the northern mountains of the country who wanted to avoid an arranged marriage chose to become "sworn virgins," which required them to live as men for the rest of their lives.

Eldridge was still so sick that as they made their way along the trail that day, people took turns walking beside him on the mule to make sure he didn't fall off. Around midday they reached a swift section of the swollen Osum River that was about fifty feet wide. The current was too powerful for anyone to wade across, and the water was deep enough that it reached the mules' bellies when they entered it. Duffy sent Bell and his radio equipment over first, followed by some of the mule skinners who were able to get the animals to backtrack across the river to pick up more of the party. When it was Eldridge's turn, they all watched in fear. If he fell over, the river would quickly sweep him away. To everyone's relief, the weakened medic held on tightly to the mule and made it safely to the other side.

With the nurses and Eldridge across, Duffy ventured ahead, leaving behind the medics and some of the mule skinners. Hayes and Abbott were the last to cross, and when they got to the other side, they had to scramble to catch up with the others on the trail. They finally found them an hour later at the next village, Gostinckë, where the locals were on guard after a partisan commander had stolen more than a thousand sheep belonging to the BK in the past week. Despite their fears of a reprisal, the villagers welcomed the Americans into their homes.

When the party headed out the following morning, they took a different route than Duffy had originally planned, to avoid BK territory. His interpreter refused to go near it, and Duffy thought traveling "at this stage without an English speaking Albanian threatened to be no fun." The new course required them to pass by large numbers of partisans who were gathering on the hills opposite from where the BK forces were positioned. Concerned that fighting would break out at any moment, Duffy rushed the group through the area.

Despite their continued difficulties and the threats surrounding them, a few of the nurses insisted on stopping on the trail to reapply their makeup before they entered a new village. The delays irritated some of the other nurses who had all kept up with the men trudging up and down the mountainsides over the many weeks, and most of the medics were baffled by it. A few of the nurses had worn makeup periodically on the journey, but none had held up the group to do so before they met the British. Duffy noted that the nurses "always managed to create an impression, either entering or leaving a village. For years to come I feel sure that certain inhabitants of Albania will never forget the 'Çupke Amerikane' (American girls), who always managed to produce the necessary cosmetics and render the necessary repairs. They used to leave the people non-plussed, including, I might add, myself; after all they were in enemy occupied territory. Amazing! Much too deep for me as a soldier."

The hours passed as the party continued walking, and Eldridge once again had to ride one of the mules. A few of the nurses and medics whose shoes were in the worst shape also hitched occasional rides. Hayes preferred to walk, though he wasn't sure his right shoe would hold out much longer. After they had first met the British, one of the nurses had put his shoes too close to the fire to help them dry, and the sole of one had cracked. Though she had been trying to help, her mistake was one he was reminded of daily; and, now, whenever he took off his shoes, he tied the laces and looped them around his neck so nothing else could happen to them.

As they plodded along that afternoon, they saw someone they never expected to see again: Gina, the partisan whom they had last seen in Berat before the German attack, along with some of his men. He had shaved off his mustache, which made him look much younger, and it took the Americans a few moments to realize who he was. He first walked over to Baggs, who had given him the machine gun as a parting gift the last time they'd been together, and asked the copilot if he had any more ammunition. Baggs shrugged his shoulders and told him he had nothing left. Gina quickly rallied from his disappointment and walked along the line of Americans and greeted each one. The party immediately asked him if he'd heard anything about the three missing nurses, but he told them he had been in Elbasan and had not yet returned to Berat. When he revealed it had taken his group of men just five days to find them, the Americans were astounded that he could track them so quickly, particularly after their long journey.

With Gina now traveling with them, they continued on their course while hearing repeated rumors of an Allied invasion at Vlorë and Durrës, the two chief ports on the coast. The rumors, Duffy wrote, had made "the two pilots slightly light-headed. They did think their walking days were over." He was much more skeptical, however, because he'd heard the same rumors seven times over the past months. "I immediately rebuked them severely, pointing out that they, like myself, were part of an organized force, namely the English and American army and not party to a rabble they had experienced in this country." When they arrived at the next village, Malind, that evening, Duffy and Bell sent a message to SOE headquarters as they had promised the pilots, though they knew what the answer would be. "Have heard persistent rumours of invasion STOP Yanks wish to hear as soon as possible any change in previous plan."

Rain and cold followed them for their roughly four-hour journey the next day to the village of Odriçan. It was a short day of walking for the party, and Duffy was glad for it because he and Bell needed to charge the set's batteries. As Duffy and Bell had expected, they received a message from Cairo hours later that the invasion was just a rumor, and they were to continue on their course.

The Americans said goodbye to Gina the next morning and set out on the trail. Unlike the other days where their destination had remained a mystery, Duffy informed them they were heading toward a town called Përmet. They would be traveling along a road sometimes used by the Germans, and he instructed the party that if they ran into trouble and were somehow separated, they were all to meet in the town. As they walked along the road, the Americans felt particularly vulnerable to attack, but luck was on their side, and they never saw another soul.

The Italians had previously burned Përmet, and the village had come under attack again just the week before by the Germans, who had burned many of the remaining houses. To protect what was left, a wooden bridge that once stretched over the Vjosë River and connected the road to the town had been destroyed and replaced with a swinging suspension bridge that would only be able to support bodies and not German tanks or trucks. The men and women, unsure of how much the bridge could handle, slowly made their way across it, spreading out their weight as they carefully maneuvered across.

When they were all safely on the other side, they boarded an old Italian truck that took them into the center of town as they passed a cheering crowd of people excited to see Americans.

CHAPTER 11

Lurking Danger

Hayes and Abbott awoke in a cold, barren room filled with straw on the morning of December 14. Their host brought them some money that Thrasher had given him earlier that morning on behalf of the two men and told them they were to go to the market to buy something to eat. The medics only had to walk a few hundred feet before they found the open-air market and others from their party. No one had eaten the night before, so Thrasher had dispersed some of the money given to him by the British and told all of the men and women to see what they could find. Hayes and Abbott had only been there for a few minutes when someone from their party told them it was time to meet the others. The men quickly scanned the choices, which seemed to be mostly cornmeal and onions, and settled on the largest head of cabbage they could find. They showed it and their money to the merchant, unsure of the value of either, and, to their surprise, the merchant took some of the money and gave the rest back to them.

Those in the market made their way to their meeting point in town, where they found Duffy, Bell, Thrasher, Baggs, and Stefa waiting for them. The only mules with them were the ones loaded down with the wireless gear, so Eldridge, who was still not feeling well despite having rallied a little, would have to walk. It was going to be a difficult day. To get to Sheper, their stop for that night, they had to take steep switchback trails over Mount Nemërçkë, whose highest peak rose more than 8,100 feet above sea level.

They were just about to leave when a group of about six Albanian men and women came out to greet them. One of the women held a jar of honey while another offered a spoonful to each person in the group. They savored the sweet taste, and the honey gave them a needed boost of energy. After weeks of mostly cornbread, onions, and sour cheese, it was a luxury.

After they all had a spoonful, they thanked their patrons and started their climb up the difficult trail, straining already sore muscles. Hayes and Abbott, who'd split the cabbage head in half, tore off leaves until there was nothing left. The steep mountain challenged even Duffy. "It took almost seven hours of what I consider the worst climbing in Albania, which is over the top of Mt. [Nemërçkë]....This was the second mountain of this type the Americans had climbed. The remarks of some of the nurses longing for the plains of their own country were really amusing." The trail was not only difficult but dangerous. Another SOE officer had a horse slip and fall while on that same trail at a different time. "But by the grace of God I had my feet out of the stirrups and slid off just in time. The horse fell down a clear drop of over 100 feet," he wrote.

*   *   *

Exhausted after a day of grueling hiking, the weary party arrived at Sheper, a village of about one hundred stone houses and roughly fifteen miles north of the border with Greece. Like every place they had been to, the threat of danger was always present. Just six months later, a bomb splinter at Sheper killed Maj. Philip Leake, head of SOE's Albania desk at the time, when two German fighter planes bombed and machine-gunned the village. The attack occurred the day Leake was supposed to head for the coast and return to Italy.

The group was soon greeted by forty-five-year-old Maj. Bill Tilman, the stocky and bristly mustached leader of the mission at Sheper, who found "the nurses in good heart and looks, the orderlies—big, stalwart men—tired, bedraggled, and depressed." The oldest SOE man sent into Albania, Tilman was also a world-famous mountaineer who had been a part of three Mount Everest expeditions and was a decorated veteran of World War I known for being able to walk faster and farther than almost anyone. A fellow officer wrote, "Once his mission had been established he climbed the local mountains every morning before breakfast, to the great discomfiture of his partisan guards who had been given strict orders to accompany him everywhere and not let him out of their sight."

Tilman and his men had created an organized life at Sheper, which, for a man who craved adventure, was rather "dull and placid" when they weren't receiving drops of weapons, clothing, and boots for the partisans. "We ate our three good meals a day, ciphered signals, visited neighbouring villages, showed the partisans how to use explosives, and argued more or less amiably with various people who came to see us," he wrote.

Given Tilman's expertise in the area and in climbing, Duffy spoke to him about the location of the sea evacuation and his planned route. Expecting another supply drop, Tilman tried to get Duffy to stay in Sheper for the next few days, but Duffy declined because he wanted to get to the coast as soon as possible.

Before the party was split into two for the evening and the medics left for the next village, Tilman announced that they had about a twenty-five-mile hike ahead of them the following day. It would be their longest walk yet.

OSS officer Lloyd Smith waited at Seaview for five days with no word over the wireless on the location of the American party. The conditions at the camp were grim and the days long. Sheep and goats had once lived in the low-ceilinged caves, and the lice they'd left behind were rampant. SOE officer Smiley, who had just been evacuated from Seaview days before, wrote, "We were desperately keen to go, for we were very rapidly running out of food and water. The mule that had carried the wireless set died, and for the week that we were there this was the only meat we ate, eked out one day by some tinned food. . . . There was no water locally, and we would have run out but for a very fortunate storm one night; after that our only meagre supply was what we could collect from puddles in the rocks with a sponge." The situation had become worse when a local appeared and tried to convince the men he owned the cave, and if they didn't pay him a sovereign a day he would turn them over to the Germans.

Unwilling to wait any longer in the bleak caves for word on the Americans, Smith decided to see what he could discover on his own. British Lt. Comm. Alexander "Sandy" Glen, a former Arctic explorer who was working from Seaview for MI6 gathering intelligence and organizing sorties, had told Smith that Tilman was in the village of Kuç and might have some information on the American party. With a .45-caliber handgun, a compass, maps, and a shepherd to guide him through BK territory, Smith set out on his mission through unfamiliar and dangerous terrain.

About noon the following day, he arrived at the village of Dukat, where more than two dozen armed members of the BK argued with him for an hour about why he should not travel through partisan territory, which was necessary to get to Kuç. They told him thirty people had recently been killed in Tërbaç, one of the villages he would pass through, after a skirmish broke out between the villagers and the partisans, and that the Germans were now thought to be occupying it. With Smith's guide scared and wanting to go back but Smith refusing to alter his plans, the BK offered him three of its men to take with him as long as he guaranteed their safety and escorted them back to BK territory. Smith accepted the arrangement, and he and his new guides headed out later that afternoon.

They had been on a rocky trail for a few hours when they ran into a band of more than two dozen partisans armed with Breda 30s, light machine guns used by the Italians, as well as several types of rifles and British and Italian grenades. Though the large group of men and their weapons must have concerned the BK guides when they first saw them, only one of them stopped and insisted on accompanying Smith and his men the rest of the way to Tërbaç.

They arrived in the early evening, and the partisan led them to a house where Smith was welcomed. As Smith talked to the men with the aid of a female interpreter, the partisans asked him why the Allies weren't making better progress in northern Italy and told him how well the Russians were doing. It wasn't long before they also told him they wanted to take the three BK guides as prisoners, quickly introducing Smith to the country's muddled politics. Smith told them he wasn't going anywhere without his guides, and if the partisans prevented him from completing his mission he would tell the U.S. government they were the cause. That was enough of a threat for the partisans, who quickly backed off. The female interpreter suggested Smith go talk to the commandant of the Fifth Partisan Brigade, whose headquarters were at Ramicë, village just a few hours to the north.

With ten partisans surrounding him, including the interpreter, Smith and his guides left for the village. On their way the party ran into the commandant, who insisted that Smith ride his horse for the rest of the journey. They finally arrived at Ramicë around midnight, only to have the commandant leave to check on some of his 1,500 men. Smith tried to get more information through the commissar, the partisan's local representative, but the partisans continued to steer the conversation toward politics.

The commandant still had not returned in the morning, but one of the SOE demolition officers arrived and informed him that Tilman had gone back to his headquarters at Sheper. With few alternatives, Smith decided he would return to Seaview to see if any news had come over the wireless.

Smith and his guides headed back to Tërbaç. When they arrived that afternoon, they learned that the partisans and Germans were fighting in the Llogora Pass, a winding road that cut through the mountains. His planned route was now blocked. With darkness only hours away, it was too late to try to cross the mountains north or south of the pass, so Smith decided he and his men would camp where they were. As he waited in the village that evening, he noticed partisans carrying German boots, army rifles, a machine gun, and three Luger pistols. "I estimated that at least ten Germans must have been killed to secure this quantity of arms, and equipment. Every Partisan I met claimed that he alone had killed from eight to ten Germans."

When he woke the following morning, he learned from the commissar's messenger that the commissar had taken Smith's three guides as prisoners and would not allow Smith to leave with them. The unexpected news didn't sit well with the American, who immediately marched down to partisan headquarters. After the two men argued, the commissar eventually agreed to let the guides go into Smith's custody with the provision that they would not be allowed to leave until the commandant gave his approval.

Those plans changed, however, when the Germans unexpectedly showed up. Smith, who had earlier noticed the villagers "getting nervous and jittery," heard gunfire that afternoon coming from a village just north of them. The commissar rushed to find Smith and tell him the Germans were coming and that he and his three guides were free to go. Having learned nothing new about the American party's location but much about Albania's civil war, Smith and his guides headed back the way they had come.

A partisan guided the enlisted men the half hour back to Tilman's mission at Sheper on the clear morning of December 15 to meet the rest of the party before they started on their grueling twenty-five-mile walk to Gjirokastër. With no place in between to stop, Duffy set a brisk pace as two in the group rode mules.

For roughly the first half of the nine-hour trip, the trail followed a river and the party passed various bands of partisans coming and going. By late afternoon, the Americans were exhausted and stopped on a hillside to rest. The hillside overlooked a large, flat valley that Duffy said had previously been used by the Italians as an airfield. As they rested, someone in the party asked Duffy why they couldn't be evacuated by air from the field rather than walk all the way to the coast. To the Americans' frustration, he replied that the plans had already been made and would not be changed.

It was about six in the evening when the party crossed the field and a wooden bridge that took them into partisan-controlled Gjirokastër, a well-preserved Ottoman town, similar to Berat, of about twelve thousand people. Set on a steep hillside with narrow cobblestone streets, it was topped by a large Byzantine castle. The town, just miles from the Greek border, was the birthplace of partisan leader Enver Hoxha, Albania's future dictator, and previously had been occupied by the Italians. It was now in partisan hands, but that would soon change.

Just seven months later, the Germans, who had gained control of the town, would hang two young partisan women in one of the town's squares with the cooperation of the locals. Twenty-year-old Persefoni Kokëdhima had been sick and wounded and was hiding in her village to the west of Gjirokastër when she was caught. The Germans had demanded that the villagers shoot her for fighting against the Germans and betraying them, but they refused. She was eventually imprisoned in the castle in Gjirokastër while awaiting sentencing and there met fellow prisoner, twenty-two-year-old Bule Naipi, who had grown up in the town. The two were sentenced to death by a panel of local men and one German for their partisan work. On July 12, Kokëdhima was brought before the gallows in front of Naipi in an attempt to force

Naipi to name other partisans and was hanged. Six days later, after Naipi refused to give up any of her fellow partisans, she too was executed.

The Americans walked through the empty streets in the dark until they reached the center of town, where they ran into a group of partisans who talked with Stefa and Duffy. The partisans then led the party to a meeting room, where they waited for several hours while partisan leaders decided where to put them for the night.

A guide led Hayes's group of six enlisted men, which included Owen and Abbott, through twisting cobblestone streets in the chilly night air until they came to a stone wall with a massive wooden gate. The guide yelled "Haki! Haki!" and a lone voice replied from behind the gate. The two men spoke through the door in Albanian before the man behind the gate asked, "English?" Owen responded, "No, we're Americans." As soon as the words came out of Owen's mouth, they heard the man start sobbing. The man rushed to unlock the gate and push open the door. When it was open, he shouted, "My friends! Come into my house" and the Americans followed him inside.

The dark-haired man named Haki led them past rooms packed with corn and finally to the guest room, where they sat on a padded bench. He continued to sob as he told them his story. Like their friend George in Berat, Haki had left Albania to seek his fortune and also ended up in Pennsylvania as a cook. When he came back to retrieve his wife and two sons, the Italians invaded, and he and his family had been trapped. Haki's wife and sons, however, refused to live with him now. As Haki told the Americans, his family had left because they didn't believe the stories he told about American luxuries—hotel rooms with private baths, milk delivered to doorsteps, and telephones in each room of a house, and they accused him of being mad. The Americans asked Haki about the piles of corn stored in the other rooms, and he explained that his tenants who farmed some of the land he owned could only pay him with part of their crop. He had been unable to sell it and had no other place to store it other than his home.

When Haki finished his story, Allen, the youngest in the group, asked Haki if he could have a pan to soak his feet, lifting his shoes so Haki could see they were in bad shape. Both of Allen's shoes had large, gaping holes in the soles, and his feet had been wet and dirty for days. Haki begged their forgiveness for being a bad host and said he would get them some water. When he came back, he brought two large pans and told them all to take off their shoes and socks. Each of the six sat in astonishment as he washed their feet, which ached from the long day's journey.

They later asked him if he had anything to eat, and again he apologized for being a poor host and asked them if they liked flap-jacks, an offering that made their mouths water. When they assured him they did, he said he'd be right back and went outside. He returned minutes later with a sack of sugar—a true extravagance in war-torn Albania that must have cost him a considerable amount. They went to the kitchen, where he lit a fire on the stone floor, set a ring stand over it, and added fat to a pan. He then mixed water and wheat flour into small clumps of batter and dropped them into the hot grease. When each deep-fried flapjack was ready, he took it out, dropped it briefly into the sugar, and handed it to the ravenous men. They each ate three before Haki ran out of batter.

The men slept better than they had in a long time. In the morning, when Haki woke them from the padded benches they'd slept on, he said he was going out to see what he could find for breakfast. He came back a short time later holding a large orange for each of them. The men had not had any fruit since they'd been in Albania other than the quinces some of them had shared after the attack on Berat, and they thanked him profusely as they ate the juicy, sweet oranges, and asked him where he had found them. When he told them he bought them in town but they came from an orange grove just beyond the nearby mountains, Hayes thought for a brief moment about going to find the grove so he could have as many as he wanted.

After they'd eaten, Haki told them it was time to meet the rest of the Americans, but before he finished, he started sobbing again and begged the Americans to take him with them. They explained that the British were helping them and decided who could go, but he continued to plead. "I'll clean your floors. I'll wash your clothes. I'll do anything for you if you will take me with you. You see what my life is like here. You see how I cook here. I think of my fry kitchen in America. I wonder what has become of it. Please, take me with you." It was an awkward and difficult moment for the young men who wished they could help the man who had been so kind to them, but they were powerless to do anything for him.

A layer of frost covered the ground that morning as they followed a somber Haki to a neighbor's house where some of the other enlisted men had stayed and were now eating breakfast at a cloth-covered table. Hayes's group was still hungry and they looked longingly at the others eating, but the host never offered them any and they had learned from Stefa not to ask.

When the others were ready, Haki led them to a meeting place at the northern edge of the city. The rest of their party was waiting there along with some three hundred and fifty troops from the First Partisan Brigade who were organizing for a mission. Some of their leaders shouted orders and men scrambled in response, while mules were loaded down with various parts of a cannon and other supplies.

By midmorning, the partisans moved out, heading north. Duffy, who had stayed up well into the night decoding several messages from Cairo with Bell, told the Americans he was staying in Gjirokastër but was sending them to Mashkullorë, a village about three hours away, that he thought was safer. The road that ran in front of Gjirokastër and the wooden bridge connecting it to the town made it too easy for the Germans to reach it. He assured them he would catch up with the group the following day. Several of the American men who had heard that a member of the Gestapo in Gjirokastër had sent word for German troops to come and capture the Americans wondered if the rumor was true.

At Duffy's order, Stefa and the Americans, who were headed the same way as the partisans, waited until late morning to leave so the two parties wouldn't be traveling together. If the partisans ran into the Germans or the BK, Duffy didn't want his group in the middle. The trail was fairly level and the pace relaxed as the temperature rose.

When they arrived at Mashkullorë, however, they found that only about a dozen houses were still standing from previous Italian and German attacks. The town had very little food, though Thrasher was able to buy some fresh meat for the group before they were split among houses for the evening. The party decided to move on to the nearest village, Zhulat, in the morning, but they soon found that it too had seen its share of war.

*   *   *

Duffy and Bell had received messages from Cairo while waiting at Gjirokastër that indicated there was a new German drive from the seaport of Vlorë headed in the same direction as their evacuation point at Seaview. Despite the grim news, Duffy was pleased to learn that Cairo indicated he should continue to press on with the party but to "take all precaution." When he and Bell left Gjirokastër in the morning, it took them longer to find the party than they had expected because the men and women had moved on to Zhulat. When the two groups finally reunited, Duffy decided they would stay in the village for another night.

CHAPTER 12

Breaking Point

In the brutally cold morning, the party continued on the trail toward the coast. The Americans had already spent five weeks in Albania, but they were still hopeful that the end was near. They were also growing impatient, and more and more of their shoes were giving out after walking so far for so many days. The stitching that held the soles onto Owen's shoes was coming apart just as the group's endurance was also giving way. In one of the villages they had just passed through, the partisans saluted the Americans in Albanian with "Death to Nazis!" instead of the usual "Death to Fascists!" Hayes, who'd had enough of the salute and the politics that were holding them hostage, on top of being exhausted and hungry, came very close to replying, "Death to Communism!" Fortunately for everyone, he stopped himself.

As the hours passed they continued to make progress, briefly marveling at two women dressed in long, black dresses, each carrying large bundles of firewood on their backs while spinning wool and walking. The group eventually arrived at another badly damaged village that afternoon, and Duffy and Stefa tried to arrange housing, but the village council refused to allow them to stay. A band of partisans had arrived the night before and eaten all the villagers' food.

The party carried on and came to the village of Progonat about an hour later—the only place in the nearby area that was still intact. The villagers welcomed the Americans, and Owen, Wolf, and Hayes were soon led to the guest room of their assigned house. In the corner of the room with bare walls and piles of straw on the floor stood an ancient-looking cot with missing springs and no mattress. Their host, another man who had learned English at the Albanian Vocational School, served them cornbread and sour cheese and excitedly asked them who wanted to sleep in the bed he proudly owned. Though they didn't want to insult their host by refusing the cot, it looked so uncomfortable that they each preferred the hard floor. Finally Owen piped up and said, "We'll draw straws! Short straw gets the cot." Owen picked up a few blades, and, after each took their chance, they held the results in front of one another. Hayes cringed at the small piece of straw he held in his hand, while Owen and Wolf both grinned.

The three medics awoke the next day to a Muslim imam chanting a call to prayer. The family they'd stayed with the previous night had no other food to offer, so the men were moved to another house. With no word that the party would be leaving the village soon, the men gestured to their new hosts that they were going out for a walk.

The dirt streets were muddy from the rain the night before and few people were out, though they passed a group of men sitting outside and talking as they held prayer beads in their hands. As the medics milled about, they came across Baggs, who told them that Duffy and Bell had left that morning to find out if the local partisan leaders had gathered any new information.

Duffy and Bell returned that night, however, without having been able to locate the local leaders. While the two men sent and received their daily messages from SOE Cairo, Hayes, Owen, and Wolf were in their assigned house watching a young boy as he stoked the fire, giggled at the American men, and played the kaval for them. The long day ended with Owen going outside to go to the bathroom and being attacked by a dog, from which he managed to escape without any injuries.

Duffy told Thrasher the next morning that he was going ahead of the group and would meet them in Gusmar to the west of Progonat two hours later. When he arrived, however, he found the village in chaos. The improvised partisan hospital was being evacuated in anticipation of the German drive. Duffy knew then that he had no choice but to stop the party's progression to the coast and backtrack. It was too dangerous to continue forward.

When the party arrived, they told Duffy of passing dozens of badly wounded partisans. Some were unable to walk and had to be carried. Stefa had learned that these were the men from the First Partisan Brigade they had seen gathered at Gjirokastër a few days before. They had run into a German patrol of roughly twenty-five soldiers, and the ensuing battle left them with the casualties they were now seeing.

Duffy gathered the group together and explained as calmly as he could that they had no choice but to turn back. "They were at this point only two days from their goal—so heartbreaking surely," he wrote. The change in plans was hard for the group to grasp, since everything had gone according to their plans since they'd met the British officers. They thought they were finally on their way home, though they didn't realize just how close they were. "We were washed up," Abbott later wrote. "We could climb mountains on our hands and knees, we'd done it; we could live on cornbread and sour milk, we'd done that; we could sleep with the lice and fleas chewing us, march in the rain and go barefoot if we had to. All these things we could do, where there was ahead of us the hope of the blue sea, the hope of getting back to our lines, the hope of home! Now that hope was gone.... There was nothing left in us that said, 'Keep on.' We'd made a good fight of it, but, the fight was over."

Though the group was devastated by the turn of events, Duffy's decision likely saved them from disaster. "As events proved later, the German drive was an avalanche, dispersing the first brigade," he wrote. The dejected party moved eastward to another village about a half hour away.

At some point that day, Monday, December 20, the Americans' forty-third day in Albania, Thrasher asked Bell to send a message on his behalf over the wireless while Duffy was on a reconnaissance mission. Like many in the party, the pilot's patience had run out. Thrasher's message, which he asked to be sent to the commanding officer of the Twelfth U.S. Army, said that the road to the coast was completely blocked and the entire party was exhausted. Half of them were sick and their shoes were nearly gone. He asked for a C-47 with an escort to pick them up at the airfield in Gjirokastër on Wednesday and added that he could ensure that there were no enemy aircraft in the area, and they would have partisan protection at the field, which was in perfect condition. Cairo received the message and forwarded it to the AAF with the following message: "Inform most urgently (one) airforce view as to feasibility (two) airforce signal and other requirements (three) dates on which pick up sortie possible. Have asked Duffy's views."

If the air evacuation happened, it wouldn't be the first in the Balkans in recent months. OSS's Cairo branch had conducted a special operation in Greece in October when it evacuated fourteen American fliers by air. It wouldn't be the last, either. The following summer, Operation Halyard, an Allied airlift operation, began after downed airmen constructed a landing strip for a fleet of C-47s. More than five hundred Allied airmen trapped in Nazi-occupied Yugoslavia were rescued.

The party turned back from Gusmar and arrived in Kolonjë as rain turned the roads into mud. They would be stuck there for two nights as Duffy and Bell tried to figure out their next move. On their second day in the village, Hayes and Owen started getting restless and hungry. They hadn't eaten in almost forty-eight hours and wanted to see if any of the others had been any luckier. Some of the enlisted men, including Hayes, were convinced the officers were getting more food than they were. Cruise even tried to stay with the nurses because he thought the villagers were more generous when the women were present.

As the two men walked through the village, Allen, the youngest of the group, called to them to come over to the one-room house where he and another medic had stayed. When the men entered the tiny house, they saw two women standing in the back, while two men lay by the fire. None of them spoke English. Hayes and Owen asked Allen if he'd had anything to eat, and Allen told them he'd only had a little corn that the family had heated for him in the fire. Hayes picked up one of the pieces of hard field corn lying on the dirt floor and started to roast it. When the kernels were brown, he removed it and took a bite. Though it was tough and tasted like scorched popcorn, it was something to eat.

When he finished, one of the women walked over to a chest and took a key from a cord around her neck and unlocked the box. She reached in and pulled out something wrapped in a rag. As she removed the cloth, the surprised Americans saw a skinned sheep's head. The woman placed the head in the coals, where it roasted for about an hour. With nowhere else to be, Hayes and Owen stayed to watch. The woman eventually removed the head from the heat with a stick before she took an ax and split it into two with one solid whack. The Americans watched wide-eyed as the two women each took one-half of the head and ate everything, including the eyeballs. Nothing was wasted. Though the Americans were famished, this was one time when they were glad to have not been offered food.

After the Americans spent a second cold and wet night in Kolonjë, Duffy told them that the fighting had gotten even worse over the past few days. Instead of going back to stay in Gjirokastër, they were going to travel to the far side of the valley, which included crossing a road that the Germans had started using in the past week as well as the Drino River, where a small boat would be waiting for them. It was too risky to cross either the road or the river in the daylight, so they would travel to a nearby village and wait until nightfall.

It was still raining when they started walking that afternoon. The soles of Allen's and Owen's shoes and some of the nurses' shoes were almost entirely gone. The leggings that Owen wore over his shoes and pants were keeping the soles of his shoes from completely falling off. They stayed on the muddy trail until they arrived at the village shortly before dark and waited.

As night started to fall they headed out, and by the time they reached the road, it was completely dark. The relentless rain continued to drench them as Duffy told them he would send them across one at a time. When they reached the other side, they were to keep walking until they reached the riverbank, where a few at a time would be taken across in the boat. When it was finally Hayes's turn, he felt more alone than he ever had in his life. He couldn't see anyone ahead of him or behind him, and it felt to him like the rest of the world had disappeared. He walked as fast as he could in the blackness of night until he reached the riverbank, where another medic was waiting for the boat. They couldn't see anything, but they could hear the oars slicing through the water as others joined them. When the boat arrived, it was a simple vessel made of wooden sides and a bottom constructed out of sheet metal. Though Hayes was sure it would leak, it proved its sturdiness, and he and the others were safely escorted across. The boatman motioned for them to continue on a trail, where a villager from Kolonjë met them and took them to a nearby house.

Duffy and Bell, who likely carried the wireless set across in the boat and arranged for fresh mules to carry it the rest of the way, soon joined the party at the house. Each person was given his own plate and silverware for the first time since they'd been at the hotel in Berat, and they enjoyed a meal of boiled potatoes. It wasn't long, however, before Duffy told the party they had to keep going. The village was too close to the road to be safe.

They finally stopped for the night a couple of hours later at the village of Karjan, and Hayes, Owen, and Wolf were once again placed together. When their hosts gave them blankets, and their son told them in stilted English to take off their wet clothes, Owen had to convince Hayes to part with his. The men spent a warm night wrapped in blankets in front of a fire, and when the family gave them their clothes the next day, the men were over-whelmed to find they were not only dry but clean.

Smith, the American OSS officer, along with his three BK guides who had been released from the commissar as the Germans approached Tërbaç, left to go back toward Seaview. After climbing a snow-covered mountain about sixty-five hundred feet high, the men finally arrived in the late afternoon on the outskirts of Dukat, the village where Smith had first met them. He had fulfilled his promise to their commander to return them unharmed.

He sent one of the guides into the village to find an English speaker, and when the two returned, they informed him that thirty German soldiers now occupied the village. They were sure, however, that they could get Smith through so he could continue on to Seaview. They dressed him in a shepherd's hat and cloak, and he boldly walked through the village, where he passed a German squad before he reached a truck that drove him to safety. It was a risky move, but it worked. Had he been caught out of uniform, he would have been executed as a spy.

After spending the night at a house owned by a man known to those at Seaview, he made his way back to the sparse base camp.

That afternoon, he received word over the wireless from Cairo that the American party had left Progonat and were expected to be at Kuç on December 21.

As he had done just nine days earlier, Smith once again set out the next morning with hopes of finding the party. This time he headed southeast on the coastal trail rather than using his first route, which would require him to go through villages now in German control. The new course was difficult but passable, and he ended the day finding shelter from the cold night air in a shepherd's cave.

The next morning he met the commissar from Vuno, who had a car and offered Smith a ride to his village. Smith spent the night in Vuno, where he arranged for two guides to accompany him the rest of the way in the unfamiliar terrain. They left the next morning, but when he and his guides were within a mile of their destination, the partisans informed them that the Germans had just occupied the village that morning. The men had no choice but to retrace their steps on the rough trail in heavy rain. After spending the night in another small village, they backtracked the following morning.

When they were once again close to Vuno, Smith studied the village and the road from a hill using field glasses and observed two German tanks moving through the village. He continued to watch until he was sure the Germans were just passing through before he headed to the partisans' headquarters. He stayed in the village for several hours, where he observed "six heavy trucks drawing 75mm guns and one command car full of Germans pass through going north." He left Vuno that evening and spent the night at the next village.

His clothes were still wet from the rain, and he decided to stay put the next day as the bad weather continued. Late that afternoon, he received word that the Germans were searching every home in Vuno looking for partisans. Concerned that the Germans would make their way to his village next, he positioned himself in a house at the western edge of town so that he could get away quickly if necessary. His instincts were right. At around ten p.m. that night, he was alerted that about eighty Germans had entered the village and were conducting house-to-house searches. He immediately fled and spent another night sleeping in a cave that he shared with a shepherd and his flock.

He arrived the next day at Seaview, having spent more than two weeks in the cold and treacherous landscape of Albania — no closer to finding the Americans than when he first arrived.

The party continued on in the rain until they arrived in Dhoksat, a mountain village overlooking the valley, late in the afternoon on December 23. There they once again met Tilman, the famous mountaineer, based at Sheper. They also were introduced to a wireless operator named Willie Williamson. The twenty-eight-year-old Scot had been among the first group of men, including Duffy, into Albania. The last few months for him had been particularly difficult since Smiley and McLean had left, and he was hoping to be evacuated soon. Just two weeks earlier, Williamson had written in his diary, "The long wait here with no certain knowledge of what is to happen to me is getting on my nerves. I feel so miserable and fed up. These wet days too. I am confined indoors with nothing whatever to occupy my mind." The arrival of the Americans, however, offered him some distraction, and he considered the nurses "the finest women [he'd] ever met."

That night, Duffy and Bell stayed with the other British in a stone house operating as their headquarters, while Thrasher, Baggs, Stefa, and the nurses were divided among the houses in Dhoksat. The enlisted men were sent to Qeserat, another village about fifteen minutes up a steep mountain trail.

While Tilman and Williamson enjoyed "an excellent lunch with the Yank officers" on Christmas Eve, the enlisted men did not fare as well. After a night crammed together in a single room in a large house without any blankets, the men watched as a few villagers brought a beef carcass into the kitchen and hung it on a hook. The Americans eyed it with great anticipation and wondered when the meal would be served. The man who would prepare it was an English-speaking Albanian cook hired by the British they'd met the night before. Almost immediately, the cook had told them that they would not be given any bedding because the female owner of the home had heard they had lice. The Americans certainly couldn't deny it; they were all still infested. Even Hayes, who had run out of louse powder, was now scratching as much as the others.

As the men looked forward to the meal, they spent the day watching German trucks drive along the road that ran in front of Gjirokastër. They noticed the partisans coming in and out of the kitchen that afternoon, but they didn't give it much thought. When they finally sat down to eat, the cook dished out small scraps of meat onto their plates. The ravenous men were incredulous and asked him what had happened to the rest of it. After some back and forth, the cook finally admitted that the partisans had eaten most of it. The men ate what was in front of them, grumbling through much of the meal, and when they retired to the cramped room where they would all sleep, they decided to post two men in the kitchen the following day to keep an eye on the cook. They also decided to send a few men to talk to the British about the food and to remind them how much they needed new shoes.

That same night, the nurses, Duffy, and Stefa joined the pilots at the house where they were staying for a Christmas Eve celebration. Someone had found a small tree branch, decorated it with some red ribbons, and put it in the corner of the room. The group spent the evening singing Christmas carols, talking, and trying to put petty arguments of the past few weeks behind them. One argument had broken out when it was discovered that two of the nurses had kept for themselves cigarettes that the British had given them at their mission headquarters at Krushovë, which others contended were for everyone to share. Some had even recently squabbled over their favorite meal and what they would eat first when they got back to Allied lines. Most wanted steak, but when one nurse said she wanted a steaming bowl of oatmeal with peaches, the others had mocked her.

The next day, Wolf won his bet with Jens. They were still in Albania on Christmas Day. She and some of the others housed with her woke early to attend a church service with their hosts in the small village. Jens had bathed the night before — a Christmas present in itself, as it was only her second bath in seven weeks — but she still had to put on her filthy uniform. Stefa met them outside the small Greek Orthodox church on frost-covered ground. They went inside and huddled in the back while the priest gave the service. It would be the last Christmas service the priest would perform. When the Germans and the BK learned his son was a partisan, they burned the church and killed the priest in an attack the following year.

That night, Duffy and Bell invited the pilots and nurses to the home they shared with Tilman and Williamson. The group ate chicken, drank wine and raki, made toasts, and danced to records on a phonograph to celebrate the holiday.

As the first shift of enlisted men monitored the cook that Christmas morning, Hayes and two others walked down the trail connecting the Americans' two village hideouts to talk to the British. Hayes carried his musette bag with him. He not only wanted to protect his belongings from being stolen, he also wanted them near in case something unexpected happened and they had to flee.

When they arrived, the British were finishing breakfast, and Hayes couldn't take his eyes off the honey and jam they had spread on their cornbread. His mouth watered at the sight of food until he remembered why he was there. The enlisted men pleaded their case regarding the cook and their shoes and then asked about the possibility of an air evacuation. They'd heard rumors about it, but no one had told them that Thrasher had sent a message. Tilman said they were on their own to work out the problems with the cook, but he would see what could be done about their shoes. He then showed the men a message he'd received over the wireless from SOE Cairo. The words, jotted down on a piece of white paper, simply said, "Men are expendable. An airplane is not." Refusing to give up the idea of an air evacuation, the Americans asked if a note could be sent to the AAF, thinking that if the British wouldn't help them, maybe the Americans would. Tilman told them a request had already been sent to the AAF; they were still waiting for a reply.

The men walked back to their village and shared the news

with the others, but most simply shrugged their shoulders. Few, if any, expected much good news at this point, and they didn't want to get their hopes too high.

The day passed slowly, with the men taking turns supervising the kitchen and turning away the partisans who came by until the cook finally refused to continue working if the Americans kept watching him. They left him alone, hoping they had staked their claim to the beef; but when dinner was served, they were each given a bowl of broth with small pieces of meat floating in it. The men asked the cook what it was, and he replied, "Something special. Sheep intestine soup." They were hungry enough that they ate it, but most of them swallowed it without ever tasting it. When they asked the cook what had happened to the beef, he left the room without replying. Though few of the men were in good spirits after the meal, Abbott coaxed them into singing a few Christmas carols in honor of the day before they spent another uncomfortable night crammed together.

While the Americans in Albania were hoping their luck would change, President Roosevelt's stirring Christmas message was delivered to the armed forces. "Two years ago Americans observed Christmas in the first dark hours of a global war. By sacrifice and courage and stern devotion to duty, you accepted the challenge boldly. You have met and overcome a determined enemy on the land, on the sea and in the air. Fighting with skill and bravery, you have already destroyed his dream of conquest. This Christmas I feel a sense of deep humility before the great courage of the men and women of our armed forces. As your commander-in-chief I send my greetings, with pride in your heroic accomplishments. For you the nation's prayers will be raised on Christmas day. Through you at last the peace of Christmas will be restored to this land in our certain victory."

The 807th in Sicily celebrated the holiday that night with a party at one of the villas outside Catania. As the nurses, flight surgeons, and enlisted men gathered to eat turkey and sing Christmas carols, their thoughts were also with their missing colleagues, whom they had been told several weeks earlier were on their way back to Allied lines. While they waited for the party's return, several of the enlisted men in the squadron had volunteered to become medics to help relieve the strain on the others and had taken classes from the flight surgeons as part of their training. One medic who was offered the chance to apply for a discharge turned it down out of respect for the missing.

CHAPTER 13

Beyond Reach

W hile the miserable weather continued over the next several days, the party waited in the two villages for the rain to clear. Tilman took the opportunity to send a local to escort the enlisted men to a cobbler in their village. When the cobbler declared there was nothing he could do for Owen's crumbling shoes, Shumway, who still limped from the crash landing, took off his flight boots, which covered his regular GI shoes, and gave them to Owen. The cobbler then ripped the cracked portion of the sole of Hayes's damaged shoe and used wooden pegs no bigger than matches to attach a new piece of leather to it. It was probably the best gift Hayes had ever received.

During those few days, Duffy got word that the AAF would attempt an air evacuation, despite his reservations about the safety and feasibility of the risky mission. The AAF had asked through SOE Cairo for information on the size of the proposed site of the air evacuation, the terrain, and the prevailing winds, so

Duffy had sent the pilots to the valley to gather it. He and Bell forwarded what they had learned. Now it was just a matter of waiting for the weather to clear. "By this time, the weather was filthy, the complete valley was enshrouded in thick soup, ground visibility was not more than a hundred yards," Duffy wrote. He continued to offer daily reports to Cairo but wouldn't offer a pickup time for the air evacuation until the weather improved. He also made it known to the pilots that they were responsible if something happened to the aircraft, since they had requested the evacuation without his consent.

On December 27, the already hazardous mission faced a new threat when a small group of German soldiers came from a town south of the valley and looted several shops in Gjirokastër. As the Germans left with their plunder in a truck and motorcycle, the partisans attacked them. Some of the Germans managed to escape, and Duffy and the townspeople knew that it was only a matter of time before more German troops came back for retribution. Duffy and Bell tried to contact SOE Cairo that night to let them know what had happened. Though they could hear Cairo, Cairo could not hear them.

Duffy and Bell tried to reach Cairo again the next day but couldn't get through. The weather had suddenly cleared, and despite their best efforts, they weren't able to make contact until that evening. Once again they could hear Cairo, which came "blaring in," but their signal was not received.

While Bell scribbled down messages, Duffy started to decode the first one: "The following arrangements will hold for [pickup] of Yanks. [Pickup] between 1100 GMT and 1300 GMT Wed Dec 28th. If weather prevents will try again some time next two successive days[.] Have party completely ready at SE corner of field. Permit no person within mile of Airfield except your party and one strong partisan guard group to stay with your party. Confirm OK. QRZ at 2130 GMT tonight."

QRZ was a Q code, which indicated that Cairo would call again at the designated hour. By the time the two men received the transmission and decoded it, however, the time had passed for the possible pickup and for confirming receipt of the message. If planes had come that day, surely they would have heard them. The attempt had likely been delayed when the British didn't hear from them.

Duffy and Bell tried again later in the evening to reach Cairo but still could not get through. Duffy also tried to get a man in Dhoksat to go to Gjirokastër and bring back a report on the German activity. At two a.m., he was finally able to convince one local to go in exchange for a sovereign. He and Bell tried again to reach headquarters at eight a.m., their designated time, but were once again unsuccessful. Knowing that the planes were coming, Duffy decided he had no choice but to try the evacuation.

The enlisted men, who were growing tired of being in the same cramped room together, were adding wood to the fire that morning when a partisan delivered a note. One of the medics read it and yelled to the group, "The airplanes are coming today! We're supposed to be in Dhoksat at seven thirty!" before he took off running. Those who still had their musette bags grabbed them, and the men immediately ran down the trail, cutting the fifteen-minute walk in half. When they arrived in Dhoksat, the British, Stefa, and the rest of their party were waiting. Thrasher asked the men what had taken them so long, and they responded by asking him why he hadn't sent the message earlier. He had. In fact, he had sent a partisan to deliver it the night before.

The group listened with excitement as Duffy explained that if he thought it was safe for the airplanes to land, they were to make a signal on the field. They would create a large X with yellow-orange parachute panels from supply drops that the British in Krushovë had given the party. The panels were about twenty feet long and several feet across at their widest point. Hayes and Owen, who had kept theirs in their musette bags, were among those who volunteered to help.

Duffy instructed the group to meet him later, and he went ahead to the airfield. When he arrived, he surveyed Gjirokastër with his binoculars and to his frustration he "saw the place alive with Germans, tanks, armed cars, trucks and troops. They had occupied the Castle."

The Americans along with Stefa and Bell arrived at the last hill between the village and the airfield later that morning—their fifty-second day in Albania. They were still about a quarter mile away from where the planes would land, but Duffy had picked this spot to prevent any chance of the Germans seeing them.

The several-mile journey from Dhoksat to the valley had been grueling for the exhausted group. Malnutrition and the GIs continued to weaken them and slow them down. Though the cobbler had repaired some shoes, others were in bad shape. Many in the party still had blisters and sore muscles, and Shumway was still limping from the crash landing. Keeping all of them going that chilly morning was the idea of getting on a plane and getting back to freedom.

When Duffy joined them on the hill, he told them that one of the messages he and Bell had received referenced multiple planes. The two men had decoded it several times to make sure they hadn't made a mistake. They didn't know what kind or how many aircraft were coming but if he thought it was safe for the planes to land despite the German forces now in Gjirokastër, the nurses would be the first to board.

Around noon, the messenger he'd sent to scout Gjirokastër in the early morning returned with details that confirmed what Duffy had seen earlier. Duffy then noticed "three trucks and one [armored] car" driving down from the town. He watched as they parked near the main road that ran in front of the airfield. With this new development, any chance the air evacuation once had seemed to have suddenly disappeared. Duffy decided it was too dangerous for the rescue planes to attempt a landing and refused to put out the signal. He and the heartbroken group waited on the hillside to see if the planes came.

About a half hour later, they heard the roar of planes coming from the north. Thirty-one Lockheed P-38 Lightning fighters, a British Wellington bomber, and two C-47s had left Italy that morning. Ten P-38s had been assigned to escort the Wellington and would patrol the road near the field when they arrived in Gjirokastër, while another twelve P-38s had been tasked with providing cover for the Wellington and the C-47s when they landed. One of those planes had been forced to turn back when the pilot was unable to raise the flaps as they approached the Albanian coast and crash-landed on its return. Nine additional P-38s would fly to the airfield near Berat to strafe the field and prevent any enemy aircraft from taking off. It was the same airfield the Americans had crossed with Gina weeks earlier.

Those on the hillside in Gjirokastër watched as twenty-one

P-38s filled the sky, circling the area in a precise pattern. The Wellington flew fifty feet over the airfield followed by two C-47s. It was the most beautiful sight many of the Americans had ever seen, and they were overwhelmed with emotion as they watched the powerful planes. "If I live to be 100 years old I shall never forget nor be able to express my feelings when I saw that swarm of planes sent out by the 15th Air Force just to rescue us," Jens said. "We were told 'planes with escort were coming' but in my wildest dreams I couldn't believe there would be more than a transport with 6 P38's. It was almost sickening to think we couldn't fill our end of the bargain by signaling them to land after they had gone all out for us. . . . We could only lie on that hill . . . and watch [the planes] fly low over the field as if they were just begging for the signal to land."

The experience was as difficult for Duffy, who felt the weight of his responsibility for the group. He wrote, "One or two of the nurses did break down after seeing this too perfect air display, just imagine the feeling, seeing the transports make three passes at the field, so near and yet so far — it almost seemed you could touch the planes, they were so low. The nurses had unquestionably suffered a very hard time — this was indeed too much. The planes flew around for over 15 min., but I would not bring them in, never in my whole life have I been faced with such a decision."

None of them had expected so many planes, including Duffy. After several minutes of watching the display of airpower, he suddenly shouted to the men who were to help him give the signal that if he had known so many planes were coming, he would have had them ready on the airfield. At that moment, he changed his mind; with so much firepower to back them up, they would attempt to signal the planes after all. He yelled that there wasn't enough time to create the signal, but the pilots might notice the bright yellow-orange parachute panels if they started running down the hill. Duffy took off, and the others followed. Hayes was so focused on running as fast as he could that he was no longer watching the planes, but he could hear them.

By the time he and the others reached the edge of the field, however, it was suddenly quiet. The planes were gone. "If they had tried, the Germans could have rounded us up then as easy as picking sweet corn in August," Abbott wrote.

The men walked back up the hill feeling more dejected than ever and found some in their group sobbing. Though all the Americans were disappointed, some eventually took comfort in the massive effort that had been made to save them. Watson wrote, "There were so few of us yet those fliers risked their lives to attempt to rescue us. After that we just had to get back to our army."

As two of the P-38s had left the airfield, they had passed three German canopied trucks parked on a road north of the airfield and strafed them with machine-gun fire. The trucks burst into flames as someone on the side of the road using small arms fired upon the P-38s. The planes strafed the area where the shots had come from before continuing on their path back to Italy. As the formation of planes made its way toward the Adriatic, machine guns fired at them but none were hit.

Duffy wanted the group to leave the area immediately in case the Germans decided to get a closer look at the airfield, but he needed two men to stay behind to report back if they did. Hayes and Abbott volunteered. Before the others headed back to the villages,

Baggs offered his coat to Abbott, who had likely left his behind. The two friends picked a spot just behind the crest of the hill and lay down so they wouldn't be seen. About ten minutes later, the young men watched as the German equivalent of a jeep came over the bridge from Gjirokastër and stopped at the base of the hill roughly three hundred feet away from where the Americans were perched. Two enlisted men sat in the front seat while two officers rode in the back. Gripped by fear, Hayes and Abbott remained as quiet as possible, refusing even to scratch the lice that crawled across their bodies, as one of the officers got out and took a quick look around the area. Satisfied there was nothing to see, the German climbed back in and the vehicle sputtered away, as Hayes and Abbott relaxed with relief.

They spent the rest of the afternoon watching the field for any signs of trouble, but only a shepherd came to graze his flock. As the hours passed and the men thought about the failed air evacuation, Abbott reached into the coat pocket Baggs had lent him and found walnuts. He checked the other pocket and found even more. The hungry men ate them, figuring they were fair game, but the discovery made them wonder if some in the group were getting more food than they were. Late that afternoon, before darkness made the journey even more difficult, the men headed back to the village to report what they'd seen.

When Duffy returned to Dhoksat, he set up a partisan guard for the village and sent a message to Cairo. "Very regrettable [aircraft] arrived to-day. Do not [repeat] not send aircraft unless you receive all clear. Germans are now in [Gjirokastër] hence the absence of party on airfield today. Self saw four MK IV tanks also troops. As it appears to be just a looting expedition by Germans expect them to leave any time. Propose staying here until all clear. Am now with Tilman who tried to send word of Germans as did self. [Ground] signal will be five [repeat] five men on runway holding strips of yellow parachute[.] If no signal do not land. Operation flight today perfect."

Lloyd Smith spent his twenty-fifth birthday, which fell on Christmas Day, in the caves at Seaview, where he learned the Americans were retracing their steps now that German activity was blocking their route to the coast. The following day he received a message from OSS Bari telling him to take the next boat back to Italy. Plans for the air evacuation were now in place, though Smith didn't know it at the time.

While he waited for a boat, life at the base continued to present challenges. On December 29, OSS officer McAdoo described the situation in a letter to Fultz, head of the OSS Albania desk in Bari: "This job here is no cinch. It's tough as hell and a terrible strain, even when we aren't sick. As of today, we have one man [Italian] dead of pneumonia (Christmas Day); two [Italians] to be evacuated, who we thought might die two days ago; and I myself have been feeling like hell...I have had (1) dysentery — cured; (2) two bad colds — one still with me; (3) terrific rheumatic pains in both hips, which makes mountain travel a real agony...(4) conjunctivitis of left eye — seemingly cured.... The last time I did the mountain (1200 meters), one day over, next day back — much rain, some snow and ice, a wind so strong that when it comes you have to hit the ground or be blown away — it was terrific."

Not mentioned in his note was another tragic event. A few days after Christmas, SOE officer Maj. Jerry Field, who had established Seaview in early November, was seriously injured by explosives near the creek below the caves. One officer reported that an explosive detonated in his face, and Field had bounced off rocks as he fell from the blast, leaving him unconscious with broken bones, wounds to his stomach, and an eyeball that had to be "put back in with a spoon." Another officer said Field was using explosives to fish and was diving into the creek when the blast occurred. By the time of the accident, Field had become fed up with dealing with the partisans and the BK, and the SOE had already planned on replacing him. Leake, the head of SOE's Albania desk, wrote of Field: "It seems that he has so low an opinion of the character and intentions of both parties that he refuses to have any dealings with either."

Field was replaced with twenty-eight-year-old Quayle, an actor and recent SOE recruit. Quayle had joined SOE after being in the British Army for three and a half years and was desperate to see some action. After his training, he learned he would be sent to Albania. "I felt nothing but joy and relief to be going at last," he wrote. "I had all the optimism and confidence of youth; others might be captured or killed, but not me — I was immortal."

Quayle's last few attempts to reach Seaview by boat had failed. He had been waiting in Brindisi to try again when news of Field's accident reached him, and he learned he would take Field's position. "Exactly what the job was there was no time to explain," he wrote. "I would have to find that out when I got there. 'Do the best you can,' I was told. 'Send out all the Intelligence you can, and make yourself a bloody nuisance to the Germans. But whatever you do, keep open the base at Sea View [*sic*]. It is vital.' " Quayle and twenty-seven-year-old Nick Kukich, a Marine Corps gunnery sergeant from Ohio who was trained as a wireless operator, boarded the *Sea Maid,* a sixty-foot diesel-engine fishing boat, which crossed the Adriatic and delivered the men close enough to Seaview that they could row ashore. "Ahead was a narrow beach, hemmed in by precipitous cliffs and lit by an enormous fire against whose leaping flames the reception party stood silhouetted." When Quayle arrived, he saw Field with his head wrapped in bloody bandages and lying under blankets. As Field was transported by stretcher to the boat, he said to Quayle, "I wish you joy of the damned place."

In the middle of this chaos, another message had arrived from Bari, which instructed Smith to continue with the original plan. With recent reports indicating that the Germans had left most of the nearby villages, he was able to resume his search. "This is [standard operating procedure] with the Germans," Smith wrote. "They move into a village, kill a few Partisans and after a few days move out again."

The villagers were surprised to see Duffy and the Americans when they returned from the field, but they let them continue their stay, since Duffy had received a message that the aircraft would stand by in case the situation changed. By New Year's Eve, however, Duffy decided to move the party to Saraqinishtë, a village to the east that would put them closer to Sheper, Tilman's base camp, and farther away from the Germans in Gjirokastër. Not only were the villagers in Dhoksat and Qeserat running out of food, they were also fearful of a German attack. "We were not exactly thrown out of the village, but Albanians can be very passive! Very passive! Indeed," Duffy wrote.

That afternoon, the party headed to Saraqinishtë and arrived a few hours later. They were parceled out to homes, and spent a quiet evening saying goodbye to 1943. Few, if any, were in the mood for celebrating, and most went to bed early that night wondering if Duffy would signal Cairo to schedule another evacuation.

Hayes and Abbott woke on New Year's Day to find their female host entering the room wearing a black dress with colorful embroidery. She had brought some food and muttered something to them in Albanian that included the word *kishë*. She continued pointing out the window until the men finally realized she wanted them to go with her to the Greek Orthodox church. They ate quickly and followed her to the nearby stone building built on the edge of a sharp drop-off.

They entered a small, dark room lit with a few lamps and candles, and their host motioned for the two young men to take their places in the stand-up pews that lined the walls. Two other nurses, Tacina and Rutkowski, came in shortly after with their host, and the service was soon conducted by a priest with a full beard dressed in a black cassock and a stiff, cylindrical black hat. When it was time for Hayes and Abbott to receive Communion, their host walked them to the altar, where they were served a small piece of bread from a basket. As they were about to walk away, the priest held up his hand to stop them and spoke to another man standing nearby. The man ducked behind a screen and came back carrying two small loaves of bread and gave one to each of them. The men thanked him and pocketed the bread in their field jackets.

On the morning of January 2, a messenger arrived at the house telling the two medics to meet in the center of the village. When they arrived, Duffy told the party he'd had no choice but to cancel the air evacuation. Snow and heavy clouds had moved into the area, he couldn't guarantee the Germans' position, and now two of the nurses were feeling ill. With all three factors against them, he had wired SOE Cairo to tell them that the party would proceed to the coast.

With the group still far from their destination, he also told Cairo to have Smith meet them in Kallarat around January 7. Both parties would have to travel for several days; Smith would head east, while the party moved northwest. In the meantime, Duffy would send Thrasher and Stefa ahead of the group to make arrangements with the local village councils for food and shelter.

That day was one of the coldest they'd experienced in Albania. As the bone-chilling wind whipped around them, Duffy announced that Cairo had informed him that the Germans had left the area that had previously blocked their journey to the coast. He and the group would leave immediately for Dhoksat, where they would spend the night before continuing on. It was good news, but few in the party reacted to it. Most had become skeptical of any plans and couldn't help but wonder what would happen next to stop them from escaping.

The walk was mostly downhill and relatively easy, but the wooden pegs in Hayes's right shoe were coming loose after a few hours of traveling. It could be another week before they reached the coast, and he feared it would never last that long. When they reached the village, Tilman greeted the party, and Hayes and several others took the chance to ask him once again to help them get more shoes. To their surprise, he replied that he thought he might be able to help them. The men were skeptical, but all they could do was wait to see what happened.

*   *   *

The following morning, on the way to the party's meeting spot, the repair on Hayes's shoe completely gave out and the front half of the sole fell off and exposed the threadbare sock he'd recently tried to darn using suture needles and parachute risers as yarn. As he looked at the damage, he wondered just how he was going to make it to the coast.

When most of the group had gathered together, Tilman greeted them with a smile and said, "I have a present for you." Someone, likely Williamson, brought over a bag and dumped roughly ten pairs of shoes on the ground. The Americans, especially those like Hayes who was in dire need, felt like kids on Christmas morning. The shoes, along with other items, had been dropped by parachute in Sheper over the past few days. Everyone who needed new shoes, including the nurses, tried on various pairs and traded with each other when they didn't fit. Hayes had grabbed a pair that was too large for him, and Owen, who was still wearing Shumway's snug flight boots, asked if he wanted to switch on the condition that Hayes give them back at the end of the journey. He wanted to keep them as a souvenir and wear them to football games. Hayes didn't mind; he was just happy to have a pair of shoes. Tilman then brought out some leather sleeveless vests, which he gave to all the enlisted men whose field jackets didn't offer much protection from the weather that grew colder by the day. His final gifts to the group were a scoop of dried peas for each of them and a roll of toilet paper, which they'd run out of long before. They suddenly felt very rich.

CHAPTER 14

Unstoppable

The group began its journey, once again, to the coast. Though the men and women didn't know it, the next several days would require them to put forth a "super-human effort."

With reports indicating that the road to the coast was now clear, the British had decided to send the two men ahead to various villages to make arrangements for the rest of the party, using gold sovereigns provided by the British to pay for food and housing.

After hours of walking, they finally arrived at Karjan in the late afternoon. All who had gotten new shoes and leather vests were more thankful than ever for the comfort these items had already provided.

Despite assurances from the War Department that more information would be forthcoming, and after weeks of waiting for news from their loved ones, the family members of the missing had still heard nothing from them. On January 2, Watson's husband, Nolan McKenzie, wrote to the Office of the Adjutant General in Washington, DC. "After nearly a full month since your last communication neither her parents have received any communication from her, nor have I. This is a source of great worry to us, as we would like to know if she is under hospitalization, if she is well, whether she is in enemy hands, or just what her status is. I am writing you only in desperation as the terrible anxiety I am under is multiplying itself with each passing day and I am in hopes that there is surely some additional details that you can now release concerning her." Two days later, Cruise's brother also wrote the Adjutant General and pleaded for information. "As you can realize, we are very worried because we feel that if he was safe and well he would have sent us some word." Hayes's mother contacted the Red Cross, who looked into it but could find no additional information.

While the party braced for another long day of walking in frigid weather, someone brought them oranges, enough for each one of them. Hayes was still hungry after he ate his, so he tried to eat a few pieces of the peel before tossing it, while Schwant, a nurse from South Dakota, accidentally stabbed herself with a borrowed knife while trying to cut the rind. Blood oozed from her wound but she soon bandaged it and continued on with the rest of them.

The trail was fairly level, and they soon arrived at the Drino River, which they had crossed just weeks earlier in the cover of night when the Germans were active in the area. Now that the Germans had moved out, the British felt it was safe to cross the river and the road just beyond it in broad daylight. A couple of

Albanian men once again ferried three or four of the party across at a time in the same boat they had taken before, while partisans scouted the road ahead for signs of trouble. When it was determined that it was safe, the men and women each made their way across without any problems.

The trail from the road to the next village of Kolonjë was uphill, straining their muscles and nerves. Though they had planned to stay at this village, and Stefa and Thrasher had already made the arrangements, Duffy decided it was too early in the day to stop. They would continue on to Golem, which they weren't scheduled to reach until the following day.

As they moved along, the weather turned, and the party faced a torrent of rain. An hour before they reached the village, however, Duffy grew concerned that several of the women were going to "crack up" and was even on the verge of doing so himself. To keep the group moving, Duffy set the pace and then dropped back to keep the nurses walking. When they finally reached the village in the early afternoon, Duffy thought they looked like "a bunch of prisoners on the Russian front."

Thrasher and Stefa were surprised to see their party, which wasn't supposed to arrive until the following day, but the two, along with Duffy, talked to the village council, and within an hour they were divided into groups and taken to various homes.

That evening, Duffy and Bell sent a message to Cairo saying that he was "pushing the party through day and night." He asked that there be as little delay as possible in evacuating the group when they got to the coast, given the exhausted and weakened condition of the party and the extreme hardships they had been through.

*   *   *

Heavy snow fell during the night and continued the next morning as Duffy tried unsuccessfully to acquire more mules from the village. The mules they were using hadn't eaten in two days and were exhausted. When it was still dark, he called the party together and told them to prepare for another grueling day. At that point, Jens told him that Tacina had a bad ankle. Though Tacina insisted it was fine, Duffy found it swollen, and although he didn't think she would make it very far, he decided to let her try.

The sun came up, and the party set out in a swirling snowstorm, but after less than two hundred feet of trying her best to walk, Tacina collapsed. Duffy yelled for the others in the lead to stop, but the relentless wind made it impossible to catch their attention. With little choice but to put the injured nurse on a mule, Duffy had to take the gear off one mule and overload the other three. Doing the best they could with what they had, the men and women headed west and before long were climbing up the side of Mount Paradhisë rather than taking the trail they had previously traveled.

As they ascended the mountain, the storm picked up and soon they could barely see anything in front of them. The bitter cold made every step difficult, but the vests Tilman had given them helped keep them warm. After roughly a half hour of walking, the partisan leading the way stopped and sat down in the snow and started singing like the others had when the party crossed Mount Ostrovicë with Stefa. The guide could no longer see the trail and was waiting for the snow to let up. It was too much for Duffy. "For the first time I lost my temper and nearly strangled [him]; at the same time my interpreter verbally conveyed my wish," Duffy later wrote. The partisan finally got up and continued on, followed by the mule skinners and their mules, who pushed through the heavy snow, making it easier for the others behind them.

The party continued downhill, but then Tacina's mule suddenly stumbled and Tacina tumbled off. Duffy was behind her and had been holding onto the mule's tail as they traversed the path. "Below her was a gradual drop of about 15 feet," Duffy wrote. "I made a headlong dive after her, just catching hold of her belt and we both rolled down the hill together, emerging from the drift just two huge snowballs!"

The exhausted men and women were soon on their way again, yet one of the other mules, which carried the batteries for the wireless, also fell and stayed down for a half hour before getting up again.

As they moved farther downhill, the snow turned into a drizzling rain. They'd been in the thick of the storm for some three hours. More determined than ever to reach the coast, they plodded along despite being cold, wet, and sick. They quickly passed near the village of Kuç and found themselves at a fast-moving stream. While the men used rocks as stepping-stones to make their way across, many of the nurses were so weak that Duffy had to help them. He stood in the middle of the stream and "slung them" over. "Everything during this acrobatic display was going fine, until the last nurse produced a bit more energy than the others and came at me like a tornado," Duffy wrote. "Down I went backwards in the stream, receiving, as you can well imagine, a substantial drenching. She fared quite well."

By early afternoon, Hayes fell back from the party and stepped off the trail to relieve himself in the bushes. He could hear the party talking as they moved away, but as their voices faded, he was suddenly overwhelmed by the extreme sense of loneliness he'd encountered the handful of times he'd been by himself in Albania. It made him grateful for the others, and he hurried to catch up with them. Passing a lone man who offered him the partisan salute, Hayes walked for a few minutes before he caught up with the rest who had stopped along the trail. As he got closer, he could see they were talking to a bearded man wearing a U.S. Army uniform that included a captain's insignia on his cap and an AAF shoulder patch. Around his waist was a pistol belt that held a .45 automatic, and the smiling man carried a cane with a round handle. The bearded man was Capt. Lloyd Smith, the OSS officer.

When Smith received the message that he should continue with the original plan of locating the Americans, he decided to move from Seaview to Tërbaç, where he and his three BK guides had been taken after passing a band of armed partisans on the trail. With the Germans no longer active in the surrounding villages, and intelligence indicating that the Americans were once again heading toward the coast, he could set up camp there and send out scouts to find the party.

He arrived on January 2 and, with the help of an English speaker in the village, hired six men to venture out in three different directions. The men were paired up and instructed that if they found the party, one man would stay with them while the other would report back to Smith.

The scouts returned within a few days and informed Smith that the Americans had been in Golem, just east of Kuç. With only one route between Kuç and Golem, Smith felt confident he would find them, and he left as soon as possible. By January 6, he was on his way.

At about two o'clock that afternoon, he saw the weary group. "As the party came up I had noticed that it was extended over a distance of 500 yards with those in the rear very much perturbed over not being able to keep up," he wrote. "Those in the rear were kept back because of sprains, blisters, and illness." As he got closer, Smith halted and introduced himself, leaving out any mention of his work with OSS. "They were as surprised at our meeting as I was," he wrote. "They had heard that I had been recalled to Italy." Some, in fact, had never heard of him at all.

Smith smiled as the group peppered him with questions, and he did his best to answer. The very sight of Smith gave the party a much-needed morale boost. Not only was he a connection to the outside world and an American, but also he had just come from the coast and knew the terrain. Though Smith had somehow been injured and was now limping and using a cane, his presence was so commanding that the Americans immediately felt reassured. As a captain, Smith was the senior ranking officer and now in charge. Duffy had already been recommended for promotion to captain, but promotions and awards for SOE officers in Albania took as long as six months. He would finally be awarded the rank of captain in June 1944.

Smith spoke with Duffy and the pilots and decided to continue with their original plan of going to the village of Kallarat that day, which was just an hour away. Thrasher and Stefa were sent ahead to secure arrangements, while Smith moved those in the party who had been in the back to the front so they could set the pace and keep the party more together. "After this reorganization the morale of the party seemed to be much better," Smith wrote.

They were all anxious to get to their destination, and though those in front were slower than the others, they "made great efforts to set a good pace for the remainder of the party."

By six thirty that evening, the party arrived in Kallarat. With the arrangements already made with the village council by Thrasher and Stefa, the group was quickly sent to various homes for the evening. In the meantime, Smith and Duffy learned that, since the Germans had moved out, they could safely proceed to their next stop, Tërbaç.

The news would save the weary group several days of traveling. If they had learned the Germans had returned to the village, they would have taken a different route that included crossing mountains to get to a cave where Smith had stored emergency rations on one of his previous trips. From there, they would have hiked the difficult coastal route while leaving behind the mules, which three of the weakened party now relied on. It seemed that the party's luck had finally changed.

Another thick frost coated the ground as they left Kallarat around nine o'clock the next morning. Thrasher and Stefa had been sent ahead once again to organize lunch for them, and the three members of the party who couldn't walk, including Tacina, were given mules to ride.

Just as they left the village, they saw four partisans running to catch up with them. The breathless men who spoke some English told Smith that the party had one of their mules, which they needed right away to haul ammunition. Smith replied that though he was sorry, he could not give them the mule unless they were able to find another at the next village. The men continued to argue with him, but they finally realized Smith wasn't going to give in and took off in the direction the party was headed.

The Americans' journey to the next village was slow-moving. One of the mules kept falling, knocking off the gear it carried as it went down, which then had to be repacked. By the time they arrived, the partisans whom Smith had just argued with had a mule waiting for them, and they traded animals. Though some of the nurses asked if they could rest at the village, Smith told them they had to keep moving.

When they arrived at Tërbaç, their destination for the day, in the midafternoon, they found that the Germans had almost completely destroyed the village. Only women and children remained. Hayes's group of four was taken to a home, but the room they were put in had a hole in the wall almost big enough to walk through. They were offered olives from a barrel in the corner of the room and ate a few, until they realized they were rotten. With the temperature outside dropping, they wondered how they would make it through the night with essentially no shelter.

Smith suggested to Duffy, Thrasher, and Baggs that they should continue on, given that the village had no blankets and almost no food. It was a cloudless night with almost a full moon, and if they left soon they would be able to cross the coastal highway in darkness. The three men opposed the idea but agreed with Smith that they should let the whole party decide. Smith gathered the group together on a hillside and presented his proposal. He explained that if they left then, there would be no stopping until daybreak; if they didn't go then, they would have to wait until the following night. Though most were unaware of just how close they were to the coast, the entire party voted to keep going.

While Smith talked, he noticed one of the mule skinners starting to take off the radio equipment from one of the mules at the bottom of the hill. Despite his limp and the cane he was using, he took three giant steps forward and took his .45 out of its holster. When he reached the Albanian, his gun was underneath the man's chin. Without concerning himself with a translator, Smith said the mules were going with them to the next village. If the man wanted his mules, he could come with them or he would wait here and they would send them back. Despite the language barrier, the mule skinner immediately started retying the lines that secured the equipment to the packsaddle.

Though the man and the other mule skinners gave them the use of their mules, they would not go any farther because they were approaching BK territory. No amount of arguing would convince them, and the men left. Determined to get the party to the coast as quickly as possible, Smith found other partisan muleteers from the village after a local told the men that Smith had protected his BK guides from the partisans and would do the same for them.

Late that afternoon, with the new mule skinners ready to go, Smith briefly accompanied the party on the trail before he and a guide raced ahead to the next village to make sure that German soldiers hadn't suddenly returned. The others walked as fast as they could, but their progress was slow, as the trail seemed to get steeper with each step and the night air grew colder. They were soon trudging through snow, and by the time they reached the crest of the mountain trail around eleven o'clock that night, they were wading through knee-deep snow.

The crest was the dividing line between partisan and BK territory, and Stefa stepped to the side of the trail and said it was time for him to turn back. He shook hands with each member of the group as they passed by him. He had been with them since their time in Berat, and despite their suspicions of him and the long journey to the east, he had secured food and shelter for them and kept them out of German hands at great risk to himself. He had helped save their lives, and they were grateful to him for what he had done. Jens felt particularly close to him, since she and Lytle, one of the three missing nurses, had been to his home. Jens gave Stefa the pin she had received when she became a flight nurse and told him to give it to his young son who had admired it when she met him. Stefa then passed along the addresses of his family in the States and asked her to let them know he was safe.

Only a few days later, members of the BK would arrest Stefa and torture him for two days. His sister's husband finally won his release by speaking to a German officer, who agreed to let Stefa go if he left Berat immediately.

Smith and his guide had been at the village of Dukat for nearly four hours before Duffy and the others arrived with the help of two additional mules Smith had sent back to help those who were in the worst shape. He had already met with the BK's commissar to arrange for food. Smith kept his word to the partisans as well, and after the men and the mules were fed, they were allowed to return to their territory.

The group gathered in the middle of the village in the early morning hours after they'd been given some food and were overjoyed to see a truck that Smith had found to carry them to a safe house along the Vlorë–Sarandë highway. The truck, which had high side rails but lacked a canopy, would save the party four and a half hours of walking. Smith told them they would take two trips with the nurses going first, but he quickly learned that there was only enough gasoline for one trip, and they all had to pile in as best as they could. They squeezed in by standing shoulder to shoulder. Smith then explained that since the Germans frequently used the road, it was very possible that they would encounter them. If they did, the truck would briefly stop and the party was to quickly jump off and hide far enough from the side of the road not to be seen. The truck would come back for them when it was safe. If something happened to the truck, they were to follow along the path of the road far enough away not to be seen until they came to the next village. Hayes and Wolf volunteered to carry the radio and the generator if they had to leave the truck, since Duffy, Smith, and Bell would be manning their weapons.

It was just after two in the morning when Smith and Duffy hopped into the cab with the driver, and the truck barreled down a rough and winding road leaving the village behind. They were soon on a wider and smoother road and continued on for a few more minutes until they spotted a light ahead of them. The truck stopped, and Smith told them all to get out and hide. As they waited in the brush and crouched behind a few boulders, hearts pounding, a German soldier drove by on a motorcycle. They waited a few minutes before getting back on the truck but soon had to repeat their efforts when another light was spotted. The truck driver stopped about a half mile down the road and pretended to have engine trouble as the others hid, and the vehicle eventually passed by. They crammed themselves into the back of the truck once again, only to have to scurry for cover a few minutes later at the sight of a German truck. This time the truck stopped where the group had gotten out, and a passenger used a large spotlight mounted over the cab to twice pore over the area they were hiding in as they all attempted to stay as still as possible. The seconds passed slowly before the light was extinguished and the truck continued down the road. When the party got back on the truck for the third time, the driver went at breakneck speed for the next half hour until they reached the safe house.

They parked the truck and the men and women walked about a quarter mile through high weeds as Wolf and Hayes carried the radio and generator, which seemed to get heavier with each step. They finally reached a stone farmhouse owned by Xhelil Çela, an English-speaking Albanian who had worked with the American and British officers to establish Seaview. Like many of the group's benefactors along the way, Çela too had attended the Albanian Vocational School. He frequently brought the men at the base camp additional food from his home, and his house was often used as a stopping point for those being evacuated by the Allies, including hundreds of Italians. The recently arrived Quayle, who was sleeping in a back room when the party arrived, had immediately liked Çela and trusted him, as did many of the Allied officers.

The party's rest at the safe house was brief, and Smith instructed those who still had musette bags to leave them and the radio behind. They left the farmhouse in the dark and almost immediately faced a steep switchback trail. The hike was grueling, but they couldn't stop to rest. They had to climb as far up the mountain as possible before sunrise in hopes that the Germans wouldn't spot them from the road. As they made their way up, Rutkowski asked, "What are all those lights?" Smith calmly replied, "That is [Vlorë]." That's when many in the party realized they were finally nearing the coast, their long-awaited destination. The higher they went, the more snow they encountered underfoot, until they finally reached the summit at nine thirty the next morning.

CHAPTER 15

Escape

The shimmering waters of the Adriatic reflecting the morning light meant one thing: they had made it. After sixty-two days of setbacks and near catastrophes, they were overjoyed to reach the summit — and the coast. As soon as Owen saw it, he was so sure that their rescue was imminent that he asked Hayes to give him back the flight boots that he wanted to take home as a souvenir. The two men sat in the snow and traded shoes as Hayes reminded Owen of his promise to roll all the way to the water when they got to the coast. Owen replied, "That was seven weeks ago. Now I'm too tired." They were all tired. In the past four days they'd only been able to sleep for a total of about eight hours as they pressed toward the coast, but the promise that they would soon be escaping Albania had kept them going.

Smith immediately dispatched a shepherd to Seaview with a message to tell the men to prepare for the party's arrival before he and the others slowly made their way down the mountainside.

Jens's knees threatened to buckle under her as they descended the trail. Watson's knees gave in and she tumbled several times.

When they reached the caves, the men at Seaview rushed to greet them, and at least one gave out chocolate and cigarettes to celebrate with the weary but ecstatic party. "I cannot remember any group ever looking happier," Smith wrote later.

That happiness didn't last long, however. The British told them that a boat probably wouldn't be sent right away because the bright moonlight expected that night made boats easy targets for the German patrols. Burdened with the sudden bad news on top of their exhaustion, many of the nurses fell asleep in the cots the British kept in the caves, while the men found places to sleep outside. Hayes settled himself in the sun on a large rock outside the caves until one of the British offered him his own bed made from some boxes covered with a thin mattress and blanket. Hayes fell asleep right away.

American lieutenant David Brodie, who was in charge of communications at OSS headquarters in Bari, was lying in a bed at his station recovering from the infectious hepatitis that had swept across the Mediterranean when an operator at the base yelled, "Lieutenant! They have arrived at the pinpoint!" Brodie had been on alert for days waiting for the message, and his two operators at the base, as well as Orahood, whom Brodie had sent to Seaview, had been pounding away at their keys for some forty-eight hours.

After hearing the operator's announcement, Brodie jumped out of bed and grabbed a Handie-Talkie, a newly invented portable radio that could fit in his hand rather than in a backpack, which he had planned to use for the operation. He had already sent a courier over to Albania to deliver two handheld radio transceivers to Orahood along with plans to signal the boat. "I . . . instructed our operator that, on the night we came over, to pull [the receivers] out, and when we were approximately a mile away, I would start counting 'one-two-three' in German and he should answer 'three-two-one' in German."

With his radio in hand, Brodie and his driver hopped into a jeep and headed for the armed boat that had been held in port waiting for word from the party. Though the crew was mostly British, Lt. Jack Taylor, an American working for OSS who had first delivered Lloyd Smith to Albania in early December, was in charge of the operation.

While the Americans celebrated their arrival at the coast that afternoon, disaster befell Brig. Davies, who had first learned of the stranded party through his interpreter, and other SOE men working near Bizë. They were under attack and fighting for their lives after several devastating weeks on the run. The men had been camped out at a mountain hideout belonging to one of the local village council members, a large, bearded man who was a Muslim priest. About midday, a partisan had reported that the Germans were in Kostenjë, a village about an hour away down a steep trail. Realizing it would take the Germans some time to reach them, Davies ordered everyone to stay where they were while they finished cooking precious meat that was too valuable to abandon. About an hour later, the local commissar told Davies he had not received any reports of Germans. "It is impossible, my General, we have spies in every village, every track is watched, we are bound to get at least two hours' warning. I have heard nothing." Just then, a burst of machine-gun fire came from a ridge about six hundred yards away as two large groups of BK, led by Germans, climbed toward them from the south.

Davies gave the order for everyone — British personnel, partisans, Albanians, and a few Italian soldiers — to climb the ridge to the northeast, which would lead them to a forest that would provide cover. They struggled single file through heavy snow up the ridge, while thirty-two-year-old Lt. Col. Arthur Nicholls, Davies's chief of staff, leaned on a stick for help. His feet were so badly blistered and infected that he could barely walk. Some of the partisans and mule skinners fired occasionally toward their pursuers to slow them down, but Davies wanted to wait to reach higher ground before making a stand. As they continued to climb, bullets hit the snow on each side of them, but miraculously no one was hit. They were nearing the forest and it seemed they were going to make it when a round of machine-gun fire came from their right front. "I felt as though a horse had kicked me hard in the ribs," wrote Davies, who had been shot twice in the stomach and once in the heel. "I spun round and fell into a snowdrift in a gully on my right." A British major was hit in the thigh, an Italian colonel took a bullet in the neck, and a partisan was shot through both thighs. All three fell into the gully with Davies. "We were all struggling to avoid being smothered in the drift, the snow stained scarlet in patches from our blood," Davies wrote. Another British sergeant collapsed in the snow away from the others.

Davies yelled for Nicholls to take charge, and though Nicholls was shaken by the turn of events and still very weak and in severe pain, he followed Davies's orders and replied, "Very good, sir, goodbye." Davies had made it clear to his men earlier that they would only end up wounded or captured if they stayed behind with an injured man in a situation like this one, and they would have to leave him behind. A British captain stopped briefly, as if contemplating what to do, but Davies yelled at him to keep going.

In a few moments, the same sergeant who had risked his life in early November trying to save a wireless operator when he was shot in the head and torso was at Davies's side. Despite Davies barking at him to leave, he stayed. "Brig, you're in no position to give me orders," he said. "I'm your bodyguard and I'm stopping with you. You'll need me before you have finished." Realizing the young man wasn't going anywhere, Davies told him to look for some shelter to get them out of the cold. The sergeant left for a few minutes and came back with news that he'd found a sheep pen down the gully. Two Italians from their party also joined them as the sergeant "started a small avalanche, so that all the wounded tobogganed down the gully."

The three men carried the injured to a small stone hut, where the sergeant wrapped the major's thigh with field dressings to stop the heavy bleeding and put some plaster over one of Davies's wounds. It was all he could do for either of them. The Italian colonel was hallucinating and moaning, and Davies yelled at him to "pull himself together and shut up that bloody noise," while the partisan who'd been shot in both thighs lay quietly.

As the sergeant lit a fire using a piece of wood he tore from the roof, bullets hit the stone walls of the building. It sounded like they were being attacked on the south and west sides by about eighty men in each company. Davies wondered if the attackers thought he and the others had positioned themselves in the hut to mount an attack. The sergeant, who must have thought the same, went outside, and as bullets hit the ground around him, he walked around the hut. Unable to speak Albanian, he yelled in Italian, "English wounded here," but the attackers continued to fire.

When he came back in, he told Davies it looked to him as if they were "massing for the kill.... It would be all over soon."

For a few moments it was quiet, with an odd bullet hitting the wall. "Then hell was let loose," Davies wrote. "The supporting party opened rapid fire with all their weapons, the attacking party threw grenades and charged, shrieking at the top of their voices." The sergeant fired his .38 revolver from the door until all six rounds were gone and then threw the gun as the attackers moved in on him. With his fists flying, he was able to run across the room to try to protect Davies, but there were too many of them. Even so, when one man pushed his rifle into Davies's ribs, the sergeant took a swing at him. Another man tried to take Davies's boots. The chaos only ended when an officer ordered his men to leave and through the Italian interpreter learned that Davies was a brigadier. Now in the hands of a BK officer, Davies and the others would soon be German prisoners of war.

Hayes slept until sundown. When he awoke, he learned that Orahood, the wireless operator, had received a message indicating that a boat had already left Italy, and the party should be at the water's edge ready to leave at midnight. It was the best possible news the men and women could have hoped for. Now all they had to do was wait a little longer. The hours passed slowly, however, as the mild coastal temperatures turned a little cooler. Those who were awake ate food out of tin cans the British gave them and wondered if they were really going to make it out or if something else would get in their way. It was hard to believe they could be back in Italy in a matter of hours after having endured so much.

At about ten thirty that night, British Lt. Comm. "Sandy" Glen, who worked for MI6 and was also leaving Seaview that night, told them it was time to move. Williamson, the wireless operator who worked with Tilman at Dhoksat and was anxious to leave Albania, also joined the group.

As the party plodded down the steep trail to the small beach, Orahood, who carried one of the Handie-Talkies Brodie had sent over, tried desperately to get in touch with Brodie and the crew. He pointed the antenna in various directions and even banged the unit on his knee while muttering that he needed a walkie-talkie, referring to the large backpack radios that were more widely used at the time. He finally picked up a transmission about halfway down the trail. "I'm getting something. They're out there!" he said.

The rescue boat had left Bari at two o'clock in the afternoon. As it made its way toward Albania and the crew tested its guns, Brodie tried to figure out whether he felt sick from the boat ride or the infectious hepatitis. As the hours passed and moonlight began to bathe the boat and the coastline, Brodie went up to the fly-bridge with his Handie-Talkie and watched as the boat moved closer to the snow-capped mountains along the coast. The engines now barely whispered, and the gun crew stood on alert as Brodie called Orahood on the Handie-Talkie and counted to three in German. To the relief of all those on board, he soon heard Orahood reply, "Drei, zwei, ein — is that you, Captain B?"

About forty-five minutes after the party left the caves, they reached the small patch of beach that was barely large enough for all of them. As they stood in the sand, they couldn't help but still wonder if their time to leave had finally arrived. Assured by Orahood that the boat was somewhere nearby, the British lit a few signal fires that flickered in the night air. As the Americans waited anxiously and strained for any sight of their rescuers, three men in an inflated rubber boat suddenly appeared at the shoreline. A surge of relief washed over the group; at long last, the rescue was happening.

The crewmen took four or five women and men at a time in the small craft to the larger boat that sat idling in the water in case a quick departure was needed. It took a few hours to transport everyone, and the last two to leave the shore were Hayes and Wolf. As the medics neared the larger boat, they waited for the crest of a wave to lift their rubber boat higher into the air so they could grab on to the large boat's netting and climb up. Hayes had just put one leg over the railing when the British captain asked him if he was the last one. Still standing astride, Hayes answered that he was, and the boat lunged ahead.

It was about two fifteen in the morning on January 9 when the boat began its journey back to Italy. After sixty-three days trapped in Albania, twenty-seven Americans were returning to Allied lines. Three nurses remained behind.

Most of the nurses, and likely the pilots, immediately went to the officers' quarters and slept in the bunks, while at least one nurse was seasick from the waves that rocked the boat back and forth. By the time Hayes and Wolf boarded, the enlisted men who'd gotten there before them had already devoured crackers and strawberry jam given to them by the crew and were sleeping in bunks. The table was sticky and covered in crumbs, but Hayes and Wolf sat down and ate what was left.

When Hayes got up to look for a bunk, he realized they were all taken and was preparing to sleep on the table when the boat's radio operator offered him his bed in the tiny radio room. The room was only about four feet wide and included the operator's equipment and a bunk above a locker, but as soon as Hayes stretched out he fell asleep.

By morning, the boat had neared the Italian port of Brindisi and was following the coastline north to Bari. As those in the party awoke and ate breakfast in their quarters, they marveled at their incredible journey and rescue. At last they'd finally made it out of Albania.

Hayes spent the morning camped out on the bridge talking to the helmsman. They were soon joined by the captain and another crewman, who said, "Sir, it's time to splice the main brace!" referring to the nautical tradition of giving an extra drink to sailors after they had completed the dangerous task of fixing the main brace of the sail if it was broken in battle or a storm. The skipper replied, "Yes it is. Since today is a special occasion we'll put in a double splice!" The crewman opened a locker at the back of the bridge and removed a glass and a small cask of rum. He then filled the glass and handed it to Hayes. "Since you are here, you get the first splice!" he said. Hayes took a sip and, though it was as strong as the raki he detested, he happily toasted their freedom.

When Hayes returned to the enlisted men's quarters, he found most of the men from the 807th and several crew members talking. The radio operator who had let him sleep in his bunk tugged on Hayes's sleeve and asked, "How about giving me your jacket?" Hayes, who'd become so protective of his belongings while in Albania, immediately said no, but Owen told him, "Go on! Give it to him. You can always tell the supply officer you lost it in

Albania." Within a few minutes, all of the 807th men had given their jackets to the crew members who wanted an American coat. It was a gesture of thanks for what the men had done for them, and they were feeling generous now that they were on their way back to Allied lines. They may also have passed on the lice they still carried.

Shortly after, someone announced that they were entering Bari's harbor, the site of the German attack in early December and their original destination on November 8. The men joined nurses — some of whom had dabbed on their last bits of makeup — on deck, and the helmsman guided the boat into a dock. As the boat approached, the party saw their commanding officer, McKnight, along with dozens of military photographers and a host of other people waiting to greet them.

While the boat was being secured to the dock, the Americans thanked Duffy, Bell, Smith, and the boat crew for all they had done for them and said their goodbyes. They were so excited to get off the boat when it was time to leave that they forgot to salute McKnight as he greeted them.

Without delay, the entire group was put in a fleet of new staff cars that were usually reserved for officers. Duffy and Bell found a military truck waiting to take them to SOE's new Bari headquarters, and Smith found his way to OSS headquarters in Bari.

The Americans were driven immediately to the 26th General Hospital, which had only been open since December 4, two days after the attack on Bari. Because much of the equipment for the hospital had sunk with the Liberty ship *Samuel J. Tilden,* the 26th had to open using a hundred borrowed beds.

Thrasher and Baggs were immediately escorted to another

area to be debriefed, and the nurses and medics never saw them again. The rest of the party, still wearing lice-infested clothes, were put into a small room with enough chairs for each of them to sit. A lieutenant colonel soon arrived and announced that he was a G2 officer, or Army Intelligence officer, and explained that they were being detained in the hospital while decisions were made as to their next assignments. Theater policy dictated that anyone who had been in enemy territory for more than eight days would be sent back to the States rather than risk being treated as a spy if caught again behind enemy lines. In the meantime, he said, the nurses and enlisted men would be housed in an isolated ward.

He then picked a nurse and a medic to be the first to be debriefed. The two were sent with an escort to an interrogation room, while Hayes, Jens, and the others signed papers indicating they understood that, to protect their benefactors and future downed troops, they could not reveal where they had been or who had helped them. When Jens was called in, she took from her coat pocket the diary she'd kept to help her remember the names of the villages. When she'd finished with it, the officer insisted on keeping it, though he said it would be returned after the war.

When half the party had been interviewed, the officers decided that the stories were consistent enough that they wouldn't need to continue. The lieutenant colonel returned to the room where the main party was seated and pulled out a map that had been created from the interviews. He showed them that the distance between the crash site and Seaview was about sixty miles, while their estimated route was about three hundred forty miles. Given the mountainous terrain, the Intelligence officer surmised they had walked two to three times that amount—roughly six hundred fifty to one thousand miles.

The officer also explained that, because of their journey back to allied lines, they were now members of the unofficial Late Arrivals Club. The Club was originally created by a British public relations officer in the Royal Air Force in July 1941 during the desert campaigns in the Middle East. British personnel who were forced to abandon their aircraft, who were shot down, or who crash-landed in enemy territory and returned to their squadrons on foot were issued a badge with a winged foot on it and a membership certificate to the "club" detailing their journey. The certificate came with the words, "It is never too late to come back." Covered in the media, the badge soon became legendary, and when an unknown American evader returned to England and started wearing it in 1943, others followed. The AAF never approved the designation, so the unofficial members had to wear a winged-foot pin under their lapels. The intelligence officer then showed a pin to the Americans and gave them the name of a jeweler in Ohio who sold the pins for less than two dollars.

Even more important to the group, the officer told them that when President Roosevelt learned that thirteen nurses were trapped in Nazi-occupied Albania, he'd insisted on daily briefings on what was being done to rescue them.

Late that afternoon, Smith had just finished writing his report on the evacuation at OSS Bari and was shaving in the bathroom when he was surprised by a visit from OSS director "Wild Bill" Donovan. Donovan congratulated him on the success of the evacuation and told him he was sending him back to Albania to rescue the other three nurses. Before he left, Donovan added that when he got back to Washington he would personally tell President Roosevelt of Smith's achievements in helping to save the party.

The following day, when a medical officer examined the men and women who were still in seclusion and unable to let even their family members know they were safe, he diagnosed Cruise with pneumonia. Jens had a boil on her leg that needed treatment, and Zeiber was also ill, but the others were in good shape considering all they had been through. For the next five days, the men and women were sequestered in the two-room ward, and though they were served many of the foods they had craved in Albania, it took them several days before they could eat more than three or four bites without feeling full. The men had been given razors to shave, but some decided to keep their new goatees and mustaches and showed them off in photos taken by Army photographers.

On January 14, while Jens, Cruise, and Zeiber remained hospitalized, the others were released and flown back to their headquarters in Catania. Hornsby of the 802nd was allowed to stay with the 807th for a few days while the squadron celebrated.

Not everyone was happy to see them. When Owen, Wolf, and Hayes arrived at their old quarters, they found it occupied. One of the men asked the three medics, "What are you doing in here?" After Owen explained it was their room, someone responded that it wasn't anymore. It wasn't the homecoming they had expected. A better reception came the following day when they joined the rest of the 807th at the officers' villa and celebrated with food and dancing — though the knowledge that three of the nurses were still missing overshadowed the party.

*   *   *

The AAF kept the story of the Americans' return from the papers through January as Hornsby was sent back to the 802nd, and the nurses and medics finally were allowed to write letters to their families to let them know they were safe. Cruise, Jens, and Zeiber were released from the hospital in Bari over the next few weeks and sent back to the 807th in Sicily, while MacKinnon, the medic from California, was admitted to the Catania hospital for dysentery, and Kanable, the nurse from Wisconsin, suffered from malaria.

On January 26, most of those who'd been in Albania and were well enough to travel flew to Casablanca, Morocco, for the first leg of their journey back to the States. From there, they joined whatever flights were available and were soon separated. Though they would forever be bonded by their shared experiences during their sixty-three harrowing days in Albania, this was the last time many would be in one another's presence. Some assumed they would see each other again at Bowman Field, but only a few ever did.

CHAPTER 16

Left Behind

The three nurses separated from the others in the attack on Berat on November 15, 1943, were thirty-two-year-old Ann Maness, a tall, blue-eyed redhead with freckles; thirty-year-old brunette Helen Porter from Hanksville, Utah, who had been reassigned to the 807th at the last minute with Jens; and thirty-one-year-old Wilma Lytle, also a brunette, from Butler, Kentucky. They had last seen the others in their group the night they watched an Italian movie in Berat on their seventh day in Albania. A guide and two medics had escorted them to their assigned home after the movie, and they'd all had a glass of raki together with their hosts before saying goodnight.

When the three nurses awoke to the sound of gunfire the next morning, their hosts, a married couple named Nani and Goni Karaja, motioned for them to come down to the basement, which they used as a cellar to store the wine they made and sold. Nani's stepmother, whom they called Mama Ollga and who always dressed in black, and Nani's seven-year-old nephew, Koli, also lived with the couple and huddled with them in the basement throughout the attack.

Several hours later, when the streets had quieted, the family and nurses came upstairs and learned the Germans and the BK had won the battle. The nurses watched in horror through the window as German vehicles passed along the main road of the town. As they wondered what had happened to the rest of their party, they also wondered what would happen to them.

In an effort to protect their hosts, the nurses decided they should give themselves up and tried to convey their intentions to the family, but the family refused to let them surrender. Instead, Nani went to get his brother Kiçi, who had worked as a waiter in a hotel in Boston before the war and spoke some English. Kiçi was also the father of Koli, the seven-year-old boy who lived with Nani and Goni because the couple did not have any children of their own. When Nani returned with his brother, Kiçi told the Americans that he knew a high-ranking member of the BK who he thought might be able to help when some calm was restored to the town. Kiçi then left the house to see if he could learn what had happened to the rest of the Americans. When he returned, he brought the three nurses the good news that the other Americans had gotten out by truck before the Germans arrived.

Later that afternoon, two German soldiers, one of whom spoke Albanian, entered the house and searched it. When they saw the nurses, they pointed at their clothes and asked them what type of uniform the women were wearing. Unsure of what would happen next and most likely terrified, Maness replied, *"Infermiere,"* the Albanian word for nurse. One of the soldiers picked up the box of airplane spotter cards used to help teach military personnel types of planes that Maness had been using earlier to play solitaire. He looked at the B-25 on the cover of the box for a moment, put it down, muttered something, and left with the other soldier, leaving the nurses to wonder why they'd been spared.

While the nurses waited downstairs, the women of the house, Goni and Ollga, cried as they followed the soldiers upstairs. The soldier who spoke Albanian patted Goni on the shoulder and, to her surprise, told her to keep the nurses inside and to feed them. What the Albanian women and the nurses didn't realize was that because Nani and Kiçi were in the wine-making business and had done business with some of the Germans, Kiçi had been able to speak with them and convince them to overlook their guests.

A day or two later, Kiçi returned with his friend from the BK, who reassured the nurses that they were safe and would be taken care of. That afternoon, a hole barely large enough for an adult to squeeze through was dug between Nani's house and his cousin's house next door. The nurses were told that if the Germans came to search the house, they were to crawl through the opening and hide in the adjoining house.

It wasn't long before the nurses also received a visit from Kadre Çakrani, the BK commandant of Berat, who came to see if they needed anything. The nurses asked for some clothes, which they were given, and they also received deliveries of sugar and rice. Çakrani told them that if they needed anything else, they were to send Nani and he would make sure they got it. The commandant was true to his word, and he even returned several times to check on them.

The days, however, soon turned to weeks, and the nurses grew restless in the small home that lacked plumbing or running water. They played bridge and helped with housework to pass the time.

They even spent part of every evening next door listening to the radio before going to bed on pallets in the living room next to Mama Ollga. Kiçi and his family came almost every day to see them, and someone let them borrow an Albanian–English dictionary, which they pored over in an effort to communicate better with their hosts. They even taught Nani's nephew, Koli, the lyrics to the popular British World War I song "It's a Long Way to Tipperary." The nurses were well fed and were free to go about the house, but the days were long.

Occasionally Nani was alerted that someone was coming to search the house. At that point, the nurses would retreat to the wine cellar and stood ready to flee to the neighbors' house through the small opening, but there was never a need. Eventually the commandant arranged for a notice to be placed on the house indicating that it was reserved for his use.

By early December, however, the commandant ordered the family to tell their friends who had heard about the nurses that they had left Berat. He also told the American women that they were now to hide whenever they heard anyone approach the door. The isolation was difficult, but at Christmas, Nani's cousin's daughter next door sang carols to them, and Kiçi brought them each a pair of socks and a cake to celebrate. The nurses spent New Year's Eve watching through a window as German soldiers moved into a jail across the street from them.

On January 6, 1944, three days before the large party of Americans was evacuated at Seaview, SOE officers Victor Smith and Alan Palmer tried unsuccessfully to get the three nurses out of Berat. As they tried to make their way through a BK village, a local leader betrayed their plans to the Germans. The men were warned ahead of time and were able to narrowly escape capture in an ambush before returning to their mission.

Lloyd Smith received his orders to rescue the remaining three nurses about three weeks later. When he left on his mission, code-named Churn, he thought he had been promoted to the rank of major, but promotions were slow during the war, and his was delayed until the summer. Two other men, a wireless operator and a cryptographer, were scheduled to accompany Smith into Albania, but by the time they arrived in Bari, Smith had already departed for the country, taking the American boat *Yankee* from Brindisi to Seaview on February 2. He would have left even sooner if naval operations hadn't held up the boat.

Smith arrived at Seaview around eleven o'clock that night and was rowed to shore before he climbed the steep path to the caves. At the base camp, he found McAdoo, the American officer who had established a network of informants along the coast while operating out of Seaview. McAdoo told Smith that several prominent BK members were working to deliver the three nurses to the coast within the next ten days and suggested he wait at the caves to see what happened before venturing to Berat.

Ten days later, as the winter weather continued to make the men in the caves miserable, more Italians arrived at Seaview hoping to be evacuated. The nurses still had not arrived, and local BK representatives were now telling the Allied officers that they were worried that Seaview and Grama Bay, another base camp, would soon be attacked. Quayle, the officer in charge since Field had been evacuated after his fishing accident, had established Grama Bay shortly after his arrival to ensure that his men had two bases from which they could operate. Grama Bay, which was also dubbed "Sea Elephant," was a half day's journey to the south of Seaview and was as lice-infested and barren as the other. The members of the BK were convinced the Germans knew of both camps and would attack.

Smith set out on a reconnaissance mission to the north of Seaview to find possible hideouts and new bases and came across a group of Germans living in a house north of Orso Bay near Vlorë. He posted shepherds as guards to alert him and the other men if the Germans moved south toward them. When he returned from his reconnaissance mission, he learned that Skender Muço, the BK member from Vlorë who had promised to deliver the nurses, had told McAdoo he was unable to do it. "The situation was rather critical at this time because we were expecting the Germans any day," wrote Smith. "I did not care to risk leaving the base, pick up the nurses, and return to find it in German hands."

On the night of February 13, McAdoo and Orahood, the wireless operator involved with the evacuation of the larger American party, left Albania by boat on the orders of Fultz, the head of OSS Albania in Bari. During the evacuation, three Italians drowned when the canvas boat carrying them to the larger boat capsized from the violent surf.

Needing help, Smith was able to convince Hodo Meto, a BK member from Vlorë who spoke English and whom Smith had met on his previous mission, to come to Grama Bay later that month and assist him with the evacuation of the three remaining nurses. Meto was one of the men who had worked with Karapiçi and McAdoo in creating an intelligence network along the coast.

With Meto translating, Smith wrote a letter to Midhat Frashëri, the leader of the BK, and Kadre Çakrani, one of his top men and the commandant in Berat. Smith already had intelligence that the nurses were in the care of these two men. In his letter, Smith informed them of his mission and reminded them "that several members of their organization had promised to bring the nurses to the base and had done nothing, that the United States Army knew the nurses were with them and under their care and if they were not evacuated within a certain length of time [Smith] would be asked for reasons and would be obliged to state that [his] failure was due to a lack of cooperation on the part of [the BK]."

Meto gave the letters to his cousin, a man named Tare Shyti, who was neither a partisan nor a member of the BK. Shyti was given money to secure credentials and to purchase civilian clothes for the nurses if they needed them. Smith also included a letter to the nurses that told them it was their decision whether to take the trip by car, where they would have to change into civilian clothes and if caught would be treated as spies, or have Smith bring them back on foot. Meto was opposed to the idea of bringing the nurses by foot from Berat because he didn't want to go into partisan territory. He also didn't think the nurses should have any say in the decision. "We always tell our women what to do," he told Smith.

That night Quayle was warned that four Germans were coming their way and were only one hour north of Seaview. Quayle immediately ordered the Allied men to evacuate Grama Bay and move two hours east. Smith and Marine Corps gunnery sergeant Nick Kukich, who was trained as a wireless operator and had arrived in Albania the same time as Quayle, had agreed earlier that if the Germans came, they would travel together with Kukich's wireless set so they could communicate with Bari and arrange for a pickup along the southern coast. The next morning the two men met at their hiding place with Kukich's wireless set in tow.

The Germans moved into Grama Bay the following morning, and the Allied men anticipated that more would be coming to join them from the south. Quayle divided the men into three groups and ordered them to meet on the other side of the mountain in Dukat. "[Meto] wanted to know if we should proceed with our plans for the evacuation of the nurses," wrote Smith. "After assuring him that we could still evacuate the nurses successfully in spite of the Germans, he started for the village of [Dukat] to send his cousin to Berat with the messages."

Kukich and Smith traveled together up to the mountain, with Kukich carrying his wireless equipment and Smith carrying both of their packs. After struggling through deep snow and a hard rain through the night, they spotted six Germans coming south from Orso Bay near Vlorë the next morning. Believing they'd been seen, they pretended to backtrack down the mountain first before continuing over the top, hoping they'd lost the Germans.

For the next three days, Smith and Kukich lived off a few K rations as they made their way to Dukat, where they met other Allied men. Though the Germans had somehow overlooked Seaview, they now knew the Allies were operating in the area. Quayle decided that from then on Seaview would be used only to receive sorties and would no longer house personnel for long periods of time.

By March 10, some six weeks after arriving on his second mission in Albania, Smith still had no word on the nurses so he sent another messenger to Berat. Meto continued to assure Smith that his cousin would arrive any minute with the nurses. "If my cousin does not return within ten days, you can shoot me," he told Smith. "I'll bet my life on him."

By this time, he and Kukich had been living for several weeks "in a combination uniform of Italian, Albanian, English, and American clothes" and had sent a note alerting OSS they were both in need of "complete kit." Smith also requested ammunition for the M1 carbine he carried on this mission.

On March 14, Smith received a wireless message that said, "If nurses can be successfully evacuated in next thirty days continue, if not, return to Bari without further instructions." Smith decided at that point that he would give Meto's cousin until March 21 to arrive. If he and the nurses weren't there by then, he would start his journey to Berat.

Kadre Çakrani, the BK commandant in Berat, gave the three nurses various updates on the rest of their party, and in January he came with news that the other Americans had finally escaped from Albania. By February, however, the restless women had become increasingly suspicious that their Albanian friends weren't doing enough to help them escape and decided they had to do something themselves. They told Nani and his brother Kiçi that they were going to try to walk out on their own.

When Çakrani came to see them that night, the worried men told him what the nurses had said. His immediate solution was to take them for a ride to get them out of the house they'd been hiding in for some three months. The commandant's driver picked them up outside the door leading from the wine cellar and drove them and the commandant up to the hills, where they spent the evening looking at the moonlight in a field and talking. A week or so later, he invited them to dinner at his house. The outings helped break up the monotony of the long days, but the women were still anxious and determined to get back to Allied lines.

Shyti, Meto's cousin, had finally arrived in Berat, and on his next visit, likely in early March, Çakrani told the nurses plans were under way. To prepare, he needed the nurses to make black headscarves and blouses and skirts for themselves to wear during their escape. The plan was for someone to drive them as close to the coast as possible and, from there, they would meet Lloyd Smith and walk to Seaview to be evacuated by boat.

Goni bought the material for the women from a shopkeeper, insisting it was for a bride who didn't wish to be seen. She bought navy-blue material for Maness, blue-gray for Porter, and tan for Lytle and helped them make the clothes. Two men, likely Shyti and Sulejman Meço, another of Meto's cousins, who would act as their interpreter, then came to the house and told the women they would take their pictures the following morning so they could finish creating their official passes with fake identities. Shyti had arranged for the passes in Tiranë where he lived and included the appropriate stamps from Berat. It had taken a while to make the arrangements, which had delayed the escape plans, but the passes would hold up under scrutiny if necessary. The nurses were given their fake Albanian names that night so they could practice their pronunciation. Lytle's name was Arife Hamitaj.

The following morning the men came and took the women's pictures, and that evening the commandant brought their finished passes. Lytle's included her actual birth date and indicated she was a Muslim housewife who'd been born in Gjirokastër and lived in Berat. The commandant and his driver took them out for one last secret drive that night. As they passed the airfield that the American planes had strafed during the failed air evacuation, they had a flat tire, momentarily causing great concern. Fortunately, the driver was able to fix it and no one bothered them.

The following afternoon, March 18, Meço arrived earlier than scheduled. The women dressed anxiously in their new clothes, wrapped their uniforms and personal items in bundles to carry, and left behind the clock someone had taken from the plane's instrument panel. They wouldn't need it anymore.

With everything ready, the party used the passageway connecting the basement to the neighbor's house, and a car, driven by a BK soldier, and a pickup truck were waiting for them outside. The women and Meço piled into the car, carrying cookies from Goni and the neighbors. Maness, who sat in the passenger seat, was given a rifle and told to rest it between her knees with the barrel pointing up in case they had any trouble. Lytle and Porter rode in the back while their personal belongings and uniforms were placed in the truck with Shyti, the commandant's driver, and other BK soldiers.

Luck was not with them as they started their journey. The driver of the car got lost on the way out of town, and they had another flat tire near the airfield. The delays only added to the tension the nurses already felt. While the driver fixed the tire, several German soldiers passed by. The women continued to look down as local nurses would; their behavior also prevented anyone from noticing Porter's and Lytle's blue eyes. When the gas cap came off the truck, the BK soldiers went back to look for it, further delaying the nurses' escape.

When they finally continued on, they were stopped several times by German guards and had to offer a letter that allowed them to pass through. At the port city of Vlorë, a guard stood by Maness, who still held a rifle between her knees, as he read the letter permitting them to continue on, which almost certainly sent panic through the passengers in the car.

Hoping the worst was over, the party stopped at dusk to eat, while some of the men stood guard watching for partisan attacks. Shortly after, most in the group returned to Berat by car and truck. It was time for the women and their escorts to walk.

The small party hiked along the trail until they came to a stream, which they forded one at a time with the help of a mule. They continued walking until they came to a house where they could get some sleep in preparation for the rest of their journey the following day.

On the morning of March 19, a young British corporal woke Smith in the shepherd's hut where he was staying, so excited that Smith assumed the Germans were coming and grabbed his gun belt and pack. Instead, the corporal told him the nurses had arrived. Meto said, "See, God——, Major, I told you my cousin would bring them."

Smith met the nurses on the trail and brought them and their BK soldier escorts back to the shepherd's hut where he was staying. Two British men who were also at the hut gave each of the nurses some Albanian money as a souvenir, and the nurses, who had very little with them, reciprocated with an AAF sleeve patch. They took pictures outside the hut and waited for night to come so they could cross the same German-patrolled road where the other Americans had traveled just a few months before.

When night finally came, Smith led the party, including those who had brought them from Berat, to Xhelil Çela's farmhouse, the safe house used by OSS and SOE. They stayed for several hours, resting and drinking tea, until Smith said it was time to go.

It was about two thirty in the morning, and like their colleagues who had gone before them, they had to get as far up the snow-covered mountain as they could before daybreak to avoid being spotted by the Germans.

By eleven that morning they were at the crest of the trail, and they arrived at Seaview a little after two in the afternoon, upon which wireless operator Kukich alerted OSS Bari of their arrival. The miserable weather forced the nurses to spend the rest of the day in the caves, where they sat in front of a fire and ate stew while one of the British sang them songs. They spent their last evening in Albania sleeping in bedrolls in the lice-infested caves, but they had much to be thankful for. After months of being trapped, they were finally free.

They spent almost all of the next day, March 21, watching the rain until an Italian motor torpedo boat arrived for them around eleven thirty that evening, finally bringing an end to their 135-day journey in Albania, almost ten weeks after the others in their group had made their own night crossing of the Adriatic.

Eight days later, the three nurses left Italy for the United States to reunite with their families and celebrate their miraculous return. It would be another seventy years before their story, and that of twenty-seven others, was fully told.

Epilogue

Some of the Allied men who helped the Americans escape from Albania were honored for their work months later. Capt. Lloyd Smith, who escorted the larger party about eighty miles through enemy lines and the three nurses between twelve and fifteen miles, was first nominated for a Distinguished Service Medal but then awarded the higher Distinguished Service Cross. Exceeded only by the Medal of Honor, the award recognized Smith "for extraordinary heroism in connection with military operations against an armed enemy during the period 7 December 1943 to 21 March 1944. Captain Smith's resolute conduct in the face of great peril, throughout an extended period, in the successful accomplishment of an extremely hazardous and difficult mission exemplified the finest traditions of the armed forces of the United States."

Lt. Gavan Duffy was awarded the British Military Cross in recognition of "exemplary gallantry" for his work in Albania, including the rescue of twenty-seven Americans. Of his time with the Americans, he wrote, "For the party in general, they behaved splendidly, especially the nurses whose courage and faith were a tonic to the people escorting them on what might have been quite a disastrous journey. High tribute should be paid to Capt. Smith who did magnificent work in the latter part of the journey. Tribute should also be paid to the people of the villages through which we passed, most of whom were extremely hospitable even when a reprisal by the Germans would be the price to be paid."

Sgt. Herbert Bell, Duffy's wireless operator, was awarded the Military Medal for his service in Albania, though not specifically for the rescue. Bell had been ambushed while crossing a road in the fall of 1943, and "in the face of enemy fire and with great coolness, seized the mule carrying the wireless set which was about to bolt, and led it to a place of safety. Whenever a move was necessary owing to the close proximity of the enemy, Bell, however great the risk, devoted himself to security and packing of his W/T equipment." He was later dropped to work with local partisans in northern Italy, where he spent several months.

Lt. David Brodie was awarded the Legion of Merit for his service from October 1943 to May 1944 in which "he pioneered in planning, constructing and operating a large communications system in Italy for the purpose of communicating with undercover agents, through clandestine satellite radio station, in enemy-occupied territory." His citation specifically mentioned that he "directed, by radio, the evacuation of a group of United States Army nurses from enemy-held Albania."

Capt. Victor Smith and Maj. Alan Palmer, who became the senior British officer in Albania later that summer, both received a Mention in Despatches for their efforts to rescue the three nurses stranded in Berat.

Countless other people in Albania, as well, helped ensure that the Americans survived. Hundreds of villagers and many partisans and BK shared what little they had at great risk to their own lives. Had they not given the Americans food and shelter during that brutal winter, none would have made it back to Allied lines. The other British and American officers and noncoms, who faced unbelievable hardships with few resources, also did as much as they could for the stranded party while facing monumental tasks.

Of the British men attacked on the day the large party of Americans was evacuated, not all survived. Lt. Col. Arthur Nicholls — Brigadier Davies's second in command whose feet were already in bad shape — and a captain eventually made it to some shelter where they stayed for five days, but their condition rapidly deteriorated. Nicholls, who could no longer walk, told the captain to leave him. Though the captain survived after being on the run for more than a month, Nicholls did not.

Unable to move on his own, Nicholls sat on his coat and had two partisans pull him down the mountainside as they looked for shelter. He later found a mule and traveled at night for weeks until he finally located British major George Seymour, who was thought to be nearby. Seymour had heard of Nicholls's plight by January 14 but had been unable to locate him, while he and his men were also on the run. When the two men finally met, Seymour reported that Nicholls "was more than half-starved, verminous, exhausted, and gangrene had obtained a firm grip on his feet. He had also had an accident having fallen down a mountainside and his shoulder was dislocated. His feet were in an almost unbelievable condition. Both were festering masses and the only indication of where his toes were was where bare bones showed through gangrened flesh." Seymour was able to secure a surgeon and a doctor from Tiranë who removed toes from both of Nicholls's feet. He was too weak, however, to recover, and on February 11, five days after he turned thirty-three, he died, most likely from septicemia. Nicholls was posthumously awarded the George Cross for his actions of extreme gallantry not directly in the face of the enemy.

The British sergeant who had collapsed from exhaustion in the snow was captured by the BK, but he eventually managed to elude them shortly before they planned to shoot him by escaping from a bathroom. After weeks of hiding during the brutal winter, he made his way back to the British in March.

The wounded major, the sergeant who had stayed behind to help, and Davies were captured and handed over to the Germans a few days later. The Italian colonel and wounded partisan were separated from them while they were being transported to the Germans, and they never saw them again. The three Brits were taken to a hospital in Tiranë, and ultimately the major and sergeant were sent to a prison in Belgrade, Yugoslavia, where they were held in underground cells for six weeks before they were moved to Germany. The sergeant was then sent to a camp for captured aircrew, while the major was sent to Colditz Castle, a high-security prison.

Davies, who required multiple surgeries at the hands of German doctors and eventually recovered from his wounds, was sent to Belgrade for interrogation and then to Mauthausen Concentration Camp in Austria, a near-certain death sentence. When he arrived, the commandant tried to impress Davies by citing his long career as a soldier, but Davies refused to cower. Miraculously, the commandant told Davies he would not be responsible for him and would send him away. Davies refused to leave without the other Allied men who had come with him and was granted his request. He was eventually sent to Colditz Castle and spent the rest of the war as a prisoner until the U.S. 9th Armored Division liberated the castle on April 15, 1945.

Davies remained in the British Army after the war and posted the final draft of his book, *Illyrian Venture,* about his experiences in Albania, to his publishers the day before he died in 1951.

Hayes returned to the States on February 5 and briefly reunited with three nurses, Watson, Markowitz, and Nelson, when they traveled from Miami, Florida, to Washington, DC, to report to the Prisoner of War Office for another interrogation on February 8. There they signed more papers agreeing to not offer any details of their experience. Like the others in the Albanian group, they were then granted a thirty-day leave.

It was during their leave that Duffy's interview hit the papers. He told of the attempted air evacuation, the crossing of mountains, and fighting between the Germans and partisans, but he refused to disclose their whereabouts or how the group was rescued. "Those nurses were brave," he said. "They showed no signs of fear, even in the tightest spots." When asked if there was any "love interest," Duffy said, "Listen, if you'd been on that trip you'd have forgotten all about romance." A day later, the military announced the group's safe return; and two days later, Associated Press correspondent Hal Boyle's story, held since January 9, made the presses.

The media tracked down several in the party, who granted interviews in light of the military's official announcement, though they kept names and places to themselves. Kopsco was on her parents' farm in Hammond, Louisiana, when she was interviewed.

"If you mention the Germans to any member of a Partisan family from the children to the great grandparents," she said, "they make signs of slashing the throat." When a reporter from the *Des Moines Tribune* interviewed Hayes, he offered much of the same information already given by others and added, "If it hadn't been for Duffy and his connections with the Partisans, I doubt that we would have gotten out of there." After the article came out, people in town who didn't know him treated him as a friend and those who did know him invited him to dinner. "The owner of a gasoline service station quietly told me, 'If you need any gas come to my station. You won't need any [ration coupons].'"

When their leave was over, they spent brief stints in redistribution centers before they were stationed in various places in the country. Only Watson, who served in the 197th General Hospital in Saint-Quentin, France, during the Battle of the Bulge, was again sent overseas.

A few, like Jens, Rutkowski, Maness, and Porter, were sent back to Bowman Field as instructors. Jens also helped sell war bonds and found herself in another crash landing when one of her plane's engines failed while they were flying over Spirit Lake, Iowa. She and the others on board walked away uninjured. In July 1945, Jens visited Stefa's brother in Cleveland, as she had promised Stefa she would when they last saw each other in Albania more than a year earlier, and told him what she knew about Stefa, unaware that he had been tortured when he returned to Berat.

After Hayes's required time at the Army Air Forces Redistribution Station in Miami Beach, Florida, he was assigned to the station's medical unit. In May 1945, he graduated from Officer Candidate School at Carlisle Barracks in Carlisle, Pennsylvania, and, as a second lieutenant in the Medical Administrative Corps, became a hospital registrar at Camp Cooke, California. By then the war was almost over.

The Allies had accepted the unconditional surrender of Germany on May 7, less than a month after Roosevelt's death, which formally ended the war in Europe — and ended the drive to pass legislation that allowed nurses to be drafted. Roosevelt had "urge[d] that the Selective Service Act be amended to provide for the induction of nurses into the armed forces" in his State of the Union speech in January 1945, leaving the nation stunned. He explained the "need is too pressing to await the outcome of further efforts at recruiting." The bill had passed in the House, and on March 28, the Senate Military Affairs Committee recommended it. But in late July, the Allies gave Japan an ultimatum to surrender, and when it was ignored, the United States dropped two atomic bombs: one on Hiroshima on August 6 and one on Nagasaki on August 9. On September 2, 1945, Japan formally surrendered.

As the years passed after the war, some in the group stayed in touch with occasional visits, letters, or phone calls, but many never saw each other again. Eldridge, who became the vice president of an Indiana electric company, was the first to pass away in 1966 at the age of forty-five; and Porter, one of the three nurses hidden in Berat for months, died three years later at fifty-six years old. She had retired just five months earlier from the Air Force as a major.

When Hayes, who became an aeronautical engineer after going to college on the GI bill, learned from Owen of Abbott's death in 1982, he decided to organize a reunion. In August 1983, six of the nurses—Jens, Watson, Dawson, Tacina, Stark, and Lytle—and five of the medics—Hayes, Owen, Cruise, Zeiber, and Hornsby—along with OSS officer Smith were together again after thirty-nine years. It was then that Smith revealed he had been working for OSS when he rescued them. While they talked of their experiences in Albania and their lives after the war, they also mourned one of their own, lost far too recently. Kanable, the nurse who'd come down with malaria and was the last to leave Catania, was killed in a car accident on her way to the reunion.

Jens, whose diary was mailed back to her after the war, and Maness organized another reunion in 1988, but none of the organizers for either reunion tried to find Duffy, the SOE officer, because, back in 1945, Thrasher, the pilot, had run into Jens at an airfield and told her that Duffy had been killed parachuting into Berlin. In 1993, she learned that he had actually died just three years before at seventy years old. She was distraught at the thought that she and the others could have reconnected with him but comforted by the letters she was then able to exchange with his widow.

In 1995, just a few years after the communist government in Albania crumbled, Jens returned to the country with her two adult children. While there, she met with Stefa's wife, Eleni, and learned that the communist government had executed Stefa on March 3, 1948, for collaborating with the British and Americans during the war. It had been his youngest daughter's third birthday. After being arrested in September 1947, he had been given a trial without a lawyer and behind closed doors in January 1948. Eleni had fought for his release and been told that his life would be spared, though he would serve a 101-year sentence. Happy at the news that her husband would live, she had sent her fourteen-year-old son Alfred to the jail in Berat to deliver cake to the

guards, who announced to the boy that his father had been executed that morning for being an American spy.

Jens also learned that Gina, the partisan leader who had met
the Americans minutes after the plane crash-landed and escorted
them to Berat, had already died. He had passed away in 1986
at the age of sixty-five. Gina's family had paid dearly for his partisan activities. After Gina returned to his home, he learned that
the Germans and the BK had tortured his father, a well-known
Albanian lawyer, for a week during his absence, and his father
had succumbed to his injuries shortly after. The Germans and the
BK had been looking to capture Gina and his brother, who they
knew to be partisans.

Lloyd Smith, who became close to Jens and her family over the
years and had retired from the Army with the rank of lieutenant
colonel in 1962 after twenty-one years of service, decided to return
to Albania in 1996 to see the country again. Shortly after his
return, Qani Siqeca, the young partisan called Johnny by the
Americans who had led some of them after the attack on Berat,
contacted the American Embassy. He was eventually put in touch
with several in the group, including Hayes, Rutkowski, and Cruise,
and they exchanged letters about their perilous time together.

Hayes, now ninety-one years old, is the only remaining survivor
of the thirty personnel who were on board the C-53D the morning of November 8, 1943. Almost all of the men who served in
Albania with SOE and OSS have passed away. Hayes remembers
the details of his difficult months behind enemy lines clearly and
still has many items he carried with him on that journey, including the leather vest Tilman gave him and the yellow scarf he made
from a parachute. There are parts of the experience, however,

he'd like to forget. When he first returned to Allied lines, he had nightmares of being continually chased. Those faded with time, but as was true of many in the group, he rarely talked about his ordeal over the years, even to his family. Other than with his wife, he never discussed the nightmares he had when he first returned to Allied lines or the hunger, loneliness, and frustration he endured in Albania. The experience, however, shaped him when he was a twenty-one-year-old medic from Indianola, Iowa, just as it shaped so many of the others.

Watson worked as a psychiatric nurse at a veterans hospital in Topeka, Kansas, after her children were grown and often drew on her experiences in Albania to talk with the men she helped. She told her daughter that she wasn't the same lighthearted person when she returned to Allied lines because she'd seen too much of human nature. After Watson's death, her family found a letter to them in which she described being in Albania. She wrote, "One night while I was missing I couldn't sleep. I remember it as silently crying for my mother—wanting her there. Finally I was able to think more clearly. If she was there what could she do? She'd be only another mouth to feed! So from then on I realized that I was me and I had only myself to depend on. I guess that was the point when I accepted responsibility for my actions and put more thought into what they would be. Probably the reason my mother said when I came home I wasn't the same. 'You are so cynical. You weren't like that before.'"

Lebo, the radio operator, returned to the States and almost immediately got married, as did Bob Owen, to the woman he'd met at Bowman. Lebo was so impressed by OSS agent Lloyd Smith and what he had done for them that he and his wife spent part of their honeymoon in early 1944 driving to Smith's parents' house to tell them he was okay. When Smith died in March 2008, eighty-eight-year-old Lebo attended his funeral at Arlington National Cemetery.

Abbott, who died in 1982 from complications after heart surgery, wrote about his experience in Albania as soon as he returned to the States, though he changed names and places in the story to protect the identities of the Americans' benefactors. His son, who had only heard his father mention his time in Albania once, didn't know his father had written a book until 2000. Ten years later, his son self-published it.

Rutkowski, who was proud that her daughter had followed her into the military by becoming a reserve officer with the 917th Tactical Fighter Wing, wrote a letter to her in the 1990s about her time in air evacuation and the lessons it taught her. "I learned that although I could get scared, I didn't freeze, but gave it my best shot. I had wondered what my reaction to severe stress would be. Without military experience I may not have known I could do it. I made the decision that fear would not be permitted to decide my action. Through the years it has served me well."

Jens, who died in 2010 and is inurned at Arlington, was so moved by her experience in Albania that when she was almost eighty-five years old, she published her memoirs of that time. She, like some of the other nurses, continued to wear the gold sovereign given to her by the British agents, made into a necklace, as a reminder of their remarkable journey and their secret rescue.

Notes

The author conducted all interviews unless otherwise noted.

Because interviews with Harold Hayes were conducted at his home in Oregon, during visits in November 2011 and February 2012 and in almost daily communications over a year and a half, information provided by him is not further dated.

In instances where none of the available accounts match in details and cannot be verified through records or any other means, the author has relied on Harold Hayes's account given that so much of the information he provided that could be verified proved to be accurate. If the discrepancies are significant to the story, the author has included a note.

The ages of the members of the 807th and the flight crew were determined through family interviews, the Social Security Death Index, the National Personnel Records Center, and obituaries.

Village names were determined through a report by copilot James Baggs, a diary kept by Agnes Jensen and returned to her after the war, interviews and notes from Harold Hayes, statements made by the returning personnel, and reports by the British and American officers who helped them.

Abbreviations of key source materials:

AFHRA   Air Force Historical Research Agency
ETOUSA   European Theater of Operations, United States Army

NACP	National Archives at College Park, Maryland
NPN	No publication named
NPRC	National Personnel Records Center
RG	Record Group at NACP
TNA	The National Archives of the UK

A Note to the Reader

Duffy...account "13 U.S. Nurses Dare Nazis' Guns, Planes, Wilds—Escape!" NPN, February 15, 1943, newspaper article, Harold Hayes papers; "Chutist Leads Adams, Mates Through Nazi Balkan Lines," NPN, February 16, 1943, newspaper article, Harold Hayes papers.

Boyle's story Hal Boyle, "U.S. Nurses Tell of 60-Day Trek Across Nazi-Held Land," *Bee* (Danville, VA), February 17, 1944 (delayed from January 9).

could not reveal "Safeguarding of P/W Information," ETOUSA Headquarters, memo; James P. Cruise personnel file, NPRC; Hayes, interview.

"Too many lives" "Adams, Mates Behind Nazi Lines after Balkan Landing," NPN, 1944 newspaper article, Harold Hayes papers.

reunited twice in the 1980s Hayes, interview; Karin Welzel, "Wilderness Survival Trek Recalled," NPN, August 31, 1983, Harold Hayes papers.

Mangerich...memories Agnes Jensen Mangerich, *Albanian Escape: The True Story of U.S. Army Nurses Behind Enemy Lines* (Lexington: University Press of Kentucky, 1999).

Abbott...memoir Lawrence O. Abbott, *Out of Albania: A True Account of a WWII Underground Rescue Mission,* ed. Clinton W. Abbott (Lulu Press, 2010).

Prologue

[failed air evacuation] Duffy, "Report on Evacuation of American Party"; Hayes, interview; Agnes Jensen Mangerich, *Albanian Escape* (Lexington: University Press of Kentucky, 1999), 162–167; Abbott, *Out of Albania,* 144–149; 1st Fighter Group mission reports, December 29, 1943, from the files of Jim Graham, 1st Fighter Group, 71st Fighter Squadron, as copied from NACP and found in Roll A6544, AFHRA; Operational Records Book of 150 Squadron RAF, TNA, AIR 27/1011. Though Duffy's report said the planes arrived "just after 1200 hrs," two mission reports indicate they arrived about 12:30 p.m. The mission reports also indicate twenty-one P-38s arrived, but Hayes remembered counting eighteen. British officer H. W. Tilman also recalled seeing eighteen: *When Men and Mountains Meet* (1946), collected in *The Seven Mountain-Travel Books* (1983; repr., London: Bâton Wicks, 2010), 367.

[realized air evacuation was possible] Hayes, interview; Richard Lebo, statement, Roll A6544, AFHRA; Abbott, *Out of Albania,* 147. Though Duffy's report made no mention of the last-minute effort to attract the pilots' attention, Hayes vividly recalled the scene, which was further backed by Lebo's account in a 1944 intelligence report. He said, "We thought it would be too dangerous to signal the planes but at the last minute we did try to signal them." The description in Abbott's book supports Hayes's claim as well, except Abbott wrote they used "parachute scarves" to try to signal the planes rather than panels from parachutes used in supply drops.

They were amazed Debriefings of nurses and medics from Army Intelligence, Roll A6544, AFHRA; Duffy, "Report on Evacuation of American Party from Albania"; Hayes, interview; Mangerich, *Albanian Escape,* 162–167; Abbott, *Out of Albania,* 144–149.

Chapter 1

More than ninety personnel Grace H. Stakeman, "807th (US) Medical Air Evacuation Squadron Unit History," Roll A0323, AFHRA.

second week of August 1943 Ibid.; Hayes, interview.

more than one million troops "Winged Angels: USAAF Flight Nurses in WWII," February 7, 2011, National Museum of the U.S. Air Force, http://www.nationalmuseum.af.mil/factsheets/factsheet.asp?id=15457.

Eisenhower deemed Bruce Green, "Challenges of Aeromedical Evacuation in the Post–Cold War Era," *Aerospace Power Journal* 15 (Winter 2001): 14–26.

McKnight William P. McKnight, Jr., e-mail interview, October 14, 2012.

School of Aviation Medicine 807th Medical History Memo, August 24, 1944, Roll A0323, AFHRA; History of the School of Air Evacuation, Roll B2061, AFHRA.

flight surgeons...primary duty Robert F. Futrell, *Development of Aeromedical Evacuation in the USAF, 1909–1960* (Air Force Research Institute, 1960), 86; Hayes, interview.

squadron's twenty-four other flight nurses World War II Flight Nurses Association, *The Story of Air Evacuation 1942–1989* (Dallas: Taylor Publishing, 1989), 53; Stakeman, "807th (US) Medical Air Evacuation Squadron Unit History."

rank Carolyn M. Feller and Constance J. Moore, eds., *Highlights in the History of the Army Nurse Corps* (Washington, DC: U.S. Army Center of Military History, 1995), 11–19; Mary T. Sarnecky, *A History of the U.S. Army Corps* (Philadelphia: University of Pennsylvania Press, 1999), 147, 290–291.

sixty dollars per month Sarnecky, *A History of the U.S. Army Corps,* 252.

car accident Rudy Stakeman, e-mail interview, August 25, 2012.

squadron also included Stakeman, "807th (US) Medical Air Evacuation Squadron Unit History."

technician third grade David W. Hogan, Jr., Arnold G. Fisch, Jr., and Robert K. Wright, Jr., *The Story of the Non-Commissioned Officer Corps: The Backbone of the Army,* U.S. Army Center of Military History, Pub. 70-38. The Army abolished the technician grade title on August 1, 1948.

He and the three other young men Hayes, interview.

Owen Bob Owen (son), e-mail interview, August 25, 2012.

"Windy" Clint Abbott, e-mail interview, July 6, 2012.

she and Helen Porter Agnes Jensen Mangerich's undated and unpublished notes about her experiences in the 807th.

fiancé went missing "Detroit Nurse Is Missing in Italian Area," NPN, 1943 newspaper article, Harold Hayes papers.

Watson Lois Watson McKenzie, lecture, Nurses in War symposium, Washburn University School of Nursing, February 7, 1991, McKenzie family papers.

first…of its kind Futrell, *Development of Aeromedical Evacuation,* 93.

first two MAETS squadrons Ibid., 80–81.

[training for 807th's nurses] Ibid., 88; Historical Record of 807th, February 5, 1944, Roll A0323, AFHRA; History of the School of Air Evacuation; Mangerich's undated and unpublished notes about her experiences in the 807th; McKenzie, lecture, Nurses in War symposium, 1991.

"I won't get airsick" McKenzie, lecture, Nurses in War symposium, 1991.

Blanchfield "History of the Army Nurse Corps: World War II," U.S. Army Medical Department, Office of Medical History, http://history.amedd.army.mil/ANCWebsite/slpr/slpr5.html.

Their specialized instruction Futrell, *Development of Aeromedical Evacuation,* 89; History of the School of Air Evacuation; Hayes, interview.

To test their skills Hayes, interview.

medical evacuation Futrell, *Development of Aeromedical Evacuation,* 1–50; "Jonathan Letterman," Civil War Trust, http://www.civilwar.org/education/history/biographies/jonathan-letterman.html.

Schimmoler Mary C. Smolenski, Donald G. Smith, Jr., and James S. Nanney,

A Fit, Fighting Force: The Air Force Nursing Services Chronology (Washington, DC: Office of the Air Force Surgeon General, 2005), 24; Barbara Brooks Tomblin, *G.I. Nightingales: The Army Nurse Corps in World War II* (Lexington: University Press of Kentucky, 1996), 80.

"hardly makes for...entertaining fare" "Movie Review: Parachute Nurse (1942)," *New York Times,* July 27, 1942.

United States' strategy Futrell, *Development of Aeromedical Evacuation,* 70–71.

38th Medical Air Ambulance Squadron Peter Dorland and James Nanney, *Dust Off: Army Aeromedical Evacuation in Vietnam* (Washington, DC: U.S. Army Center of Military History, 1982), 8.

By the summer Futrell, *Development of Aeromedical Evacuation,* 72; "Winged Angels," February 7, 2011.

designated responsibility Futrell, *Development of Aeromedical Evacuation,* 72–80.

Before the Second World War "Air Force History Overview," U.S. Air Force, http://www.af.mil/information/heritage/overview.asp.

so alarmed...Roosevelt Futrell, *Development of Aeromedical Evacuation,* 54; Message of President Roosevelt to the Congress, January 12, 1939.

In June 1941 "Air Force History Overview."

By 1945 Ibid.

MAETS Futrell, *Development of Aeromedical Evacuation,* 78–80; Sarnecky, *A History of the U.S. Army Corps,* 252–255.

7,043 available nurses Sarnecky, *A History of the U.S. Army Corps,* 175.

"I ask for my boys" "The Time Is Now!" *American Journal of Nursing,* August 1942, 924.

Five hundred nurses History of the School of Air Evacuation.

Hall "Lt. Burton A. Hall Killed," *The Shield of Phi Kappa Psi,* November 1944, 11; World War II Flight Nurses Association, *The Story of Air Evacuation 1942–1989,* 17.

Gardiner World War II Flight Nurses Association, *The Story of Air Evacuation 1942–1989,* 17; Feller and Moore, *Highlights in the History of the Army Nurse Corps,* 17.

Bataan Feller and Moore, *Highlights in the History of the Army Nurse Corps,* 6; "History of the Army Nurse Corps: World War II."

To help ensure History of the School of Air Evacuation.

"taken aloft" Sarnecky, *A History of the U.S. Army Corps,* 252.

port of embarkation Stakeman, "807th (US) Medical Air Evacuation Squadron Unit History"; Hayes, interview.

Chapter 2

Camp Kilmer "A Historical Sketch of Camp Kilmer," National Archives Records Administration, Northeast Region (NYC), http://www.archives.gov/nyc/public/camp-kilmer.pdf.

soot Hayes, interview.

During their six-day stay Ibid.; Grace H. Stakeman, "807th (US) Medical Air Evacuation Squadron Unit History," Roll A0323, AFHRA.

"I wrote my boyfriend today" Agnes Jensen Mangerich's undated and unpublished notes about her experiences in the 807th.

"Many fellows took advantage" Untitled and undated account, Roll A0323, AFHRA.

like Jens and Rutkowski Mangerich's undated and unpublished notes about her experiences in the 807th; Eugenie Rutkowski to her daughter, undated and unpublished letter.

Close to midnight Stakeman, "807th (US) Medical Air Evacuation Squadron Unit History"; Hayes, interview; Mangerich's undated and unpublished notes about her experiences in the 807th.

nightly dim-out "Aurora of Lights Dims Out in City for the Duration," *New York Times,* April 29, 1942.

U-boat attacks A. Timothy Warnock, *The Battle Against the U-boat in the American Theater: December 7, 1941 to September 2, 1945* (Washington, DC: Office of Air Force History, 1992), 7; Nathan Miller, *War at Sea: A Naval History of World War II* (New York: Scribner, 1995), 291–295.

Casablanca Conference "Mr. Churchill's Speech in Parliament on Feb. 11, 1943," *Bulletin of International News* 20, no. 4 (February 20, 1943), 152–154; A. Timothy Warnock, *Air Power Versus U-boats: Confronting Hitler's Submarine Menace in the European Theater* (Washington, DC: Air Force History and Museums Program, 1999), 9.

"Pistol Packin' Mama" Mangerich's undated and unpublished notes about her experiences in the 807th.

coffee and doughnuts Stakeman, "807th (US) Medical Air Evacuation Squadron Unit History"; Hayes, interview.

staterooms Mangerich's undated and unpublished notes about her experiences in the 807th.

in the brig Eugenie Rutkowski to her daughter, undated and unpublished letter.

medics bunked Hayes, interview.

next twenty-four hours Ibid.; Mangerich's undated and unpublished notes about her experiences in the 807th.

lines to the pier Untitled and undated account, Roll A0323, AFHRA.

Navy airplanes and blimps Hayes, interview.

including Rutkowski Eugenie Rutkowski to her daughter, undated and unpublished letter.

convoy entered the open sea Stakeman, "807th (US) Medical Air Evacuation Squadron Unit History"; Hayes, interview; Mangerich's undated and unpublished notes about her experiences in the 807th.

poker games Hayes, interview.

To avoid sleeping Ibid.

sweated in their fatigues Mangerich's undated and unpublished notes about her experiences in the 807th.

olive-drab bags Hayes, interview.

Bay of Bizerte Ibid.; Stakeman, "807th (US) Medical Air Evacuation Squadron Unit History"; Mangerich's undated and unpublished notes about her experiences in the 807th.

movie featuring . . . Alice Faye Untitled and undated account, Roll A0323, AFHRA.

[description of attack] "[807th] War Diary for September 1943," Roll A0323, AFHRA; Hayes, interview; Mangerich's undated and unpublished notes about her experiences in the 807th.

torpedo fired by a submarine "[807th] War Diary for September 1943."

luck ran out Samuel Eliot Morison, *History of United States Naval Operations in World War II: The Atlantic Battle Won* (Champaign: University of Illinois Press, 2002), 263; "1700 on Transport Picked Up at Sea," *New York Times,* July 1, 1944; "Grace Line Gets $6,875,000: WSA to Pay for Santa Elena and Santa Clara," *New York Times,* October 12, 1944; Cynthia Toman, *An Officer and a Lady: Canadian Military Nursing and the Second World War* (Vancouver: UBC Press, 2007), 77. The July 1, 1944, *New York Times* article reported that three men died, whereas the October 12, 1944, article reported that four men died.

Santa Elena arrived "[807th] War Diary for September 1943"; Stakeman, "807th (US) Medical Air Evacuation Squadron Unit History."

five other ships Hayes, interview.

stood in awe Stakeman, "807th (US) Medical Air Evacuation Squadron Unit History."

Bizerte's strategic location "Bizerte," *Britannica Online Encyclopedia;* "To Bizerte with the II Corps," U.S. Army Center of Military History, 1990, CMH Pub. 100-6.

handful of men Hayes, interview.

McKnight and the others boarded Ibid.; "[807th] War Diary for September 1943"; Mangerich's undated and unpublished notes about her experiences in the 807th.

temporary desert campsite "[807th] War Diary for September 1943"; Hayes, interview; Mangerich's undated and unpublished notes about her experiences in the 807th.

only women at the camp "[807th] War Diary for September 1943"; Stakeman, "807th (US) Medical Air Evacuation Squadron Unit History."

sick tent "[807th] War Diary for September 1943"; Stakeman, "807th (US) Medical Air Evacuation Squadron Unit History."

"Still being rookies" Untitled and undated account, Roll A0323, AFHRA.

One of the flight surgeons "[807th] War Diary for September 1943."

Jens crawled into Mangerich's undated and unpublished notes about her experiences in the 807th.

As Rutkowski ran Eugenie Rutkowski to her daughter, undated and unpublished letter.

Watching the raid Ibid.; "[807th] War Diary for September 1943."

One bomb "[807th] War Diary for September 1943"; Hayes, interview.

dug foxholes "[807th] War Diary for September 1943"; Hayes, interview.

"The great news that you have heard" Franklin Delano Roosevelt, *The Fireside Chats of Franklin Delano Roosevelt* (Teddington, UK: Echo Library, 2007), 136.

climbed in the back of military trucks "[807th] War Diary for September 1943"; Hayes, interview; Mangerich's undated and unpublished notes about her experiences in the 807th.

Roman arches and a German fighter plane Hayes, interview.

twenty-five nurses Ibid.

While most in the 807th "[807th] War Diary for September 1943"; Stakeman, "807th (US) Medical Air Evacuation Squadron Unit History."

old apartment building Hayes, interview.

women spent their days Mangerich's undated and unpublished notes about her experiences in the 807th.

three weeks after their arrival "[807th] War Diary for October 1943," Roll A0323, AFHRA.

successfully delivered [patients] Untitled and undated account, Roll A0323, AFHRA; Stakeman, "807th (US) Medical Air Evacuation Squadron Unit History."

turned the tide Bruce Robinson, "World War Two: Summary Outline of Key Events," BBC, History, http://www.bbc.co.uk/history/worldwars/wwtwo/ww2_summary_01.shtml; "Timeline of World War II: 1943," PBS, http://www.pbs.org/thewar/at_war_timeline_1943.htm.

medics were stationed Hayes, interview.

so picturesque Mangerich's undated and unpublished notes about her experiences in the 807th.

four flight surgeons Robert F. Futrell, *Development of Aeromedical Evacuation in the USAF, 1909–1960* (Air Force Research Institute, 1960), 79.

up to twenty-four patients per flight Hayes, interview; "Douglas C-53D Skytrooper," Aerospace Museum of California, http://www.aerospaceca.org/museum_aircraft/douglas_c-53d_skytrooper.html,

responsibility for the patients Hayes, interview; Futrell, *Development of Aeromedical Evacuation,* 92.

required the teams to split up Stakeman, "807th (US) Medical Air Evacuation Squadron Unit History"; Futrell, *Development of Aeromedical Evacuation,* 79.

807th's primary responsibility Futrell, *Development of Aeromedical Evacuation,* 197; "[807th] War Diary for October 1943."

casualties pouring in "[807th] War Diary for October 1943."

On one of Hayes's first flights Hayes, interview.

On one of Rutkowski's flights Eugenie Rutkowski to her daughter, undated and unpublished letter.

on their own Hayes, interview; Mangerich's undated and unpublished notes about her experiences in the 807th.

caught rides on combat planes Untitled and undated account, Roll A0323, AFHRA; Lois Watson McKenzie, lecture, Nurses in War symposium, Washburn University School of Nursing, February 7, 1991, McKenzie family papers; Hayes, interview.

1,651 patients "[807th] War Diary for October 1943."

Chapter 3

November 8 Missing Air Crew Report (MACR) No. 1147, Roll A6544, AFHRA; operations officer 61st Troop Carrier Squadron to commanding officer 314th Troop Carrier Group, memo attached to MACR No. 1147, November 13, 1943, Roll A6544, AFHRA; "[807th] War Diary for November 1943," Roll A0323, AFHRA; statements by returning personnel, Roll A6544, AFHRA. Hayes believes the plane crash-landed in Albania on November 7, 1943, and the AAF did not consider the thirty Americans missing until November 8 because they were present for the November 7 Morning Report, which recorded units' personnel changes.

boarded jeeps Agnes Jensen Mangerich's undated and unpublished notes about her experiences in the 807th; Hayes, interview.

sky was clear for the first time in days Hayes, interview; World Data Center for Meteorology, http://www.ncdc.noaa.gov/oa/wdc. Agnes Jensen Mangerich, *Albanian Escape* (Lexington: University Press of Kentucky, 1999), 10, indicated that it was raining while the nurses were driving to the airfield, but data for that day in Catania shows no precipitation.

galoshes Hayes, interview.

Simpson Ibid.; Mangerich, *Albanian Escape,* 10; Robert L. Simpson, 90, "District Pediatrician," *Washington Post,* January 13, 2002.

Storms had grounded the 807th Hayes, interview.

Bari and Grottaglie Untitled and undated account, Roll A0323, AFHRA.

807th's medics dressed in Hayes, interview.

military leggings Ibid.

On one of the mornings Ibid.

former medic who refused to fly Ibid.; "[807th] War Diary for October 1943," Roll A0323, AFHRA.

Hornsby Hayes, interview; "[807th] War Diary for November 1943."

C-53D Skytrooper Missing Air Crew Report No. 1147; Hayes, interview.

C-47 Skytrain "C-47 Skytrain Military Transport," Boeing, History, http://www.boeing.com/history/mdc/skytrain.htm; Jim Winchester, ed., *Aircraft of World War II* (San Diego: Thunder Bay Press, 2004), 80-81.

the C-47 was considered by Eisenhower Dwight D. Eisenhower, *Crusade in Europe* (Baltimore: Johns Hopkins University Press, 1948), 163–164.

every theater Norman Polmar and Thomas B. Allen, *World War II: The Encyclopedia of the War Years 1941–1945* (Mineola, NY: Dover Publications, 2012), 183; "C-47 Skytrain Military Transport," Boeing.

Almost identical Polmar and Allen, *World War II,* 183; "Douglas C-53D Skytrooper," Aerospace Museum of California. http://www.aerospaceca.org/museum_aircraft/douglas_c-53d_skytrooper.html.

Among a few other planes Futrell, *Development of Aeromedical Evacuation in the USAF, 1909–1960* (Air Force Research Institute, 1960), 95; Bruce Green, "Challenges of Aeromedical Evacuation in the Post–Cold War Era," *Aerospace Power Journal* 15 (Winter 2001): 14–26.

never flown together Hayes, interview; Lawrence O. Abbott, *Out of Albania,* ed. Clinton W. Abbott (Lulu Press, 2010), 10.

61st Troop Carrier Squadron Missing Air Crew Report No. 1147; 61st Troop Carrier Squadron War Diary, Roll A0984, AFHRA.

dropped paratroops 61st Troop Carrier Squadron History, Roll A0984, AFHRA.

pilot…had canceled the trip Charles Thrasher, statement, Roll A6544, AFHRA.

prominent Daytona Beach, Florida, family David F. Mitchell, e-mail interview, July 17, 2012; Dana Ramsey, e-mail interview, June 4, 2012.

Bolles Military Academy David F. Mitchell, e-mail interview, July 17, 2012; *The Eagle* (Bolles Military Academy Yearbook), 1939, 29.

enlisted in 1941 Charles B. Thrasher record, U.S. World War II Army Enlistment Records, 1938–1946, NACP, http://aad.archives.gov/aad/series-list .jsp?cat=WR26.

promoted the previous month 61st Troop Carrier Squadron History.

Baggs William Hunter Baggs, phone interview, December 20, 2011; James A. Baggs record, U.S. World War II Army Enlistment Records, 1938–1946.

Foster Field "Commissioned at Randolph Field," *Savannah Morning News*, February 16, 1943.

one hundred missions "Lieut. Baggs Has an Unusual Record," *Savannah Morning News*, December 21, 1945.

Shumway Bill Shumway, e-mail interview, May 24, 2012.

filled in for Hayes, interview.

Lebo Clifford M. Lebo, Craig D. Lebo, Gayle A. Yost, e-mail interviews, August 26, 2012.

first of the medical personnel Mangerich, *Albanian Escape,* 9.

Headstrong and independent Mangerich family video; Jon Mangerich, Karen Curtis, interviews, Naples, Florida, February 18–19, 2012.

training of ANC nurses Robert J. Parks and William S. Mullins, eds., *Medical Training in World War II* (Washington, DC: Office of the Surgeon General, Department of the Army, 1974), 127–130.

dinner dates and dancing Mangerich's undated and unpublished notes about her experiences in the 807th.

including Rutkowski Lee Whitson, telephone interview, October 11, 2011; "Detroit Nurse Is Missing in Italian Area," NPN, 1943 newspaper article, Harold Hayes papers.

required stewardesses to be nurses Futrell, *Development of Aeromedical Evacuation,* 91.

Dawson "Former Stewardess Missing in Action," *The Era* (Bradford, PA), November 30, 1943.

Kanable "Serves Overseas: Lieut. Pauleen J. Kanable," *Wisconsin State Journal,* September 30, 1943.

Kopsco Mangerich, *Albanian Escape,* 27.

Others who piled into the plane Kathi Jackson, *They Called Them Angels: American Military Nurses of World War II* (Lincoln: University of Nebraska Press, 2006), 2.

"Tassy" Mangerich, *Albanian Escape,* 40.

one of five children "Three Nurses from Michigan Reported Safe," NPN, 1944 newspaper article, Harold Hayes papers.

younger brother Willard Bette Newell, e-mail interview, December 7, 2012; Mangerich, *Albanian Escape,* 172.

"Marky" Mangerich, *Albanian Escape,* 26; Hayes, interview.

Hayes Hayes, interview.

sat across from Mangerich, *Albanian Escape,* 9.

Pennsylvania Railroad William Eldridge personnel file, NPRC.

medics who were married Hayes, interview; Wanetta Wolf, obituary, February 12, 2006, http://www.clinehansonfuneralhome.com/sitemaker/sites/clineh0/obit.cgi?user=wanetta; Kristin Zeiber-Pawlewicz, e-mail interview, June 19, 2012; Elva Brooks, e-mail interview, January 20, 2013.

easygoing Kristin Zeiber-Pawlewicz, e-mail interview, June 19, 2012.

whose brother had been taken prisoner "Adams, Brother of Wake Captive, Lost Near Italy," NPN, 1943 newspaper article, Harold Hayes papers.

Abbott had switched places Abbott, *Out of Albania,* 9.

Rutkowski had learned Mangerich, *Albanian Escape,* 26.

roughly two-hour flight Hayes, interview; Agnes Jensen, statement, Roll A6544, AFHRA.

Simpson...had also boarded Mangerich, *Albanian Escape,* 10.

Bari was open Charles Thrasher, statement, Roll A6544, AFHRA.

Shumway secured Hayes, interview.

Around eight thirty a.m. Several passengers, statements, Roll A6544, AFHRA. Though the Missing Air Crew Report listed 9:00 a.m. as the departure time, and Thrasher's statement gave 7:30 a.m., several of the passengers, including Dawson, Kanable, Owen, and Jensen, said the plane took off between 8:15 a.m. and 8:30 a.m. Mangerich, *Albanian Escape,* 13, said the plane was flying with two others that morning. Though Lieutenant T. E. Yarbrough described piloting one of those planes in a letter to Mangerich many years later, neither Mangerich nor Hayes remembered seeing any other planes flying with them that morning. Lieutenant Joseph Rogers, the other pilot mentioned by Yarbrough, mentioned the flight in a family history and included a newspaper reference, but no other sources could be found.

within fifteen minutes Hayes, interview.

paged through magazines or books Ibid.

Watson read a book Lois Watson McKenzie, lecture, Nurses in War symposium, Washburn University School of Nursing, February 7, 1991, McKenzie family papers.

control tower at Bari Missing Air Crew Report No. 1147.

classified as confidential "Pilots' Information File," War Department, April 9, 1943, PIF 3-3-1.

[experiences during flight] Hayes, interview; Charles Thrasher, statement, Roll A6544, AFHRA; Mangerich, *Albanian Escape,* 11–19; Abbott, *Out of Albania,* 10–14; McKenzie, lecture, Nurses in War symposium, 1991; Eugenie Rutkowski to her daughter, undated and unpublished letter.

IFF Hayes, interview; "Pilots' Information File," War Department, April 9, 1943, PIF 1-3-2; Geoffrey Perret, *Winged Victory: The Army Air Forces in World War II* (New York: Random House, 1993), 74; Frederik Nebeker, *Dawn of the Electronic Age: Electrical Technologies in the Shaping of the Modern World, 1914–1945* (Hoboken, NJ: Wiley, 2009), 455.

"Look out there!" Hayes, interview.

both experienced swimmers Ibid.

airfield Charles Thrasher, statement, Roll A6544, AFHRA, identified the location of the airfield as Fushë-Krusjë.

forgotten to switch the fuel tanks Hayes, interview.

"What's that plane doing?" Ibid.

"Butcher Bird" Winchester, *Aircraft of World War II,* 94–95.

less than a few hundred feet from the waterline Hayes, interview.

black eye McKenzie, lecture, Nurses in War symposium, 1991.

Chapter 4

picked up Shumway Hayes, interview.

shot of morphine Ibid.

[crash aftermath] Ibid.; Charles Thrasher, statement, Roll A6544, AFHRA; Agnes Jensen Mangerich, *Albanian Escape* (Lexington: University Press of Kentucky, 1999), 11–19; Lawrence O. Abbott, *Out of Albania,* ed. Clinton W. Abbott (Lulu Press, 2010), 10–14.

[crash site] Peter Lucas and Edi Kurtezi located the crash site near the village of Çestie in the mid-1990s with a map from Lloyd Smith showing the general location. Lucas wrote of it in his book *Rumpalla: Rummaging Through Albania* (Xlibris, 2002). With this information and confirmation of the location from a document found in the German archives, the author visited the crash site in March 2012.

sandals made of old tire carcasses Hayes, interview; H. W. Tilman, *When Men and Mountains Meet* (1946), collected in *The Seven Mountain-Travel Books* (1983; repr., London: Bâton Wicks, 2010), 349.

[Albania during World War II] "Implementation Study for the Over-all and Special Program Pertaining to Albania, Office of Strategic Services," December 30, 1943, RG 226, entry 116, box 1, folder 1, NACP; Roderick Bailey,

The Wildest Province: SOE in the Land of the Eagle (London: Jonathan Cape, 2008); Bernd J. Fischer, *Albania at War: 1939–45* (West Lafayette, IN: Purdue University Press, 1999); David Smiley, *Albanian Assignment* (London: Sphere Books, 1984); E. W. ("Trotsky") Davies, *Illyrian Venture: The Story of the British Military Mission to Enemy-Occupied Albania 1943–44* (London: Bodley Head, 1952); Tilman, *When Men and Mountains Meet*.

"personally cut the throats" Smiley, *Albanian Assignment,* 56.

[Albanian history] Miranda Vickers, *The Albanians: A Modern History* (London, Tauris, 2006); Raymond Zickel and Walter R. Iwaskiw, eds., *Albania: A Country Study* (Washington, DC: Federal Research Division, Library of Congress, 1992); "Albania," *Britannica Online Encyclopedia.*

Baggs asked Gina Hayes, interview.

Draža Mihailović "Dragoljub Mihailović," *Britannica Online Encyclopedia.*

"my dear" Hayes, interview.

shoot down their plane Ibid.; Mangerich, *Albanian Escape,* 27; Abbott, *Out of Albania,* 20.

Albanian Vocational School Hayes, interview; Mangerich, *Albanian Escape,* 43; Joan Fultz Kontos, *Red Cross, Black Eagle: A Biography of Albania's American School* (New York: Columbia University Press, 1981), 17–58.

offered to lead them Hayes, interview; Mangerich, *Albanian Escape,* 23; Abbott, *Out of Albania,* 20–21.

IFF Hayes, interview; "Pilots' Information File," War Department, April 9, 1943, PIF 1-3-2; Perret, *Winged Victory,* 74; Nebeker, *Dawn of the Electronic Age,* 455.

activated a charge Hayes, interview.

"Hey, Baggs, hurry it up!" Ibid.

coats Ibid.

transport Shumway Ibid.; Mangerich, *Albanian Escape,* 23; Abbott, *Out of Albania,* 21.

carried the machine gun Hayes, interview.

small stone hut Ibid.; Abbott, *Out of Albania,* 23.

two-story house Hayes, interview; Mangerich, *Albanian Escape,* 23; Abbott, *Out of Albania,* 23.

Gjolen "Economic, Social, Political Conditions of Towns and Villages which the Party Passed Through," Roll A6544, AFHRA.

After a long discussion Hayes, interview; Mangerich, *Albanian Escape,* 25.

kaval Hayes, interview.

cheese…cornbread Ibid.; Lois Watson McKenzie, lecture, Nurses in War symposium, Washburn University School of Nursing, February 7, 1991, McKenzie family papers. McKenzie mentioned only cornbread. Abbott, *Out of*

Albania, 23, mentioned cornbread and boiled chicken. Wilma Dale Lytle Gibson, "World War II Story of Escape from Germans," *Falmouth Outlook,* May 18, 1964, mentioned cornbread, eggs, chicken, and cheese.

nurses gave the liners Gibson, "World War II Story of Escape from Germans."

Hayes stretched out Hayes, interview.

Jens...detached the hood Mangerich, *Albanian Escape,* 28–30.

the 807th in Catania "[807th] War Diary for November 1943," Roll A0323, AFHRA; untitled and undated account, Roll A0323, AFHRA.

"Someone has been in my musette bag!" Hayes, interview.

sentenced them to be shot Tilman, *When Men and Mountains Meet,* 349.

Hayes's bag Hayes, interview.

pitcher of water Ibid.; Mangerich, *Albanian Escape,* 31; Abbott, *Out of Albania,* 27.

Chapter 5

commandant Hayes, interview; Lawrence O. Abbott, *Out of Albania,* ed. Clinton W. Abbott (Lulu Press, 2010), 29.

[attempt to burn plane] Hayes, interview.

clock Koli Karaja, telephone interview through translator Albana Droboniku, December 22, 2012; Koli Karaja, interviews by Ajet Nallbani in Berat on behalf of the author, December 2012.

Hayes thought it was safer Hayes, interview.

finally set the plane ablaze Ibid.; Agnes Jensen Mangerich, *Albanian Escape* (Lexington: University Press of Kentucky, 1999), 36; Abbott, *Out of Albania,* 32.

Kahreman Ylli Personal papers of Hasan Gina, courtesy of the family of Hasan Gina.

considering two options Hayes, interview; Charles Thrasher, statement, Roll A6544, AFHRA. According to Hayes, the Americans did not learn that the British were operating in Albania until much later. They thought a British downed airman might be in the country but not organized British missions. If they had learned of British officers in the area, it seems likely that the Americans would have immediately sought their help. Thrasher mentioned in his statement that they didn't look for the British until after the attack on Berat. Mangerich, *Albanian Escape,* 34, and Abbott, *Out of Albania,* 31, both mentioned learning about British agents early on, though Mangerich later wrote about the party learning for the first time that British were working with the partisans (77).

water buffalo or ox Hayes, interview; Mangerich, *Albanian Escape,* 35; Abbott, *Out of Albania,* 30; Wilma Dale Lytle Gibson, "World War II Story of Escape from Germans," *Falmouth Outlook,* May 18, 1964. Hayes and Mangerich both reported the animal was an ox. Abbott and Gibson identified the animal as a water buffalo, as did the article "Balkan Escape," *Collier's,* April 1, 1944, which reported interviews with Lillian Tacina and Eugenie Rutkowski.

announced his decision Hayes, interview.

led the party Ibid.; Mangerich, *Albanian Escape,* 39–41.

"Never mind. Just eat it." Gibson, "World War II Story of Escape from Germans."

Besa Robert Elsie, *A Dictionary of Albanian Religion, Mythology, and Folk Culture* (New York: NYU Press, 2001), 35; Robert Elsie, *Historical Dictionary of Albania,* 2nd ed. (Lanham, MD: Scarecrow Press, 2010), 218–219; Bernd J. Fischer, *Albania at War* (West Lafayette, IN: Purdue University Press, 1999), 187; Norman Gershman, *Besa: Muslims Who Saved Jews in World War II* (Syracuse: Syracuse University Press, 2008).

churning river Hayes, interview; Mangerich, *Albanian Escape,* 42; Abbott, *Out of Albania,* 36.

possibly Poshnje "Economic, Social, Political Conditions of Towns and Villages which the Party Passed Through," Roll A6544, AFHRA.

retaliation Gavan Duffy, "Report on Evacuation of American Party from Albania," TNA, HS 5/124; Fischer, *Albania at War,* 190.

Owen, Hayes, and Abbott Hayes, interview.

led the party through the woods Ibid.

Watson kept thinking of the cake "Nurse Back with Army after Plane Is Lost in Flight," *Southtown Economist,* February 2, 1944.

nearby stream Hayes, interview.

German patrol Ibid.; Mangerich, *Albanian Escape,* 44; Abbott, *Out of Albania,* 39.

stay near the roads Fischer, *Albania at War,* 197.

Borovë Roderick Bailey, *The Wildest Province* (London: Jonathan Cape, 2008), 62; "Memorial to the Victims of the Wehrmacht Massacre of Borovë," Information Portal to European Sites of Remembrance, http://www.memorial-museums.org/eng/staettens/view/1262/Memorial-to-the-Victims-of-the-Wehrmacht-Massacre-of-Borovë; Owen Pearson, *Albania in the 20th Century: A History* (London: Tauris, 2005), vol. 2, 258.

they would arrive in Berat Hayes, interview.

six B-25s Ibid.; Mangerich, *Albanian Escape,* 46; Abbott, *Out of Albania,* 41.

bombs exploding "Excerpts from operations report," November 13, 1943, RG 18, entry 6, box 10, NACP; Kit C. Carter and Robert Mueller, comps., *The Army Air Forces in World War II: Combat Chronology, 1941–1945* (New York: Arno Press, 1980), 215; Philip Adams, "Chronological Sequence of Events in Albania, from June 15 to December 31, 1943," November 12, 1943, entry, RG 226, entry 154, box 17, folder 238, NACP.

facedown in a ditch Hayes, interview.

reminded Jens of home Mangerich, *Albanian Escape,* 46.

Chapter 6

[description of Berat] "Historic Centres of Berat and Gjirokastra," World Heritage Centre, UNESCO, http://whc.unesco.org/en/list/569.

people cheered, sang, and waved Hayes, interview; Agnes Jensen Mangerich, *Albanian Escape* (Lexington: University Press of Kentucky, 1999), 47; Lawrence O. Abbott, *Out of Albania,* ed. Clinton W. Abbott (Lulu Press, 2010), 43; Agnes Jensen, Richard Lebo, statements, Roll A6544, AFHRA.

Grand Hotel Kolumbo Ajet Nallbani, e-mail interview and photo of hotel, April 7, 2012.

Stefa Hayes, interview; Mangerich, *Albanian Escape,* 47; Abbott, *Out of Albania,* 46; Joan Fultz Kontos, *Red Cross, Black Eagle* (New York: Columbia University Press, 1981), 95.

Stefa had remained in Berat Stefa family, written statement delivered to the author in person in Berat in March 20, 2012.

pool...money Hayes, interview. Abbott, *Out of Albania,* 48, 78.

Watson, in the hotel Lois Watson McKenzie, lecture, Nurses in War symposium, Washburn University School of Nursing, February 7, 1991, McKenzie family papers.

Jens and Lytle Mangerich, *Albanian Escape,* 48–50.

Hayes was paired Hayes, interview.

milling about the town Ibid.; "Economic, Social, Political Conditions of Towns and Villages which the Party Passed Through," Roll A6544, AFHRA.

tens of thousands of Italians SOE report, RG 226, entry 144, box 97, folder 1023, NACP; Bernd J. Fischer, *Albania at War* (West Lafayette, IN: Purdue University Press, 1999), 164; Roderick Bailey, *The Wildest Province* (London: Jonathan Cape, 2008), 85; E. W. ("Trotsky") Davies, *Illyrian Venture* (London: Bodley Head, 1952), 73.

keep themselves from starving Davies, *Illyrian Venture,* 74; "Economic, Social, Political Conditions of Towns and Villages which the Party Passed Through," Roll A6544, AFHRA.

Between one thousand and two thousand SOE report, RG 226, entry 144, box 97, folder 1023, NACP.

a hundred Italians a day Fischer, *Albania at War,* 164.

Albanian bar Hayes, interview; Abbott, *Out of Albania,* 46.

raki "raki," *Britannica Online Encyclopedia.*

[George's home] Hayes, interview.

Jens and Lytle Mangerich, *Albanian Escape,* 48–50.

speech Ibid., 50–51; Hayes, interview; Abbott, *Out of Albania,* 47.

Vdekje Fashizmit...Liri Popullit Hayes, interview; Abbott, *Out of Albania,* 48; Owen Pearson, *Albania in the 20th Century* (London: Tauris, 2005), vol. 2, 205; H. W. Tilman, *When Men and Mountains Meet* (1946), collected in *The Seven Mountain-Travel Books* (1983; repr., London: Bâton Wicks, 2010), 349.

Shqipëria Shqiptarëvet...Vdekje Tradhëtarëvet Pearson, *Albania in the 20th Century,* 210.

next two days Ibid., 54; Hayes, interview; Wilma Dale Lytle Gibson, "World War II Story of Escape from Germans," *Falmouth Outlook,* May 18, 1964.

never come back Mangerich, *Albanian Escape,* 53.

"the GIs" Hayes, interview.

photographer Ibid.

[attack on Berat] Ibid.; Mangerich, *Albanian Escape,* 55–61; Abbott, *Out of Albania,* 49–59; Charles Thrasher, Richard Lebo, statements, Roll A6544, AFHRA. Though Mangerich, *Albanian Escape,* 57–58, reported that the party was aware that three nurses were missing, Hayes maintained that they did not discover the nurses' fate until much later. Abbott, *Out of Albania,* 72, confirmed this. It likely would have been very difficult, if not impossible, to count heads on the crowded truck during the chaos of the attack.

[Hayes and Jens's group] Hayes, interview; Mangerich, *Albanian Escape,* 61–63.

Siqeca Qani Siqeca to Eugenie Rutkowski, letter, September 17, 1998; Qani Siqeca to Harold Hayes, letter, March 10, 1997.

Chapter 7

memo Operations officer 61st Troop Carrier Squadron to commanding officer 314th Troop Carrier Group, memo attached to Missing Air Crew Report No. 1147, November 13, 1943, Roll A6544, AFHRA.

attended church services Untitled and undated account, Roll A0323, AFHRA.

morale was low Untitled and undated account, Roll A0323, AFHRA.

"The building housing" Untitled and undated account, Roll A0323, AFHRA.

officially missing Ibid.

signed the reports William Eldridge personnel file, NPRC.

rushed them out Hayes, interview.

Hayes, Owen, and Ebers Ibid.

Qani, Jens, and the others Agnes Jensen Mangerich, *Albanian Escape* (Lexington: University Press of Kentucky, 1999), 64–68.

"Here they are!" Hayes, interview.

one partisan lying on the floor Ibid.; Mangerich, *Albanian Escape,* 67. Mangerich mentioned one severely wounded partisan who was shot in the leg, along with two other less injured partisans who arrived later. Siqeca mentioned that two partisans were injured. Hayes believes that by the time he, Owen, and Ebers arrived, there was only one wounded man, who'd been shot in the chest.

BK Hayes, interview; Mangerich, *Albanian Escape,* 66; Roderick Bailey, *The Wildest Province* (London: Jonathan Cape, 2008), 63. Mangerich referred to the BK as Ballista. Bailey listed a variety of names used to refer to the group, including BK, Ballists, Balkom, or as the British called it, the Balli.

Italian soldiers…following them Hayes, interview; Mangerich, *Albanian Escape,* 64. Mangerich mentioned the large group of Italian soldiers following them before they were caught in the shootout. She estimated the number at one hundred fifty men; Hayes estimated the group to number around eighty.

"Look back there!" Hayes, interview.

lights of Berat Ibid.

reached a village Ibid.

mountain telegraph Ibid.; Melville Chater, "Albania, Europe's New Kingdom, *National Geographic Magazine,* February 1931, 175.

refused to let them stay Hayes, interview.

"onion strudel" Ibid.

walnuts Ibid.

Americans in Dobrushë Ibid.; Mangerich, *Albanian Escape,* 72–73.

saw some of their missing party Hayes, interview; Mangerich, *Albanian Escape,* 73–74; Lawrence O. Abbott, *Out of Albania,* ed. Clinton W. Abbott (Lulu Press, 2010), 72.

three nurses [missing] Hayes, interview; Abbott, *Out of Albania,* 72–76.

Americans' suspicions Hayes, interview; Mangerich, *Albanian Escape,* 72–76, 86; Abbott, *Out of Albania,* 64–71.

contact some of the British Hayes, interview; Mangerich, *Albanian Escape,* 77; Abbott, *Out of Albania,* 78.

SOE William Manchester and Paul Reid, *The Last Lion: Winston Spencer Churchill, Defender of the Realm, 1940–1965* (New York: Little, Brown, 2012), 273–274; Nigel Morris, "The Special Operations Executive 1940–1946," BBC, http://www.bbc.co.uk/history/worldwars/wwtwo/soe_01.shtml.

"set Europe ablaze!" Manchester and Reid, *The Last Lion,* 273–274; Morris, "The Special Operations Executive."

offices [in Cairo and Bari] Bailey, *The Wildest Province,* 35, 200; Jon Naar (former Royal Artillery captain with SOE and military intelligence officer, who worked in the Cairo and Bari SOE offices), interview at his home in New Jersey on March 7, 2012.

"Thousands of Albanian guerrillas" Bailey, *The Wildest Province,* 128; "Aid for Albanians Cited by Churchill," *New York Times,* November 5, 1943.

The day before the Americans crash-landed Bailey, *The Wildest Province,* 101–102; E. W. ("Trotsky") Davies, *Illyrian Venture* (London: Bodley Head, 1952), 93–94.

kill a sheep Hayes, interview.

bottle of raki Ibid.

Zippo lighter Ibid.

tobacco Ibid.; "Balkan Escape," *Collier's,* April 1, 1944, 66.

fleas and lice Hayes, interview; Abbott, *Out of Albania,* 78.

"foot races" Lois Watson McKenzie, lecture, Nurses in War symposium, Washburn University School of Nursing, February 7, 1991, McKenzie family papers.

books whose pages Hayes, interview; Abbott, *Out of Albania,* 84.

route was necessary Hayes, interview.

Owen had announced Ibid.

higher mountains Ibid.; Mangerich, *Albanian Escape,* 80.

streams Hayes, interview; Mangerich, *Albanian Escape,* 79; Abbott, *Out of Albania,* 71.

the GIs Hayes, interview; Mangerich, *Albanian Escape,* 82; Abbott, *Out of Albania,* 81.

shoes Hayes, interview; Mangerich, *Albanian Escape,* 83; Abbott, *Out of Albania,* 87.

clean bedding Hayes, interview.

red berries Ibid.

Hayes and Abbott Ibid.

crude bridge Ibid.

yelled across the mountains Ibid.

invaded Albania Ibid.

Hayes, Owen, and Wolf Ibid.

fourteenth day in Albania Ibid.

highly trained German soldiers Department Military Archive, Freiburg, RH-26-100-31, November 23, 1943.

Chapter 8

over several mountain ridges Hayes, interview.

village council Ibid.

Thanksgiving Ibid.; Lawrence O. Abbott, *Out of Albania,* ed. Clinton W. Abbott (Lulu Press, 2010). Abbott's memoir differs from Hayes's account, but Hayes's dates of when the party met the British in Lavdar coincide with the reports filed by the British. Agnes Jensen Mangerich, *Albanian Escape* (Lexington: University Press of Kentucky, 1999), skipped from November 22 to November 29.

imam Hayes, interview.

Mecca John L. Esposito, ed., *The Oxford Dictionary of Islam* (Oxford: Oxford University Press, 2003), 103.

sacred stone Hayes, interview; Abbott, *Out of Albania,* 87.

curse Hayes, interview; Abbott, *Out of Albania,* 87.

Qani Hayes, interview

Mount Ostrovicë [and snowstorm] Ibid. Mangerich, *Albanian Escape,* 87–90, and Abbott, *Out of Albania,* 87–89, mentioned Mount Tomorrit, which is close to Berat and not near the villages of Faqekuq and Ceramicë, which Agnes Jensen Mangerich's diary listed as the places they were before and after their crossing.

Cruise's hat off his head Jim Cruise to John Graham, letter received February 3, 1995, from the John Graham family's papers.

"Some of the girls were sleepy" "Balkan Escape," *Collier's,* April 1, 1944, 64.

lost her footing Hayes, interview; Welzel, "Wilderness Survival Trek Recalled."

village council of Çeremicë Hayes, interview; Mangerich, *Albanian Escape,* 90; Abbott, *Out of Albania,* 90.

note from a British officer Hayes, interview; Mangerich, *Albanian Escape,* 91–92; Abbott, *Out of Albania,* 91–92. "American Nurses," TNA, HS 7/70.

Not everyone knew right away. Hayes, interview.

OSS "What Was OSS?" Center for the Study of Intelligence, Central Intelligence Agency, https://www.cia.gov/library/center-for-the-study-of-intelligence/csi-publications/books-and-monographs/oss/art03.htm.

On November 27 David Brodie, "The Rescue of American Nurses from Albania," in *The OSS CommVets Papers,* ed. J. F. Ranney and A. F. Ranney (Covington, KY: James F. Ranney, 2002), 28.

[Davies was alerted] E. W. ("Trotsky") Davies, *Illyrian Venture* (London: Bodley Head, 1952), 67–68.

"an American aircraft" Davies, *Illyrian Venture,* 67.

forty-three-year-old Roderick Bailey, *The Wildest Province* (London: Jonathan Cape, 2008), 92.

Royal Ulster Rifles Ibid.

twice been awarded Bailey, *The Wildest Province,* 92.

"take all steps" Davies, *Illyrian Venture,* 67.

radiogram Colonel David R. Stinson to Major General Smith, Allied Force Headquarters, memo, November 29, 1943, Women in Military Service for America Memorial Foundation archives.

front-page wire story "13 U.S. Army Nurses Missing: Transport Plane Struck Bad Weather," *The News* (Frederick, MD), November 29, 1943; "Plane Missing with Army Nurses Aboard," *Wisconsin Tribune,* November 29, 1943; "13 U.S. Nurses Missing at Sea," *Las Cruces Sun-News,* November 29, 1943.

devastating telegrams Adjutant General James Alexander Ulio to Ralph V. Hayes, telegram, November 26, 1943, Harold Hayes papers; Adjutant General James Alexander Ulio to Peter Cruise, telegram, November 26, 1943, James P. Cruise personnel file, NPRC; Mangerich, *Albanian Escape,* 211. "Army Nurse Listed Missing," *Indiana Evening Gazette,* November 30, 1943; Nolan McKenzie to Office of the Adjutant General, letter, January 2, 1944.

Watson's husband of just a few months Lois Watson McKenzie, lecture, Nurses in War symposium, Washburn University School of Nursing, February 7, 1991, McKenzie family papers.

"I don't know what to say." Nolan McKenzie to Harry and Leila Watson, letter, November 27, 1943, McKenzie family papers.

"Your grief is mine too." Helen King McKenzie to Harry and Leila Watson, letter, November 27, 1943, McKenzie family papers.

Hayes's mother...nightmares and premonitions Virginia McCall, e-mail interview, November 3, 2011.

sent their...son, Karl Karl Hayes, e-mail interview, November 7, 2011.

Adams "Adams, Brother of Wake Captive, Lost Near Italy," 1943 newspaper article, NPN, Harold Hayes papers.

Schwant Bette Newell, e-mail interview, December 7, 2012; Mangerich, *Albanian Escape,* 172.

As the weary party...left Çeremicë Hayes, interview.

they found the British soldier Ibid.; Mangerich, *Albanian Escape,* 95; Abbott, *Out of Albania,* 98.

Lavdar Hayes interview; Mangerich, *Albanian Escape,* 95; Abbott, *Out of Albania,* 98; "American Nurses," TNA, HS 7/70.

Victor Smith TNA, HS 9/1384/6.

dropped into Albania Ibid.

spycraft techniques Bailey, *The Wildest Province,* 60.

SOE personnel attended Bailey, *The Wildest Province,* 60; Nigel Morris, "The Special Operations Executive, 1940–1946," BBC, http://www.bbc.co.uk/history/worldwars/wwtwo/soe_02.shtml.

same type of training Bailey, *The Wildest Province*, 60.

"just about the most useful course" Bailey, *The Wildest Province*, 52.

local touches Ibid., 53.

first mission into Albania David Smiley, *Albanian Assignment* (London: Sphere Books, 1984), 17–18; Bailey, *The Wildest Province*, 58.

four men had parachuted Smiley, *Albanian Assignment*, 17–18; Bailey, *The Wildest Province*, 58.

Commando Order Roderick Bailey, e-mail interview, November 19, 2012; David M. Kennedy, ed., *Library of Congress World War II Companion* (New York: Simon and Schuster, 2007), 657.

concentration camp Davies, *Illyrian Venture*, 194–196; Bailey, *The Wildest Province*, 215.

trained some eight hundred men Smiley, *Albanian Assignment,* 67; Bailey, *The Wildest Province,* 77.

Of the first fifty Bailey, *The Wildest Province*, 90.

[agents in Yugoslavia, Greece] Ibid.

knew nothing of SOE Hayes, interview.

Lancashire Fusiliers TNA, HS 9/1384/6.

"Why did you bring these people?" Hayes, interview.

list of their names Ibid.; Mangerich, *Albanian Escape,* 96.

stay in Lavdar Hayes, interview; Mangerich, *Albanian Escape,* 96. Abbott, *Out of Albania,* 98.

maps Hayes, interview.

took baths Mangerich, *Albanian Escape,* 97–98.

Chapter 9

When Smith returned to Lavdar Hayes, interview; Agnes Jensen Mangerich, *Albanian Escape* (Lexington: University Press of Kentucky, 1999), 100; Lawrence O. Abbott, *Out of Albania,* ed. Clinton W. Abbott (Lulu Press, 2010), 98. Hayes remembers that they spent two nights in Lavdar, November 30 and December 1, and arrived in Krushovë on December 2. Mangerich wrote that they spent the night of November 29 and November 30 in Lavdar and December 1 in Krushovë. Abbott indicated that they spent the nights of November 26 through November 30 in Lavdar and arrived in Krushovë on December 1. The available British records do not offer the specific date the Americans arrived in Krushovë.

left for…Krushovë Hayes, interview; Mangerich, *Albanian Escape,* 100–102. Abbott, *Out of Albania,* 99–100.

"Some individuals grated" Mangerich, *Albanian Escape,* 106.

Palmer TNA, HS 9/1139/3; Roderick Bailey, *The Wildest Province* (London: Jonathan Cape, 2008), 95.

told the...nurses Mangerich, *Albanian Escape,* 103.

War Department "13 Missing Nurses Are Reported Safe," *Joplin Globe,* December 3, 1943.

Smith was being sent "Recommendation for Award," memo, May 18, 1944, RG 226, entry 224, box 723, Lloyd Smith personnel file, NACP.

In 1943, OSS Douglas Waller, *Wild Bill Donovan: The Spymaster Who Created the OSS and Modern American Espionage* (New York: Free Press, 2011); John Whiteclay Chambers II, *OSS Training in the National Parks and Service Abroad in World War II* (Washington, DC: U.S. National Park Service, 2008); John Whiteclay Chambers II, "Office of Strategic Services Training During World War II," *Studies in Intelligence: Journal of the American Intelligence Professional* 54, no. 2, June 2010.

[OSS and SOE relations] Untitled document, RG 222, entry 144, box 100, folder 1046; Neville Wylie, ed., *The Politics and Strategy of Clandestine War: Special Operations Executive 1940–1946* (New York: Routledge, 2006), 95; David Stafford and Rhodri Jeffreys-Jones, eds., *American-British-Canadian Intelligence Relations 1939–2000* (London: Frank Cass, 2000), 22–23; Waller, *Wild Bill Donovan,* 129–139; Bailey, *The Wildest Province,* 198.

"They are not under our jurisdiction" Bailey, *The Wildest Province,* 199.

Smith Lloyd Smith, undated autobiography, Mangerich family papers.

"Unless I did something" Ibid.

Hayden Ibid.; RG 226, entry 224, boxes 308 and 320, Sterling Hayden personnel file, NACP.

"The Most Beautiful Man in the Movies" Turner Classic Movies, http://www.tcm.com/tcmdb/person/83248|142549/Sterling-Hayden.

"We have a priority job." Ibid.

three-hour briefing "Recommendation for Award."

German mines Lloyd Smith, undated autobiography.

Dubbed "the second Pearl Harbor" Eric Niderost, "Deadly Luftwaffe Strike in the Adriatic," *World War II Magazine,* February 2001, 46; Glen Infield, *Disaster at Bari* (New York: Bantam Books, 1988), 140.

"I would regard it as a personal affront" Niderost, "Deadly Luftwaffe Strike in the Adriatic," 44.

[description of attack on Bari] Ibid., 42–48; Infield, *Disaster at Bari*; Gerald Reminick, *Nightmare in Bari: The World War II Liberty Ship Poison Gas Disaster and Cover-up* (Palo Alto: Glencannon Press, 2001).

"Axis Sally" Infield, *Disaster at Bari,* 207–208; "Mildred Gillars," *Britannica Online Encyclopedia.*

[807th in Bari during attack] Grace H. Stakeman, "807th (US) Medical Air Evacuation Squadron Unit History," Roll A0323, AFHRA.

telegrams Telegram to Peter Cruise, December 4, 1943, James P. Cruise personnel file, NPRC; telegram to Jaley Eldridge, December 4, 1943, William Eldridge personnel file, NPRC.

Jens's parents Mangerich, *Albanian Escape,* 212.

Watson's parents Nolan McKenzie to Harry and Leila Watson, letter, December 5, 1943, McKenzie family papers; Nolan McKenzie to Office of the Adjutant General, letter, January 2, 1944.

would not hear anything more Jim Cruise's brother to Office of the Adjutant General, letter, James P. Cruise personnel file, NPRC; Nolan McKenzie to Office of the Adjutant General, letter, January 2, 1944.

medics in Hayes's group Hayes, interview.

shoes for the nurses Gavan Duffy, "Report on Evacuation of American Party from Albania," TNA, HS 5/124. Mangerich, *Albanian Escape,* 177, and Abbott, *Out of Albania,* 103, indicated that many pairs of shoes were given away. Hayes did not remember anyone getting shoes, and Duffy indicated that "Palmer gave the party socks, woolen garments and to two of the nurses a pair of boots, size 7."

"heavy as lead" Lois Watson McKenzie, lecture, Nurses in War symposium, Washburn University School of Nursing, February 7, 1991, McKenzie family papers.

British gave Thrasher gold Hayes, interview; Jon Mangerich, e-mail interview, February 24, 2012.

more than twenty tons of materials Bailey, *The Wildest Province,* 75.

since World War I "Gold Sovereigns: George V, the Great War, and the End of Gold Coinage in Circulation," London Mint Office, http://www.londonmintoffice .org/gold-sovereigns-george-v-the-great-war-and-the-end-of-gold-coinage-in-circulation.

over thirty thousand sovereigns David Smiley, *Albanian Assignment* (London: Sphere Books, 1984), 49–50.

"Some of the bags" Ibid.

Smiley...first supply drop Smiley, *Albanian Assignment,* 48–49.

Delivering...supplies Ibid.; Bailey, *The Wildest Province,* 68.

while the Americans were in Krushovë Jon Naar, interview at his home in New Jersey on March 7, 2012

gauze...menstruating Hayes, interview; Mangerich, *Albanian Escape,* 174.

Palmer asked the whole party Hayes, interview.

Duffy TNA, HS 9/454/8.

Bell TNA, HS 9/118/7.

no mention Hayes, interview.

team of four men Smiley, *Albanian Assignment,* 17–20; Bailey, *The Wildest Province,* 58–60.

Hasluck Smiley, *Albanian Assignment,* 9–11; Bailey, *The Wildest Province,* 36–44; Anthony Quayle, *A Time to Speak* (London: Sphere Books, 1990), 367–368.

"She was an enthusiast" Quayle, *A Time to Speak,* 367.

"loosen his revolver" Ibid., 409.

Jasper Maskelyne Smiley, *Albanian Assignment,* 15.

"produce about twenty things" Bailey, *The Wildest Province,* 52.

desolate camp in Derna Smiley, *Albanian Assignment,* 15.

plane caught on fire Bailey, *The Wildest Province,* 105; E. W. ("Trotsky") Davies, *Illyrian Venture* (London: Bodley Head, 1952), 70.

day before their departure Smiley, *Albanian Assignment,* 15.

"trussed chickens" Ibid., 17.

"We sat round the hole" Bailey, *The Wildest Province,* 58.

"We dropped" Smiley, *Albanian Assignment,* 18.

tore a leg muscle Ibid.

tried to parachute into Macedonia Bailey, *The Wildest Province,* 61.

Chapter 10

Palmer explained Hayes, interview.

American captain Lloyd Smith, "Report on Mission of Evacuation, American Rescue Party," RG 226, entry 144, box 97, folder 1023, NACP; Agnes Jensen Mangerich, *Albanian Escape* (Lexington: University Press of Kentucky, 1999), 129; Lawrence O. Abbott, *Out of Albania,* ed. Clinton W. Abbott (Lulu Press, 2010), 105.

all business Hayes, interview.

dubbed "Blondie" Ibid.; Mangerich, *Albanian Escape,* 110.

leave Albania with the party Hayes, interview.

"a kind of guinea pig" Gavan Duffy, "Report on Evacuation of American Party from Albania," TNA, HS 5/124.

"Under these conditions" David Smiley, *Albanian Assignment* (London: Sphere Books, 1984), 61.

"time to rest and refit" E. W. ("Trotsky") Davies, *Illyrian Venture* (London: Bodley Head, 1952), 66.

fourteen days Hayes, interview.

destroyed a village Ibid.

young American OSS officer Smith, "Report on Mission of Evacuation."

Taylor "Outline of Duties with Office of Strategic Services," memo, October 4, 1945, RG 226, entry 224, box 767, Jack H. Taylor personnel file, NACP.

seven sorties...ten tons Captain G. F. Else, USMCR, to Colonel Paul B. Nelson, memo, September 6, 1945, Jack H. Taylor personnel file, NACP.

rough seas Smith, "Report on Mission of Evacuation."

establish the camp Roderick Bailey, *The Wildest Province* (London: Jonathan Cape, 2008), 196.

"so they lay there" H. W. Tilman, *When Men and Mountains Meet* (1946), collected in *The Seven Mountain-Travel Books* (1983; repr., London: Bâton Wicks, 2010), 363.

temporary home Bailey, *The Wildest Province,* 41, 196–197.

Orahood RG 226, entry 224, box 575, Donald Orahood personnel file, NACP; David Brodie, "The Rescue of American Nurses from Albania," in *The OSS CommVets Papers,* ed. J. F. Ranney and A. L. Ranney (Covington, KY: James F. Ranney, 2002), 28.

Karapiçi Bailey, *The Wildest Province,* 200–201; Peter Lucas, *The OSS in World War II Albania: Covert Operations and Collaboration with Communist Partisans* (Jefferson, NC: McFarland, 2007), 13, 18–19.

"landing was duck soup" Bailey, *The Wildest Province,* 196.

shot in the back Ibid., 208–210; Lucas, *The OSS in World War II Albania,* 54–56.

Duffy explained Duffy, "Report on Evacuation of American Party"; Mangerich, *Albanian Escape,* 119–120.

wireless set Herbert Bell, "Signal Report on Colour Operation," TNA, HS 5/124.

Station IX Terry Crowdy, *SOE Agent: Churchill's Secret Warriors* (Oxford: Osprey Publishing, 2008), 10.

Brown John Brown, unpublished interview, Imperial War Museum (IWM), 1989, provided to the author by Roderick Bailey with permission from IWM.

forty-two pounds Louis Meulstee and Rudolf F. Staritz, *Wireless for the Warrior: Clandestine Radio* (Ferndown, UK: Wimborne Publishing, 2004), vol. 4.

could not use it to communicate Bailey, *The Wildest Province,* 67.

Field operators...coded messages Margaret Pawley, *In Obedience to Instructions: FANY with the SOE in the Mediterranean* (Barnsley, UK: Leo Cooper, 1999), 58, 65.

"sked" Bailey, *The Wildest Province,* 68.

two mules Duffy, "Report on Evacuation of American Party."

"I would prefer" Ibid.

bitter negotiating and price gouging Bailey, *The Wildest Province,* 71.

"After being in Albania" Duffy, "Report on Evacuation of American Party."

"propaganda and goodwill tour" Ibid.

"looked back and surveyed" Ibid.

MP40 Ibid. In his report, Duffy referred to his weapon as a tommy gun, but the pictures of the group when they are rescued show an MP40.

"looked us over" Agnes Jensen Mangerich to John Graham, undated letter, John Graham family papers.

clasped on the barrel Hayes, interview.

Sten gun Ibid.; Bailey, e-mail interview, November 8, 2012; Chris Bishop, ed., *Encyclopedia of Weapons of World War II* (London: Metro Books, 2002), 263.

cost one SOE officer Roderick Bailey, *Forgotten Voices of the Secret War* (London: Ebury Press, 2008), 282.

sprained his ankle Duffy, "Report on Evacuation of American Party"; Hayes, interview.

[description of Voskopojë] Hayes, interview.

[churches of Voskopojë] "Voskopojë Churches," World Monuments Fund, http://www.wmf.org/project/voskopojë-churches.

"It's a hell of a place" Hayes, interview.

vomited Mangerich, *Albanian Escape,* 122.

others insisted Ibid.; Hayes, interview.

curse Hayes, interview; Abbott, *Out of Albania,* 111.

"the piano roll" Hayes, interview.

Dividing the group Ibid.

bride Ibid.

young couple in love Davies, *Illyrian Venture,* 34.

"sworn virgins" Robert Elsie, e-mail interview, November 11, 2012; Mike Lanchin, "Last of Albania's 'Sworn Virgins,'" BBC News, October 22, 2008, http://news.bbc.co.uk/2/hi/europe/7682240.stm; Dan Bilefsky, "Sworn to Virginity and Living as Men in Albania," *New York Times,* June 23, 2008.

[crossing the river] Hayes, interview; Duffy, "Report on Evacuation of American Party"; Mangerich, *Albanian Escape,* 124 (quotes from Duffy's report); Abbott, *Out of Albania,* 110.

last to cross Hayes, interview.

stolen more than a thousand sheep Duffy, "Report on Evacuation of American Party."

"without an English speaking Albanian" Ibid.

makeup Hayes, interview; Abbott, *Out of Albania,* 58.

"managed to create an impression" Duffy, "Report on Evacuation of American Party."

[Hayes's shoes] Hayes, interview.

Gina, the partison Ibid. The description and timing of Gina's return in Mangerich, *Albanian Escape,* 148, differed from Hayes's.

"pilots slightly light-headed" Duffy, "Report on Evacuation of American Party."

"Have heard persistent rumours of invasion" Ibid.

message from Cairo Ibid.

goodbye to Gina Hayes, interview. Mangerich, *Albanian Escape,* 148, and Abbott, *Out of Albania,* 119, differed as to the timing and description of when Gina left. Both placed his departure slightly later in the story but are not consistent.

bridge Hayes, interview; Duffy, "Report on Evacuation of American Party"; Abbott, *Out of Albania,* 117.

truck Duffy, "Report on Evacuation of American Party"; Abbott, *Out of Albania,* 117.

Chapter 11

cold, barren room Hayes, interview; Lawrence O. Abbott, *Out of Albania,* ed. Clinton W. Abbott (Lulu Press, 2010), 117–118.

meeting point in town Hayes, interview.

Mount Nemërçkë Ibid.; Gavan Duffy, "Report on Evacuation of American Party from Albania," TNA, HS 5/124; Abbott, *Out of Albania,* 118–119.

honey Hayes, interview.

"It took almost seven hours" Duffy, "Report on Evacuation of American Party."

"But by the grace of God" Roderick Bailey, *The Wildest Province* (London: Jonathan Cape, 2008), 67.

Sheper H. W. Tilman, *When Men and Mountains Meet* (1946), collected in *The Seven Mountain-Travel Books* (1983; repr., London: Bâton Wicks, 2010), 367.

Leake Bailey, *The Wildest Province,* 244; E. W. ("Trotsky") Davies, *Illyrian Venture* (London: Bodley Head, 1952), 98.

Tilman Bailey, *The Wildest Province,* 75–76; David Smiley, *Albanian Assignment* (London: Sphere Books, 1984), 65.

"the nurses in good heart and looks" Tilman, *When Men and Mountains Meet,* 367.

"Once his mission had been established" Smiley, *Albanian Assignment,* 65.

"dull and placid" Tilman, *When Men and Mountains Meet,* 360.

"We ate our three good meals" Ibid., 361.

location of the sea evacuation Duffy, "Report on Evacuation of American Party."

twenty-five-mile hike Hayes, interview.

Smith waited at Seaview Lloyd Smith, "Report on Mission of Evacuation, American Rescue Party," RG 226, entry 144, box 97, folder 1023, NACP.

"We were desperately keen to go" Smiley, *Albanian Assignment,* 97.

a local appeared Ibid.

Unwilling to wait Smith, "Report on Mission of Evacuation."

.45-caliber handgun "Recommendation for Award," memo, May 18, 1944, RG 226, entry 224, box 723, Lloyd Smith personnel file, NACP.

[description of Smith's journey] Smith, "Report on Mission of Evacuation."

Breda 30s Chris Bishop, ed., *Encyclopedia of Weapons of World War II* (London: Metro Books, 2002), 237.

"getting nervous and jittery" Smith, "Report on Mission of Evacuation."

A partisan guided Hayes, interview.

set a brisk pace Duffy, "Report on Evacuation of American Party."

hillside Hayes, interview.

about six in the evening Duffy, "Report on Evacuation of American Party."

Gjirokastër Gillian Gloyer, *Albania* (Guilford, UK: Globe Pequot Press, 2007), 104; Gjirokastra Conservation and Development Organization, http://www.gjirokastra.org/sub_links/visiting_sub/visiting_monuments.html.

about twelve thousand "Confidential Report, City and Towns, Albania." RG 226, entry 165, box 12, folder 114, NACP.

Kokëdhima Gloyer, *Albania,* 104; Gjirokastra Conservation and Development Organization.

meeting room Hayes, interview.

[description of time with Haki] Ibid.

First Brigade Ibid.; Abbott, *Out of Albania,* 121.

decoding several messages Duffy, "Report on Evacuation of American Party."

Mashkullorë Ibid.; Hayes, interview.

member of the Gestapo Abbott, *Out of Albania,* 121; Cranson, Allen, Owen, and Ebers, statements, Roll A6544, AFHRA.

waited until late morning Hayes, interview.

[town destroyed] Ibid.; Abbott, *Out of Albania,* 122.

fresh meat Hayes, interview; Abbott, *Out of Albania,* 122.

Zhulat Hayes, interview; Abbott, *Out of Albania,* 122.

"take all precaution" Duffy, "Report on Evacuation of American Party."

finally found them Ibid.

Chapter 12

growing impatient Hayes, interview; Lawrence O. Abbott, *Out of Albania,* ed. Clinton W. Abbott (Lulu Press, 2010), 129.

two women dressed Hayes, interview; Abbott, *Out of Albania,* 129.

band of partisans Hayes, interview; Abbott, *Out of Albania,* 129; Gavan Duffy, "Report on Evacuation of American Party from Albania," TNA, HS 5/124. Duffy's report indicated that his intention for the day was Progonat.

Owen, Wolf, and Hayes Hayes, interview.

"We'll draw straws!" Ibid.

moved to another house Ibid.

Duffy and Bell had left that morning Ibid.; Duffy, "Report on Evacuation of American Party."

kaval Hayes, interview.

attacked by a dog Ibid.; Abbott, *Out of Albania,* 127. Abbott's memoir mentions the incident and that Owen's hand was "torn." Hayes believes Owen was not injured and that Abbott was not in the house with them that evening.

Duffy told Thrasher Ibid.

found the village in chaos Duffy, "Report on Evacuation of American Party."

badly wounded partisans Ibid.; Hayes, interview; Abbott, *Out of Albania,* 127.

"two days from their goal" Duffy, "Report on Evacuation of American Party."

"We were washed up" Abbott, *Out of Albania,* 128.

"As events proved later" Duffy, "Report on Evacuation of American Party."

[Thrasher's message] "Copy of Lt. Thrasher's Message of December 20, 1943 (Transmitted over BLO's Cairo Link)," Roll A6544, AFHRA.

"Inform most urgently" Ibid.

special operation in Greece William J. Donovan to Franklin D. Roosevelt, memo, October 29, 1943, FDR's Office Files, 1933–1945, Library of Congress.

Operation Halyard Gregory Freeman, *The Forgotten 500: The Untold Story of the Men Who Risked All for the Greatest Rescue Mission of World War II* (New York: New American Library, 2007); Torsten Ove, "George Vujnovich Dies at 96: Leader of Daring World War II Rescue," *LA Times,* May 1, 2012.

sheep's head Hayes, interview.

[crossing river] Ibid.

Karjan Ibid.

[Smith's journey] Lloyd Smith, "Report on Mission of Evacuation, American Rescue Party," RG 226, entry 144, box 97, folder 1023, NACP.

until they arrived in Dhoksat Hayes, interview; Agnes Jensen Mangerich, *Albanian Escape* (Lexington: University Press of Kentucky, 1999), 150; Abbott, *Out of Albania,* 134.

Williamson Roderick Bailey, *The Wildest Province* (London: Jonathan Cape, 2008), 57.

diary Willie Williamson, diary transcribed by Roderick Bailey during an interview with Williamson around 1999.

Qeserat Hayes, interview; Abbott, *Out of Albania,* 134–135.

"an excellent lunch" Williamson diary.

[events at Qeserat] Hayes, interview.

Christmas Eve celebration Mangerich, *Albanian Escape,* 151–153; "Balkan Escape," *Collier's,* April 1, 1944, 66.

church service Mangerich, *Albanian Escape,* 153–154.

priest...killed Foto Prifti, interview, March 25, 2012, Dhoksat, Albania; Foto Prifti, e-mail interview through his grandson, Klevis Haxhiaj, December 24, 2012.

ate chicken...records on a phonograph Agnes Jensen, statement, Roll A6544, AFHRA.

[meeting with Tilman] Hayes, interview.

"Something special. Sheep intestine soup." Ibid.

Christmas carols Ibid.

Roosevelt's Christmas message Franklin D. Roosevelt, "To the Men and Women of the Armed Forces," *Billings Gazette,* December 25, 1943.

807th in Sicily Untitled and undated account, Roll A0323, AFHRA; "[807th] War Diary for November 1943," Roll A0323, AFHRA.

Chapter 13

cobbler Hayes, interview.

information Ibid.; Gavan Duffy, "Report on Evacuation of American Party from Albania," TNA, HS 5/124.

"the weather was filthy" Duffy, "Report on Evacuation of American Party from Albania.

looted several of shops Ibid.

tried to contact Cairo Ibid.

"blaring in" Ibid.

decoded...message Ibid.

to go in exchange for a sovereign Ibid.

"The airplanes are coming today!" Hayes, interview.

"saw the place alive" Duffy, "Report on Evacuation of American Party."

multiple planes Hayes, interview; Agnes Jensen, statement, Roll A6544, AFHRA.

"three trucks and one [armored] car" Duffy, "Report on Evacuation of American Party"; Lawrence O. Abbott, *Out of Albania,* ed. Clinton W. Abbott (Lulu Press, 2010), 144–149. Hayes did not remember seeing any trucks or a car near the road, but Duffy's report and Abbott's agreed.

[failed air evacuation] Duffy, "Report on Evacuation of American Party"; Hayes, interview; Agnes Jensen Mangerich, *Albanian Escape* (Lexington: University Press of Kentucky, 1999), 162–167; Abbott, *Out of Albania,* 144–149; 1st Fighter Group mission reports, December 29, 1943, from the files of Jim Graham, 1st Fighter Group, 71st Fighter Squadron, as copied from NACP and found in Roll A6544, AFHRA; Operational Records Book of 150 Squadron RAF, TNA, AIR 27/1011. Though Duffy's report said the planes arrived "just after 1200 hrs," two mission reports indicate they arrived about 12:30 p.m. The mission reports also indicate twenty-one P-38s arrived, but Hayes remembers counting eighteen. British officer H. W. Tilman also recalled seeing eighteen: *When Men and Mountains Meet* (1946), collected in *The Seven Mountain-Travel Books* (1983; repr., London: Bâton Wicks, 2010), 367.

"If I live to be 100" Agnes Jensen, statement, Roll A6544, AFHRA.

[realized air evacuation was possible] Hayes, interview; Richard Lebo, statement, Roll A6544, AFHRA; Abbott, *Out of Albania,* 147. Though Duffy's report made no mention of the last-minute effort to attract the pilots' attention, Hayes vividly recalled the scene, which was further backed by Lebo's account in a 1944 intelligence report. He said, "We thought it would be too dangerous to signal the planes but at the last minute we did try to signal them." The description in Abbott's book supported Hayes's claim as well, except Abbott wrote they used "parachute scarves" to try to signal the planes rather than panels from parachutes used in supply drops.

"One or two of the nurses did break down" Duffy, "Report on Evacuation of American Party."

dejected...sobbing Ibid.; Debriefings of nurses and medics from Army Intelligence, Roll A6544, AFHRA; Hayes, interview; Mangerich, *Albanian Escape,* 162–167; Abbott, *Out of Albania,* 144–149.

"There were so few of us" Lois Watson, statement, Roll A6544, AFHRA.

strafed them with machine-gun fire 1st Fighter Group mission reports, December 29, 1943, from the files of Jim Graham, 1st Fighter Group, 71st Fighter Squadron as copied from NACP and found in Roll A6544.

Hayes and Abbott volunteered Hayes, interview. Abbott, *Out of Albania,* 151, did not mention that he stayed behind after the air evacuation but mentioned a similar scene on December 31 while he was with Hornsby (152).

"Very regrettable" Duffy, "Report on Evacuation of American Party."

[Smith at Seaview on Christmas Day] Lloyd Smith, "Report on Mission of Evacuation, American Rescue Party," RG 226, entry 144, box 97, folder 1023, NACP.

"This job here is no cinch" Roderick Bailey, *The Wildest Province* (London: Jonathan Cape, 2008), 197.

Field...injured Bailey, *The Wildest Province,* 205; Anthony Quayle, *A Time to Speak* (London: Sphere Books, 1990), 374–375.

"he has so low an opinion" Bailey, *The Wildest Province,* 206.

"I felt nothing but joy" Quayle, *A Time to Speak,* 372.

"'Send out all the Intelligence'" Ibid., 374.

Kukich Bailey, *The Wildest Province,* 209; Peter Lucas, *The OSS in World War II Albania* (Jefferson, NC: McFarland, 2007), 42.

"Ahead was a narrow beach" Quayle, *A Time to Speak,* 375.

"I wish you joy" Ibid.

"This is [standard operating procedure]" Smith, "Report on Mission of Evacuation."

move the party to Saraqinishtë Hayes, interview; Duffy, "Report on Evacuation of American Party"; Mangerich, *Albanian Escape,* 173; Abbott, *Out of Albania,* 154.

"We were not exactly thrown out" Duffy, "Report on Evacuation of American Party."

Greek Orthodox church Hayes, interview; Abbott, *Out of Albania,* 154–155.

Duffy told the party Hayes, interview; Duffy, "Report on Evacuation of American Party."

leave immediately for Dhoksat Hayes, interview; H. W. Tilman, report, TNA HS 5/128. Duffy's report told of leaving for the coast from Saraqinishtë rather than stopping in Dhoksat again, but Dhoksat is where Tilman gave the party the shoes and other supplies. In Tilman's report he mentioned seeing the party again on January 2.

"I have a present for you." Hayes, interview.

[Owen and Hayes switch shoes] Ibid.

[Supplies from Tilman] Ibid.

Chapter 14

"super-human effort" Gavan Duffy, "Report on Evacuation of American Party from Albania," TNA, HS 5/124.

arrived at Karjan Ibid.; Hayes, interview. Hayes's account and Jens's diary did not agree with Duffy's report regarding the names of the villages they stayed in. Neither Agnes Jensen Mangerich, *Albanian Escape* (Lexington: University Press of Kentucky, 1999), nor Lawrence O. Abbott, *Out of Albania,* ed. Clinton W. Abbott (Lulu Press, 2010), mentioned walking through the night, as Duffy's report indicated.

McKenzie wrote Nolan McKenzie to Office of the Adjutant General, letter, January 2, 1944.

Cruise's brother Jim Cruise's brother to Office of the Adjutant General, letter, James P. Cruise personnel file, NPRC.

Hayes's mother Hayes, interview.

oranges Ibid. Abbott, *Out of Albania,* 156, said Schwant was cutting a piece of cornbread.

Drino River Hayes, interview. Abbott, *Out of Albania,* 157, said they crossed in the dark.

"crack up" Duffy, "Report on Evacuation of American Party."

"a bunch of prisoners on the Russian front" Ibid.

"pushing the party through" Ibid.

Tacina...bad ankle Ibid.

[description of storm] Ibid.; Hayes, interview; Abbott, *Out of Albania,* 164–165; "Balkan Escape," *Collier's,* April 1, 1944, 64.

"Everything during this acrobatic display" Duffy, "Report on Evacuation of American Party."

Hayes fell back Hayes, interview.

[meeting Smith] Ibid.; Mangerich, *Albanian Escape,* 181–183; Abbott, *Out of Albania,* 166; Duffy, "Report on Evacuation of American Party"; Lloyd Smith, "Report on Mission of Evacuation, American Rescue Party," RG 226, entry 144, box 97, folder 1023, NACP.

[Smith's journey] Smith, "Report on Mission of Evacuation."

recommended for a promotion TNA, HS 9/454/8.

"After this reorganization" Smith, "Report on Mission of Evacuation."

safely proceed Ibid.

four partisans running Ibid.

olives from a barrel Hayes, interview.

Smith suggested Smith, "Report on Mission of Evacuation."

three giant steps Ibid.; Hayes, interview; Abbott, *Out of Albania,* 168.

raced ahead Smith, "Report on Mission of Evacuation."

[Stefa said goodbye] Hayes, interview. Mangerich, *Albanian Escape,* 183–185, described Stefa leaving at a different time of day and location.

arrest him Stefa family, written statement delivered to the author in person in Berat, March 20, 2012; Kostaq Stefa (grandson), e-mail interview, December 31, 2012.

Smith and his guide Smith, "Report on Mission of Evacuation."

[description of truck ride] Ibid.; Hayes, interview; Mangerich, *Albanian Escape,* 190–192; Abbott, *Out of Albania,* 170–172; Duffy, "Report on Evacuation of American Party."

Chapter 15

"That was seven weeks ago" Hayes, interview.

"I cannot remember any group" Lloyd Smith, "Report on Mission of Evacuation, American Rescue Party," RG 226, entry 144, box 97, folder 1023, NACP.

[boat delayed] Hayes, interview.

moonlight "Phases of the Moon: 1901 to 2000," NASA, http://eclipse.gsfc.nasa.gov/phase/phases1901.html.

radio in hand, Brodie David Brodie, "The Rescue of American Nurses from Albania," in *The OSS CommVets Papers,* ed. J. F. Ranney and A. L. Ranney (Covington, KY: James F. Ranney, 2002), 28.

Davies...under attack E. W. ("Trotsky") Davies, *Illyrian Venture* (London: Bodley Head, 1952), 148–153.

Orahood...received a message Hayes, interview.

tried...to get in touch with Brodie Ibid.; Brodie, "The Rescue of American Nurses from Albania," 28.

crew made their way toward Albania Brodie, "The Rescue of American Nurses from Albania," 28.

signal fires Ibid.; Hayes, interview.

last two to leave the shore Hayes, interview.

two fifteen Smith, "Report on Mission of Evacuation."

one nurse was seasick Agnes Jensen Mangerich, *Albanian Escape* (Lexington: University Press of Kentucky, 1999), 197.

Hayes and Wolf boarded Hayes, interview.

"it's time to splice the main brace!" Ibid.

"How about giving me your jacket?" Ibid.

"Give it to him." Ibid.

McKnight...photographers Ibid.; photos from 15th Air Force (USAAF), AFHRA, Roll A6544.

26th General Hospital Hayes, interview; photos from 15th Air Force (USAAF), AFHRA, Roll A6544.

open since December 4 Charles M. Wiltsie, *The Medical Department: Medical Service in the Mediterranean and Minor Theaters* (Washington, DC: Office of the Chief of Military History, Department of the Army, 1965), 333.

equipment for the hospital Ibid.

being detained Hayes, interview; Colonel C. A. Young to Brigadier General Lauris Norstad, memo, Roll A6544, AFHRA.

signed papers Hayes, interview; William Eldridge personnel file, NPRC.

half the party Hayes, interview.

Late Arrivals Club Ibid.; Lawrence O. Abbott, *Out of Albania,* ed. Clinton W. Abbott (Lulu Press, 2010), 181; *Air Forces Escape and Evasion Society* (New York: Turner Publishing, 1992), 6.

President Roosevelt Hayes, interview; Jon Naar, interview at his home in New Jersey, March 7, 2012; David Smiley, *Albanian Assignment* (London: Sphere Books, 1984), 106; Mangerich, *Albanian Escape,* 200–201. Though no historical documents confirming FDR's involvement in the story could be found at the NACP, the Franklin D. Roosevelt Presidential Library and Museum in Hyde Park, NY, the Eisenhower Presidential Library and Museum in Abilene, KS, or the U.S. Army Military History Institute in Carlisle, PA, Naar reported that Roosevelt called the Cairo SOE office to find out why it was taking the SOE so long to get the nurses out of Albania. In his book, Smiley wrote of FDR's interest, Hayes was told at his debriefing, and Mangerich wrote in her book of Donovan's telling Smith he would update FDR.

[Donovan and Smith] Mangerich, *Albanian Escape,* 200–201; Douglas Waller, *Wild Bill Donovan* (New York: Free Press, 2011), 226. Waller confirmed that Donovan spent much of January "hopping in the Mediterranean."

remained hospitalized "[807th] War Diary for January 1944," Roll A0323, AFHRA.

"What are you doing in here?" Hayes, interview.

celebrated Untitled and undated account, Roll A0323, AFHRA.

[status of personnel] "[807th] War Diary for January 1944," Roll A0323, AFHRA.

Morocco Hayes, interview.

Chapter 16

[three nurses in home in Berat] Wilma Dale Lytle Gibson, "World War II Story of Escape from Germans," *Falmouth Outlook,* May 18, 1964; Koli Karaja, telephone interview through translator Albana Droboniku, December 22, 2012; Koli Karaja, interviews by Ajet Nallbani in Berat on behalf of the author, December 2012.

Victor Smith and Alan Palmer "Honours and Awards," TNA, HS 7/70.

major Lloyd Smith, "Evacuation of Three American Nurses from Albania," March 29, 1944, RG 226, entry 154, box 6, folder 105, NACP; Hayes, interview;

"Promotion of Officer," RG 226, entry 92A, box 7, folder 92, NACP. Smith signed his evacuation report as "Major," thinking his promotion was official, as he'd been told, but on May 4, 1944, Colonel C. C. Carter wrote a memo asking for the promotion to be handled quickly as Smith was under the assumption that he had already been promoted to the rank of major.

Grama Bay Roderick Bailey, *The Wildest Province* (London: Jonathan Cape, 2008), 206.

"The situation was rather critical" Smith, "Evacuation of Three American Nurses from Albania."

McAdoo and Orahood Bailey, *The Wildest Province,* 215.

three Italians drowned Ibid., 212.

"several members of their organization" Smith, "Evacuation of Three American Nurses from Albania."

Tare Shyti Leka Bezhani, e-mail interviews, December 2012; Vojsava Bezhani, telephone interview through translator Albana Droboniku, December 22, 2012.

"We always tell our women" Smith, "Evacuation of Three American Nurses from Albania."

"[Meto] wanted to know" Ibid.

"If my cousin does not" Ibid.

By this time Letter from Lloyd Smith, March 12, 1944, RG 226, entry 92A, box 7, folder 92, NACP.

Kadre Çakrani Gibson, "World War II Story of Escape from Germans"; Smith, "Evacuation of Three American Nurses from Albania."

Goni bought the material Gibson, "World War II Story of Escape from Germans."

given a rifle Ibid.; Diane Burke Fessler, *No Time for Fear* (East Lansing: Michigan State University Press, 1996), 146.

"See, God——, Major" Smith, "Evacuation of Three American Nurses from Albania."

Epilogue

Smith...Distinguished Service Cross RG 226, entry 92A, box 7, folder 92, NACP.

Duffy...Military Cross "Honours and Awards," TNA, HS 7/70.

"For the party in general" Gavan Duffy, "Report on Evacuation of American Party from Albania," TNA, HS 5/124.

Bell...Military Medal "Honours and Awards," TNA, HS 7/70.

Brodie...Legion of Merit RG 226, entry 225, box 81, David Brodie personnel file, NACP.

Smith…Palmer…Mention in Despatches "Honours and Awards," TNA, HS 7/70.

[what happened to Nicholls and a captain] E. W. ("Trotsky") Davies, *Illyrian Venture* (London: Bodley Head, 1952), 226–227; Roderick Bailey, *The Wildest Province* (London: Jonathan Cape, 2008), 123–126.

"was more than half-starved" Bailey, *The Wildest Province,* 124.

[what happened to major, sergeant, and Davies] Davies, *Illyrian Venture,* 154–227.

final draft Ibid., 9.

Prisoner of War Office Hayes, interview.

Duffy's interview "13 U.S. Nurses Dare Nazis' Guns, Planes, Wilds— Escape!" NPN, February 15, 1943, newspaper article, Harold Hayes papers; "Chutist Leads Adams, Mates Through Nazi Balkan Lines," NPN, February 16, 1943, newspaper article, Harold Hayes papers.

Boyle's story Hal Boyle, "U.S. Nurses Tell of 60-Day Trek Across Nazi-Held Land," *Bee* (Danville, VA), February 17, 1944 (delayed from January 9).

Kopsco [interview] "Guerrillas Save 12 Army Nurses Lost in Albania," *Memphis Press-Scimitar,* February 17, 1944.

Hayes [interview] "Iowa Soldier's Own Story of Escape from Nazis," *Des Moines Tribune,* February 17, 1944.

Watson…again sent overseas World War II Flight Nurses Association, *The Story of Air Evacuation 1942–1989* (Dallas: Taylor Publishing, 1989), 142.

instructors Ibid., 19.

Hayes's [service] Hayes, interview.

[draft of nurses] Jill Elaine Hasday, "Fighting Women: The Military, Sex, and Extrajudicial Constitutional Change," Georgetown Public Law and Legal Theory Research Paper No. 1260756, 2008, http://scholarship.law.georgetown.edu/facpub/450; Doris Weatherford, *American Women During World War II: An Encyclopedia* (New York: Routledge, 2010), 20.

reunion Hayes, interview.

[Thrasher told Jens] Agnes Jensen Mangerich, *Albanian Escape* (Lexington: University Press of Kentucky, 1999), 212.

[Stefa's family learns of execution] Ibid., 212–213; Stefa family, written statement delivered to the author in person in Berat, March 20, 2012; Kostaq Stefa (grandson), e-mail interview, December 31, 2012.

Gina was helping the Americans Marjola Llogoni, e-mail interview, February 21, 2013.

Smith…return to Albania Mangerich, *Albanian Escape,* 213.

American Embassy U.S. Embassy to Qani Siqeca, letter, November 8, 1996, Harold Hayes papers.

exchanged letters Copies of letters, Harold Hayes papers.

many items he carried with him Hayes, interview.

Watson...experiences Phyllis McKenzie, telephone interview, June 7, 2012; World War II Flight Nurses Association, *The Story of Air Evacuation 1942–1989,* 142.

"One night while I was missing" Lois Watson McKenzie, letter, McKenzie family papers.

Lebo Gayle Yost, Craig Lebo, interviews, October 10, 2011; Gayle Yost, e-mail interview, December 16, 2012.

Abbott Lawrence O. Abbott, *Out of Albania,* ed. Clinton W. Abbott (Lulu Press, 2010), 190–194.

Jens Jon Mangerich, Karen Curtis, interviews, Naples, FL, February 18–19, 2012; Jon Mangerich, Karen Curtis, e-mail interviews, January 2012.

Acknowledgments

When I started this book, I had no idea that writing about the extraordinary journey of thirty stranded Americans in World War II and those who saved them would lead to such an incredible journey of my own on which I would meet countless people willing to help me uncover this remarkable story.

I am deeply grateful to medic Harold Hayes, the one remaining survivor of the fateful flight, who spent countless hours recalling events in incredible detail and sharing stories, articles, memorabilia, and photos he'd collected over seven decades. No matter how many questions I asked, Harold always answered. A special thanks goes to Betty, Harold's wife of sixty-eight years, who was as welcoming to me as Harold and who also shared her memories of those in the 807th whom she met after the war. I am thankful to nurse Agnes Jensen Mangerich and medic Lawrence Abbott for their memoirs of these harrowing events.

Dr. Roderick Bailey, historian and author of *The Wildest Province: SOE in the Land of the Eagle,* was incredibly generous with his time and answered numerous questions during the writing of this book. Rod's research and expertise on the British and Americans serving in Albania during World War II and Albania's complicated political situation proved invaluable.

I want to thank Jon Naar, who at the time of the rescue was a

Royal Artillery Captain with SOE working in Cairo and Bari, and who graciously shared his recollections of the events of 1943–44.

The many children, nieces, nephews, and grandchildren of those in the story, from the stranded Americans to the Albanian partisans, were generous with their time, memories, and photos, and I am truly grateful to them. I am particularly thankful for the assistance of Karen Curtis and Jon Mangerich, the children of nurse Agnes Jensen Mangerich, who not only shared in person and through e-mail memories, letters, photos, videos, and articles related to the story, they, along with their spouses, Bob and Beverly, continuously offered their support. My sincere thanks also extend to Hunter Baggs, nephew of copilot James Baggs, and James's son, Jim Baggs; Craig Lebo and Gayle Yost, the children of radio operator Richard Lebo; Sue Lonaker, niece of nurse Wilma Lytle; Nelson McKenzie, husband of nurse Lois Watson; Phyllis McKenzie, daughter of Lois Watson; William McKnight, Jr., son of the 807th's commanding officer, William McKnight; Bob Owen, son of medic Robert Owen; Bill Shumway, son of medic Willis Shumway; the family of partisan Kostaq Stefa, especially his wife, Eleni Stefa, daughters Elda Stefa Naraci and Vitore Stefa-Leka, and grandsons, Kostaq Stefa and Dr. Pjetër Naraci; and Lee Whitson, daughter of nurse Eugenie Rutkowski. I also thank Clint Abbott, son of medic Lawrence Abbott, who published his father's memoirs; Leka Bezhani, grandson of Tare Shyti, who helped lead the three nurses from Berat to the coast; Vojsava Bezhani, daughter of Tare Shyti; Elva Brooks, daughter of medic Gordon MacKinnon; Denis Cranson, son of medic Robert Cranson; Jim Cruise, son of medic James Cruise; Hasan Gina's family, including his children Akil Gina, Cesar Gina,

Donika Gina, Luiza Gina, and his granddaughter Marjola Llogoni; Karl Hayes and Virginia McCall, siblings of medic Harold Hayes; Koli Karaja, nephew of Nani and Goni Karaja, who hid the three nurses in their home in Berat; Mary Ann Adams Lofland, daughter of medic Charles Adams; David Mitchell, nephew of pilot Charles Thrasher; Bette Newell, daughter of nurse Elna Schwant; Dana Ramsey, daughter of Charles Thrasher; Hal Smith and Karen Smith, children of OSS officer Lloyd Smith; Rudy Stakeman, brother of the 807th's head nurse Grace Stakeman; Joe Turnage, son of nurse Ann Markowitz; Paul Voigt, son of flight surgeon Philip Voigt; and Kristin Zeiber-Pawlewicz, granddaughter of medic Charles Zeiber. I am also grateful to the many distant relatives of those in the story who helped me locate these family members.

For their invaluable expertise and assistance, I thank Col. Nancy Cantrell, Chief Nurse of the 94th Combat Support Hospital and former Army Nurse Corps Historian; Dr. Dixie Dysart, Historian, Air Force Historical Research Agency; Dr. Robert Elsie, Specialist, Albanian Studies; Britta Granrud, Curator of Collections, Women's Memorial Foundation; Ajet Nallbani, Historian, Berat Enthographic Museum; Art Reinhardt, OSS Veteran (China) and OSS Society Treasurer; and Judith Taylor, Senior Historian, Air Force Medical Service.

I am also grateful to Albana Droboniku and Blerin Rada for their generous assistance as guides and interpreters during my trip to Albania and their continued help once I returned to the States, as well as to Zeqine Droboniku and Valmira Frasheri for their hospitality in Tiranë.

Aleksander Sallabanda, former ambassador of the Republic of Albania to the United States, arranged for my meeting with

Albanian president Bamir Topi, my meeting with Kostaq Stefa's family and mayor of Berat Fadil Nasufi, and my meeting with Elbasan prefect Shefqet Deliallisi. I am sincerely grateful to him, to President Topi, and to the others for their time and efforts on my behalf. My thanks also go to Albanian journalist and researcher Dr. Monika Stafa, who put me in touch with the family of partisan Hasan Gina and who shared a document from the Albanian archives on partisan Kostaq Stefa's arrest.

Many of the villagers I met, particularly Foto Prifti in Dhoksat, and Vesel Ibrahimi and Xhevit Elezi who live near the crash site, proved to me that Albania's time-honored tradition of hospitality remains alive and well. When I showed up at their doorsteps unannounced, they welcomed me into their homes, offered me raki, and shared their stories. My thanks also extend to Klevis Haxhiaj, the grandson of Foto Prifti, who made a separate trip to Dhoksat on my behalf to ask follow-up questions.

For helping me search various archives in the United States and around the world, I thank Dr. Roderick Bailey, Dr. Gregory Geddes, Marisa Larson, Kevin Morrow, Dominik Naab, and Sim Smiley. Thanks also to author and Brig. Gen. Philip D. Caine, USAF (Ret.), and researcher Steven Kippax for sending me files. I am grateful to several people who found related newspaper articles and information on my behalf, including Betty Menges at the New Albany–Floyd County Public Library, Julia Muller at *Savannah News,* Maureen Nelson at the Mecosta County Genealogical Society, and Holly Peery at the Bolles School. For fact-checking sections of this book, I thank Michelle Harris. My thanks also go to the sons of the late John Graham, an SOE officer in Greece and a friend of Lt. Gavan Duffy after the war, who generously shared research materials on the story gathered by their father in the 1990s, to Jim Graham of the 1st Fighter Group who shared copies of mission reports, and to Robert Vrilakas of the 1st Fighter Group who shared his experiences as a P-38 pilot assigned to rescue the Americans.

I am very fortunate to have the support and guidance of my agent, Ellen Geiger, partner at Frances Goldin Literary Agency, who found the perfect home for my book at Little, Brown. I am extremely grateful for the talent, support, and wisdom of my Little, Brown editor, John Parsley. I would also like to thank my former editor at Little, Brown, Christina Rodriguez, who believed in this story from the very beginning, and publisher Michael Pietsch. My gratitude extends to Morgan Moroney and Miriam Parker as well as Malin von Euler-Hogan, Peggy Freudenthal (and freelance copyeditors Carolyn Haley and Alice Cheyer), and the rest of Little, Brown's consummate team.

I consider myself very lucky to have had the opportunity to work with and learn from an extraordinary group of people, including those at *National Geographic* magazine, *Smithsonian* magazine, *AARP The Magazine,* and the *New York Times* as well as my teachers and fellow students at Johns Hopkins University and the University of North Carolina at Chapel Hill. I am especially grateful for the continued support of Don Belt, Ken Budd, Molly Crosby, Whitney Dangerfield, Allan Fallow, Nancy Perry Graham, Gary Krist, Jess Ludwig, Candice Millard, Austin O'Connor, Leslie Pietrzyk, Bob Poole, Clay Risen, Tim Wendel, and Frank Yuvancic.

I am deeply grateful to my wonderful family, especially my parents, who encouraged me to pursue my passion for writing and whose love and support inspired me to write this book. A special thanks goes to my three brothers and my sisters-in-law, who've always cheered me on, and to the nurses in my family, including my mother, aunt, and great-grandmother, who helped so many people. I hope in some small way this book inspires the youngest members of my family, including Caleb, Katelyn, Alyssa, Taylor, Jenelle, Aaron, Kyle, Evan, Adrian, Owen, Banks, Ben, and Madelyn, to discover and follow their own dreams.

My husband and best friend, Tim Wiersma, has supported me through every step of writing this book, including traveling with me to Albania as my photographer. He continues to amaze me each and every day with his love, kindness, and sense of humor, for which I will be thankful for the rest of my life.

Index

About the Author

CATE LINEBERRY was a staff writer and Europe editor for *National Geographic* magazine and the web editor for *Smithsonian* magazine. Her work has also appeared in the *New York Times*. Originally from Raleigh, NC, she lives in the Greater Washington, DC, area.